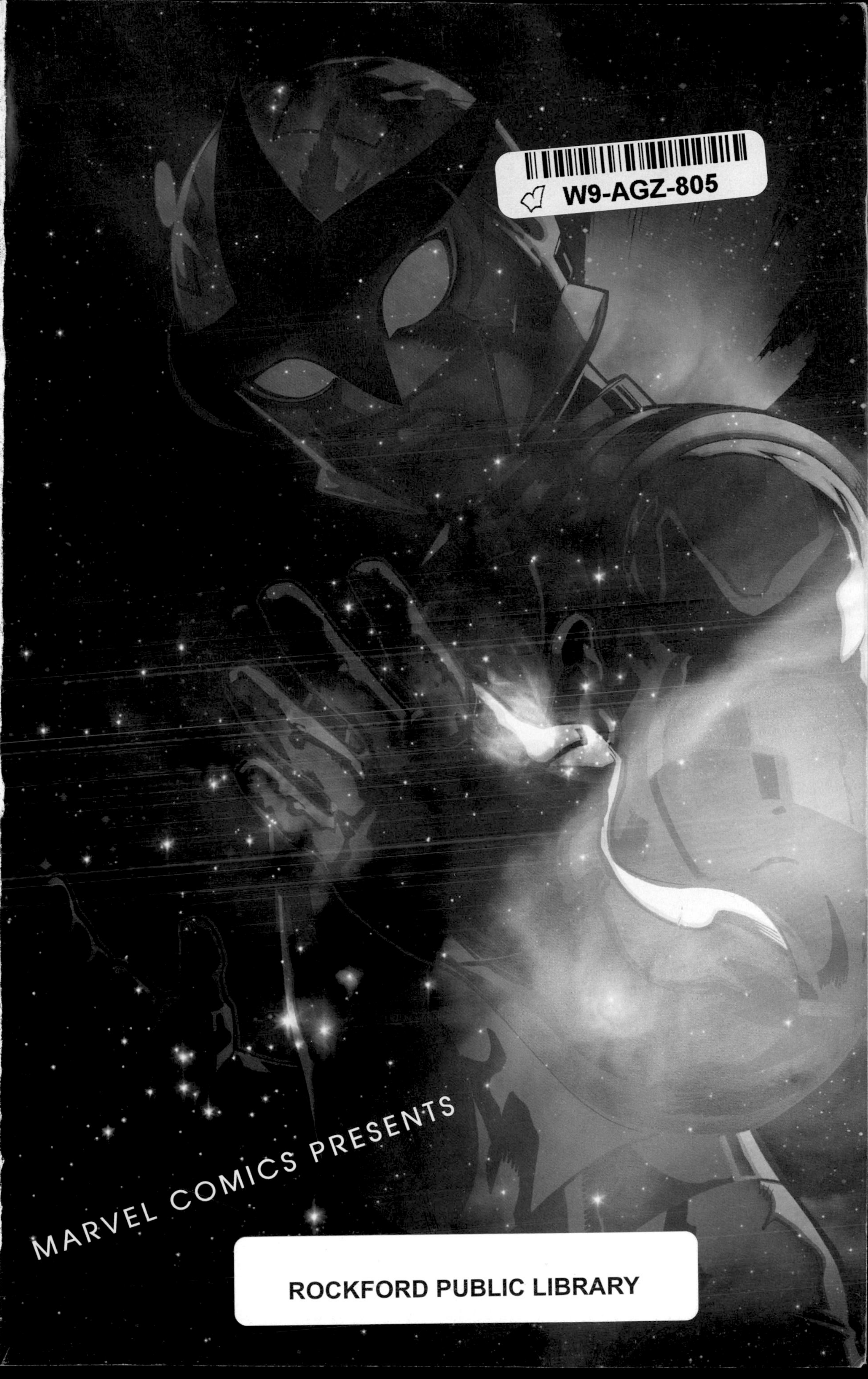
MARVEL COMICS PRESENTS

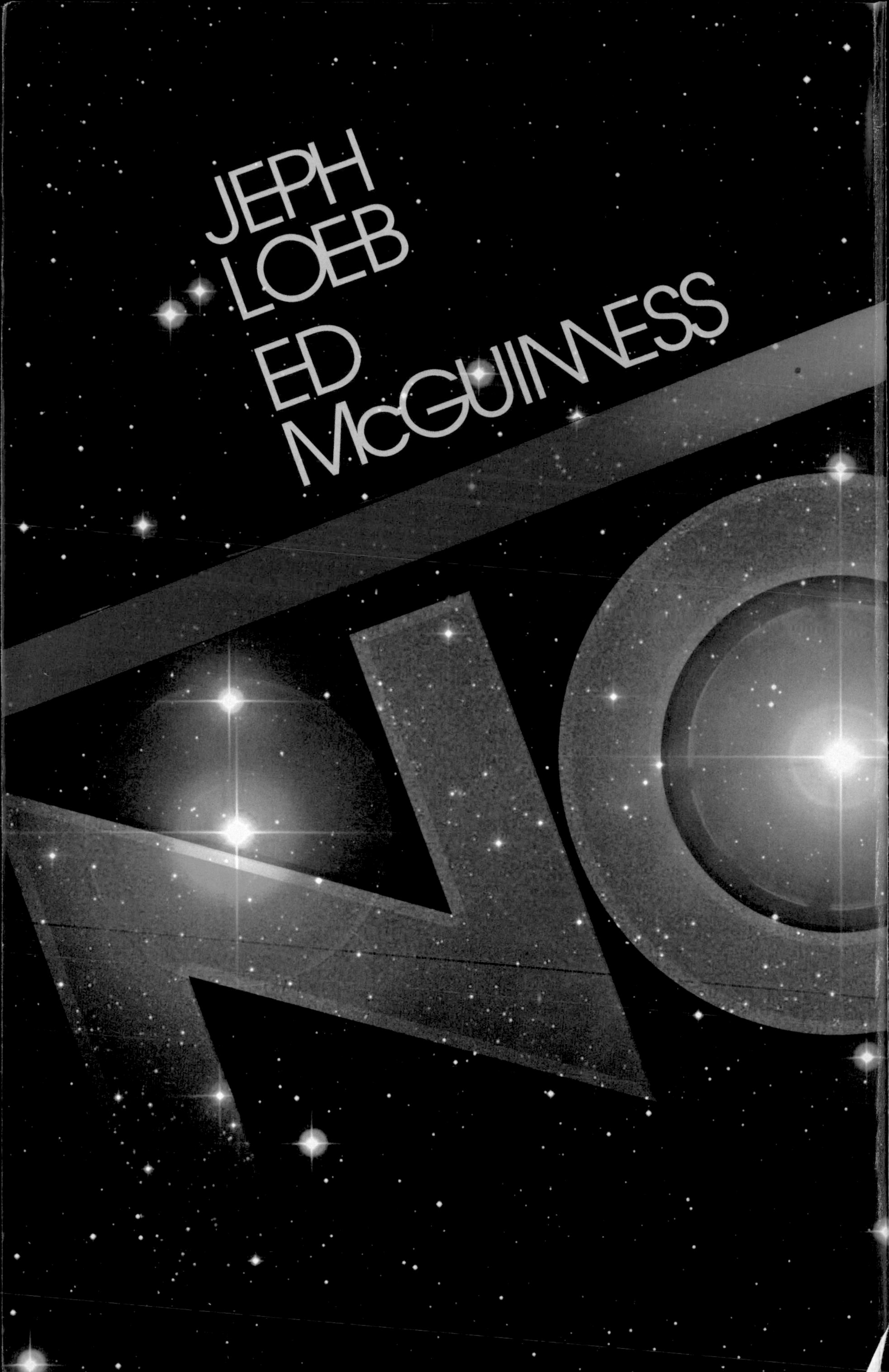
JEPH
LOEB
ED
McGUINNESS

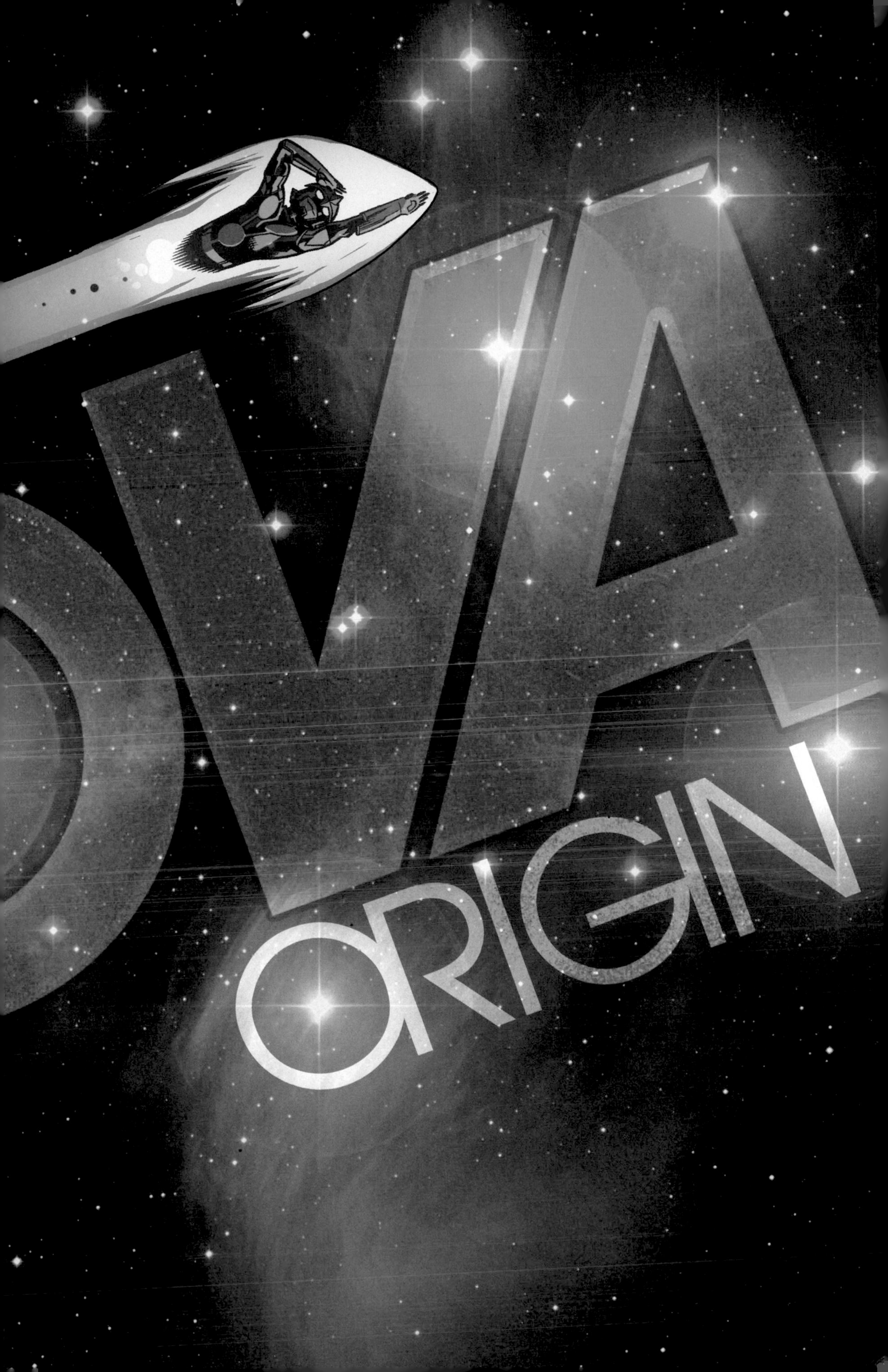
OVA
ORIGIN

WRITER JEPH LOEB
PENCILS ED McGUINNESS
INKS DEXTER VINES WITH ED McGUINNESS (#5)
COLORS MARTE GRACIA (#1-4 & "DIAMONDHEAD")
& EDGAR DELGADO (#5)
LETTERS COMICRAFT'S ALBERT DESCHESNE
COVER ART ED McGUINNESS, DEXTER VINES & MARTE GRACIA
ASSISTANT EDITOR ELLIE PYLE
ASSOCIATE EDITOR SANA AMANAT
EDITOR STEPHEN WACKER

COLLECTION EDITOR JENNIFER GRÜNWALD
ASSISTANT EDITOR CAITLIN O'CONNELL
ASSOCIATE MANAGING EDITOR KATERI WOODY
EDITOR, SPECIAL PROJECTS MARK D. BEAZLEY
VP PRODUCTION & SPECIAL PROJECTS JEFF YOUNGQUIST
SVP PRINT, SALES & MARKETING DAVID GABRIEL
BOOK DESIGN JOHN ROSHELL @ COMICRAFT
STARFIELD IMAGES COURTESY NASA/JPL-CALTECH

EDITOR IN CHIEF AXEL ALONSO
CHIEF CREATIVE OFFICER JOE QUESADA
PRESIDENT DAN BUCKLEY
EXECUTIVE PRODUCER ALAN FINE

NOVA VOL. 1: ORIGIN. Contains material originally published in magazine form as NOVA #1-5, POINT ONE #1 and MARVEL NOW! POINT ONE #1. Third printing 2017. ISBN# 978-0-7851-6605-4. Published by MARVEL WORLDWIDE, INC., a subsidiary of MARVEL ENTERTAINMENT, LLC. OFFICE OF PUBLICATION: 135 West 50th Street, New York, NY 10020. Copyright © 2014 MARVEL No similarity between any of the names, characters, persons, and/or institutions in this magazine with those of any living or dead person or institution is intended, and any such similarity which may exist is purely coincidental. Printed in the U.S.A. DAN BUCKLEY, President, Marvel Entertainment; JOE QUESADA, Chief Creative Officer; TOM BREVOORT, SVP of Publishing; DAVID BOGART, SVP of Business Affairs & Operations, Publishing & Partnership; C.B. CEBULSKI, VP of Brand Management & Development, Asia; DAVID GABRIEL, SVP of Sales & Marketing, Publishing; JEFF YOUNGQUIST, VP of Production & Special Projects; DAN CARR, Executive Director of Publishing Technology; ALEX MORALES, Director of Publishing Operations; SUSAN CRESPI, Production Manager; STAN LEE, Chairman Emeritus. For information regarding advertising in Marvel Comics or on Marvel.com, please contact Vit DeBellis, Integrated Sales Manager, at vdebellis@marvel.com. For Marvel subscription inquiries, please call 888-511-5480. Manufactured between 7/26/2017 and 8/14/2017 by LSC COMMUNICATIONS INC., KENDALLVILLE, IN, USA.

10 9 8 7 6 5 4 3

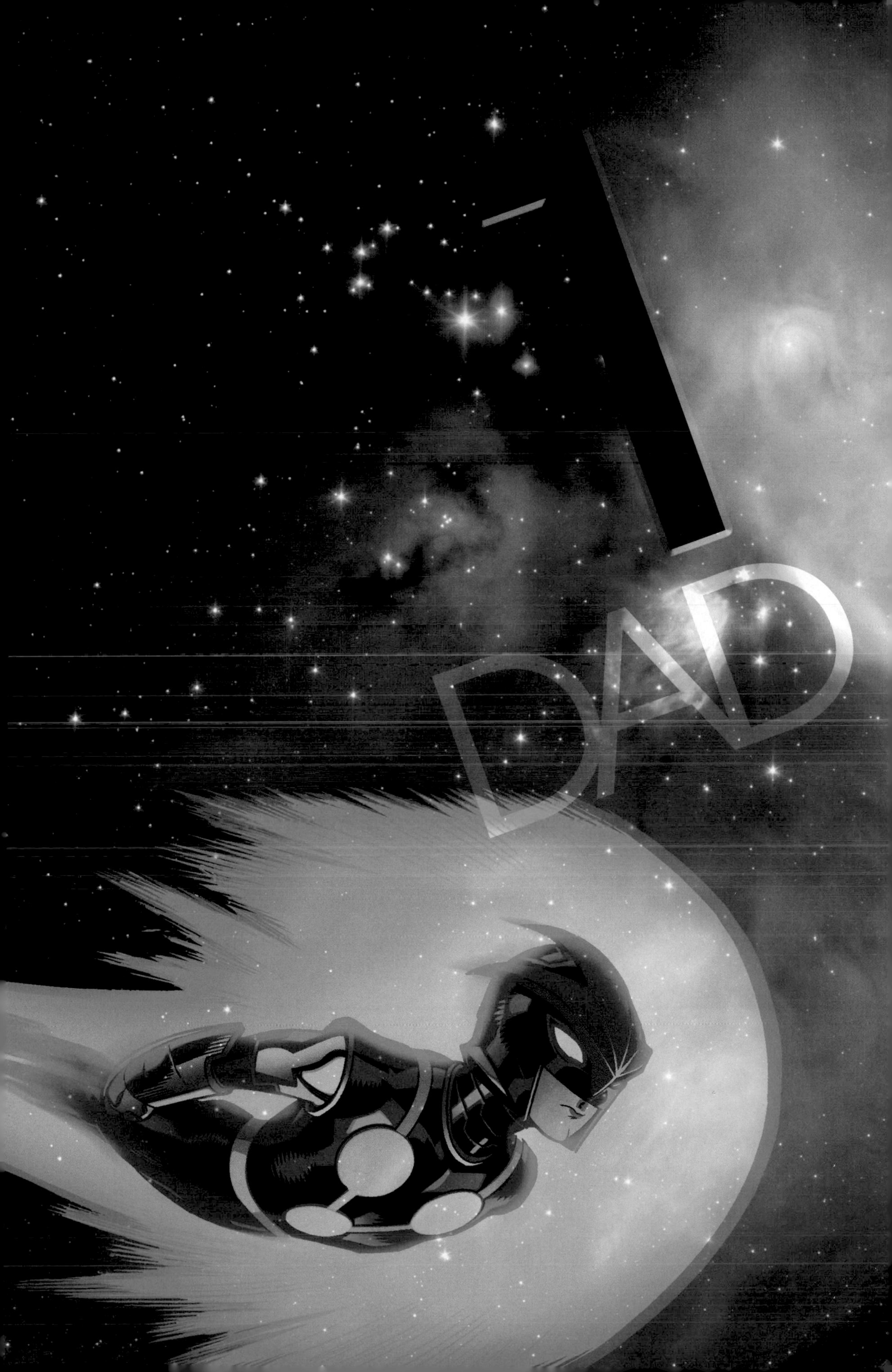
DAD

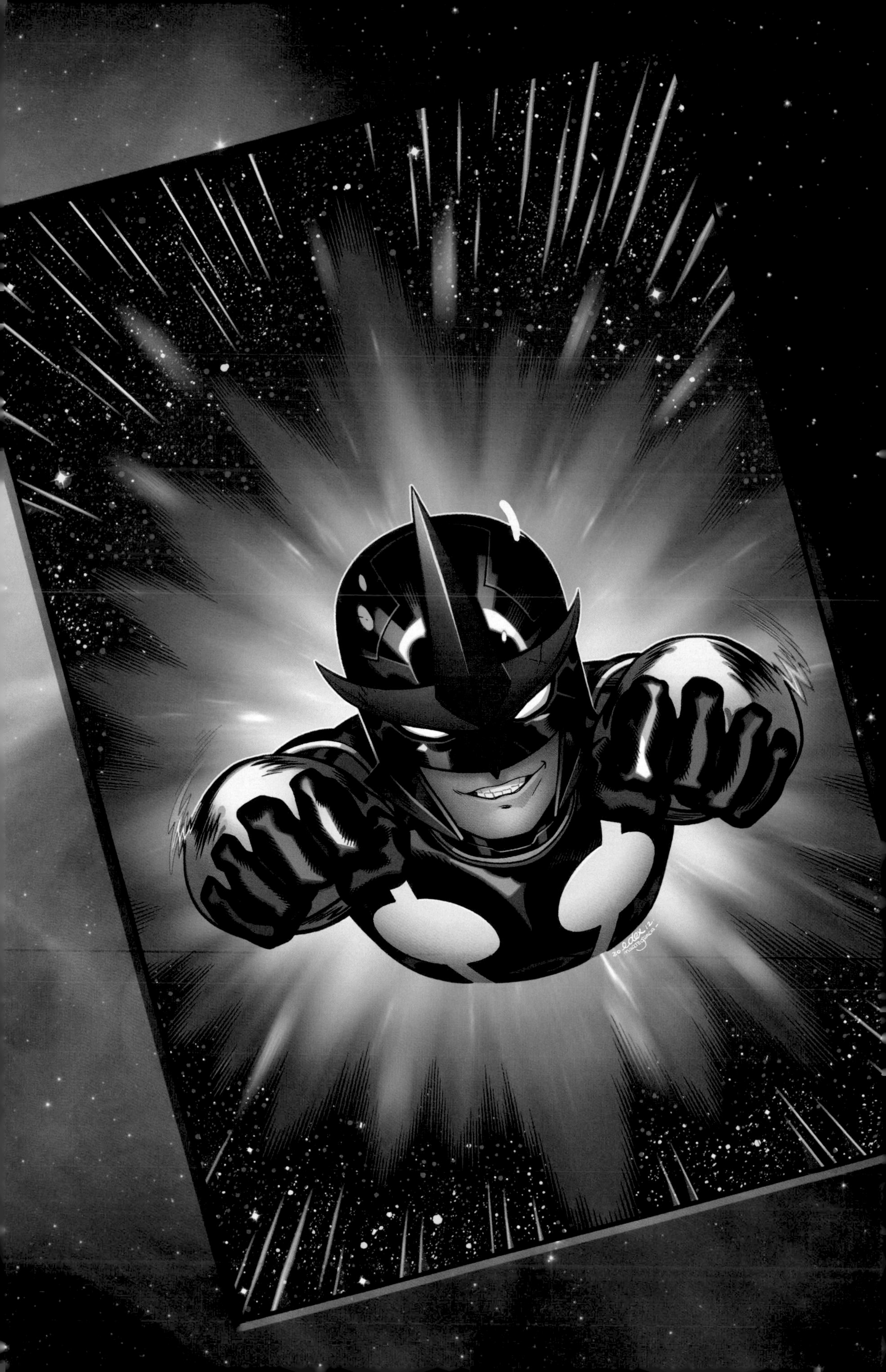

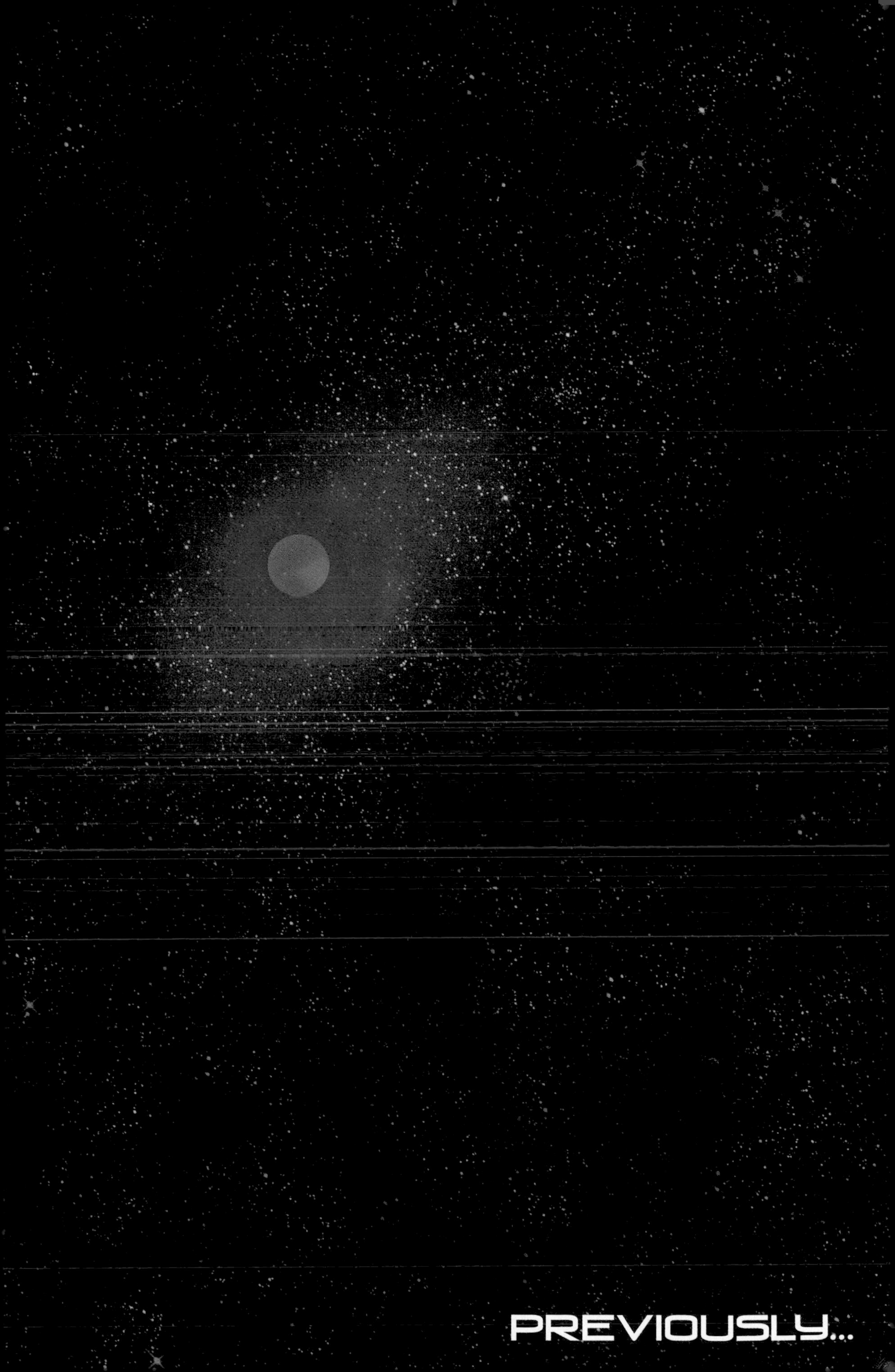

PREVIOUSLY...

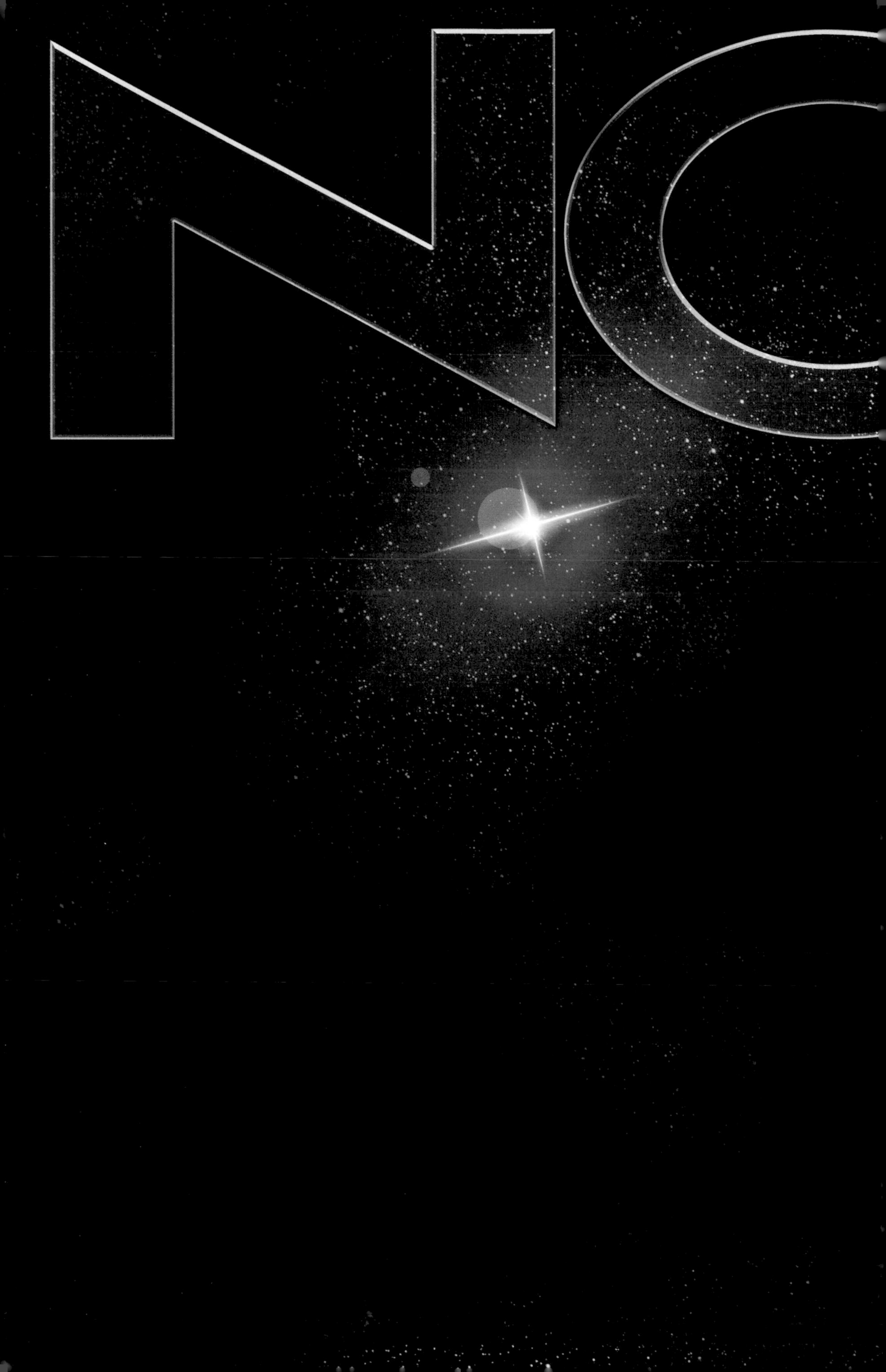

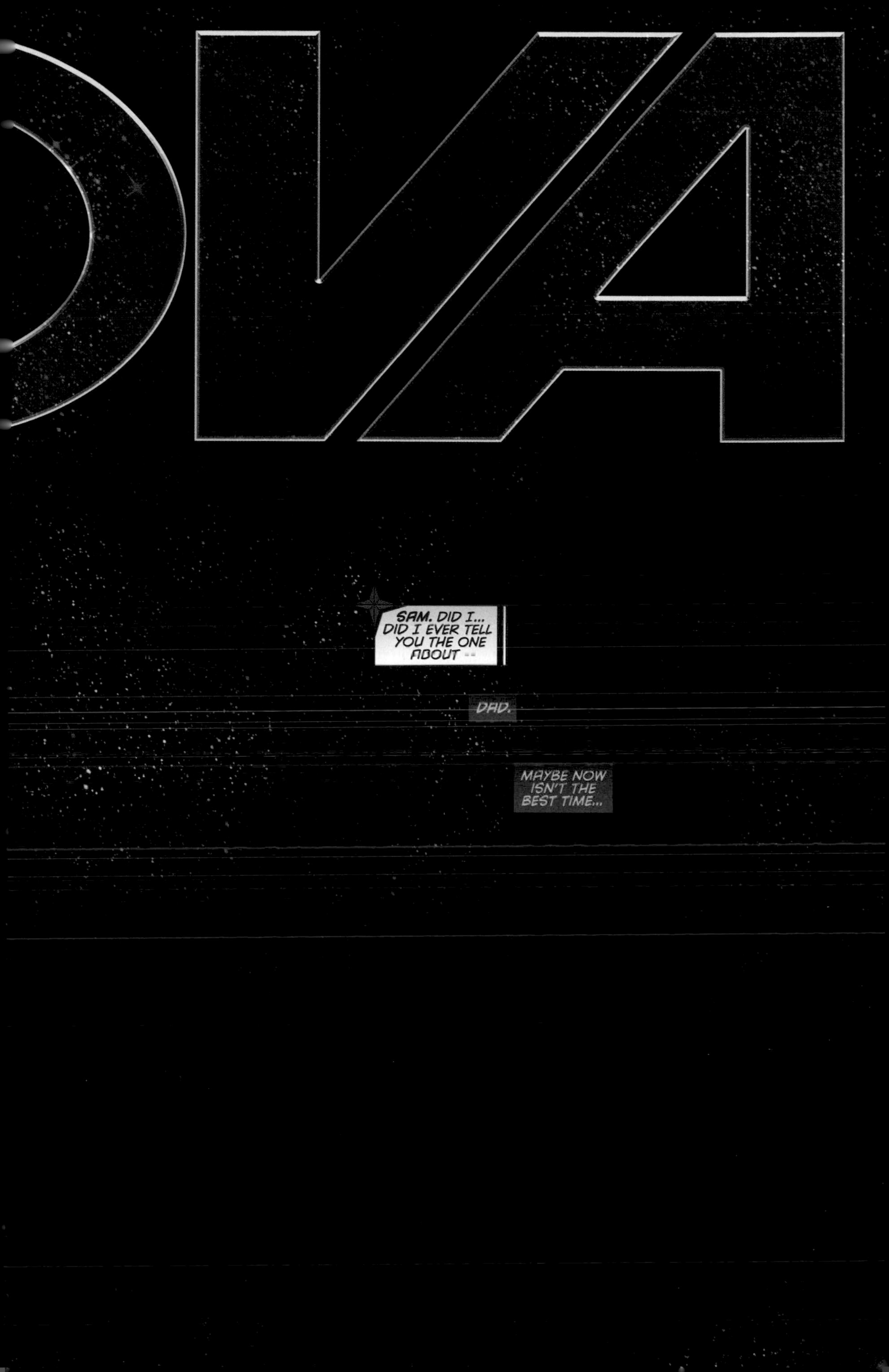
NOVA
SAM. DID I... DID I EVER TELL YOU THE ONE ABOUT --
DAD.
MAYBE NOW ISN'T THE BEST TIME...

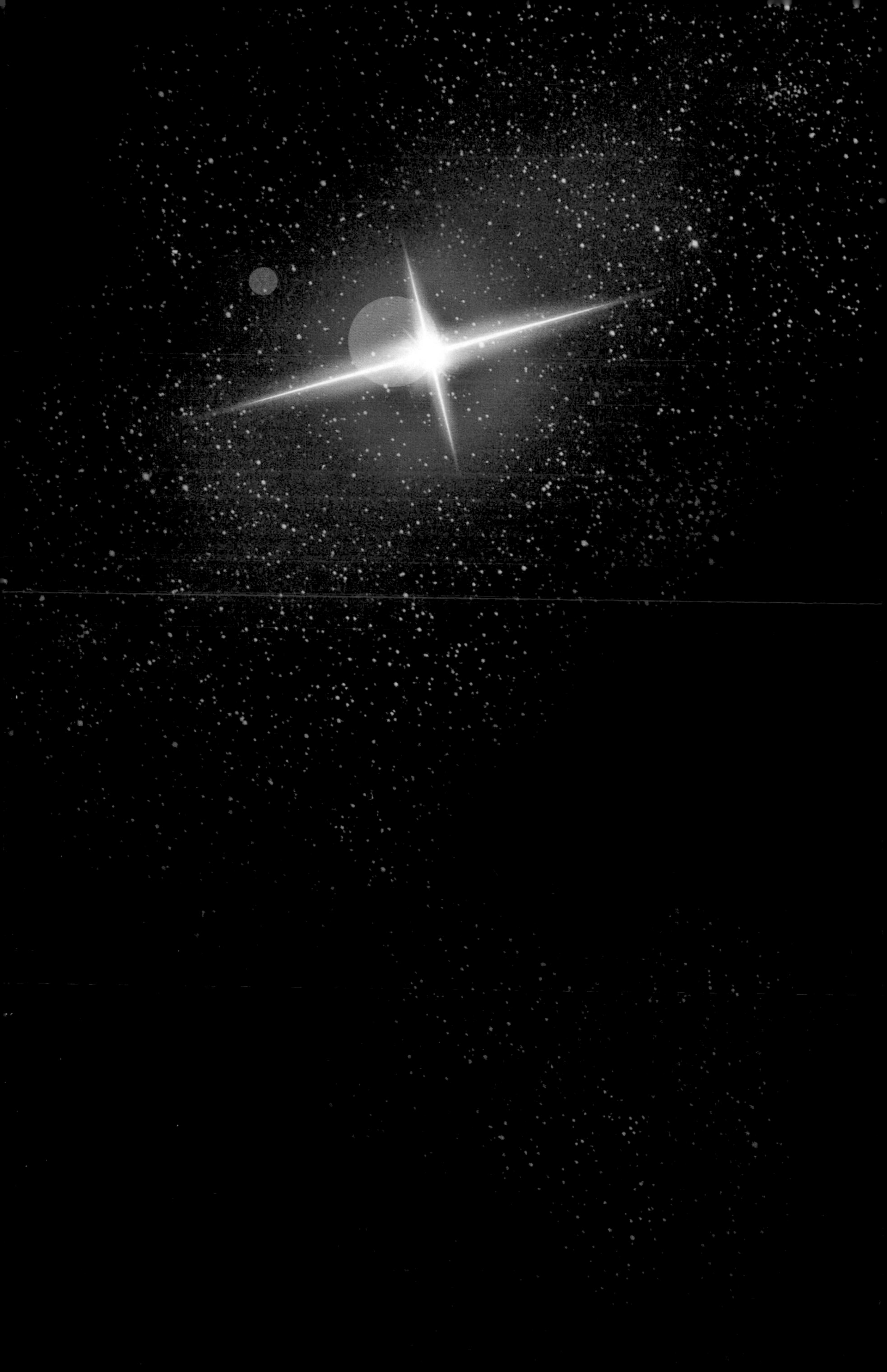

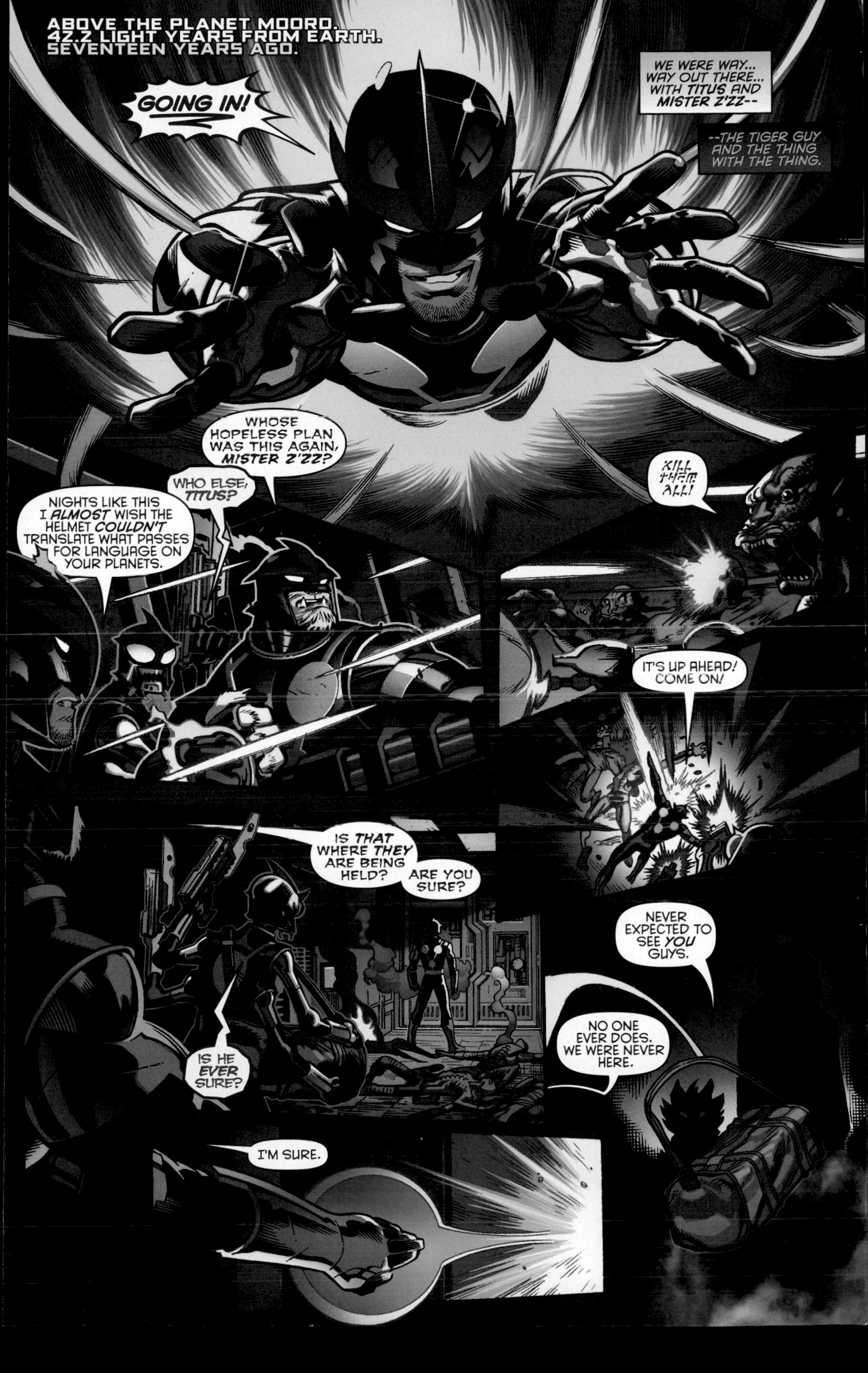
ABOVE THE PLANET MOORD. 42.2 LIGHT YEARS FROM EARTH. SEVENTEEN YEARS AGO.
GOING IN!
WE WERE WAY... WAY OUT THERE... WITH TITUS AND MISTER Z'ZZ--
--THE TIGER GUY AND THE THING WITH THE THING.
WHOSE HOPELESS PLAN WAS THIS AGAIN, MISTER Z'ZZ?
WHO ELSE, TITUS?
NIGHTS LIKE THIS I ALMOST WISH THE HELMET COULDN'T TRANSLATE WHAT PASSES FOR LANGUAGE ON YOUR PLANETS.
KILL THEM ALL!
IT'S UP AHEAD! COME ON!
IS THAT WHERE THEY ARE BEING HELD?
ARE YOU SURE?
IS HE EVER SURE?
NEVER EXPECTED TO SEE YOU GUYS.
NO ONE EVER DOES. WE WERE NEVER HERE.
I'M SURE.

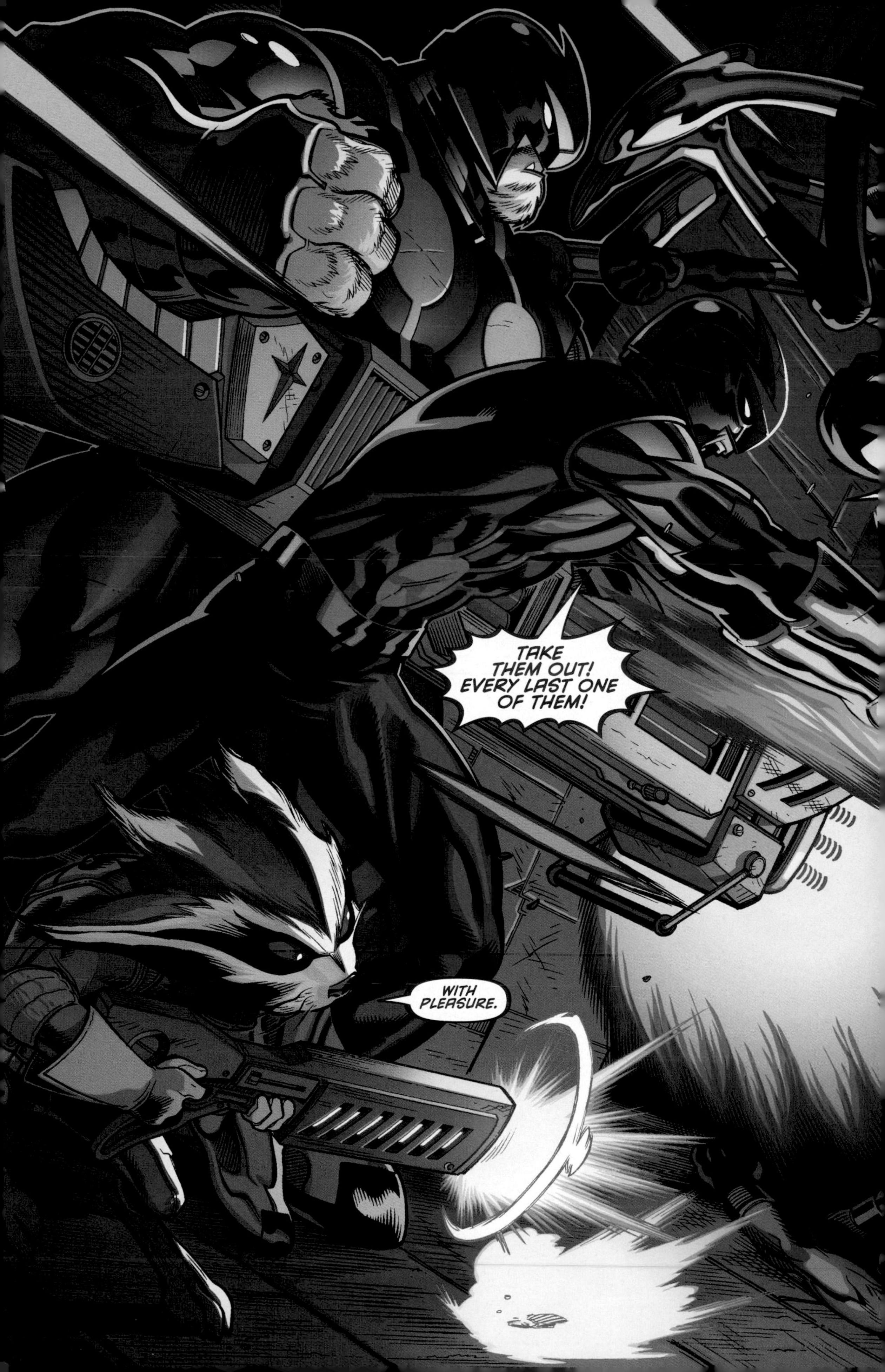
TAKE THEM OUT! EVERY LAST ONE OF THEM!
WITH PLEASURE.

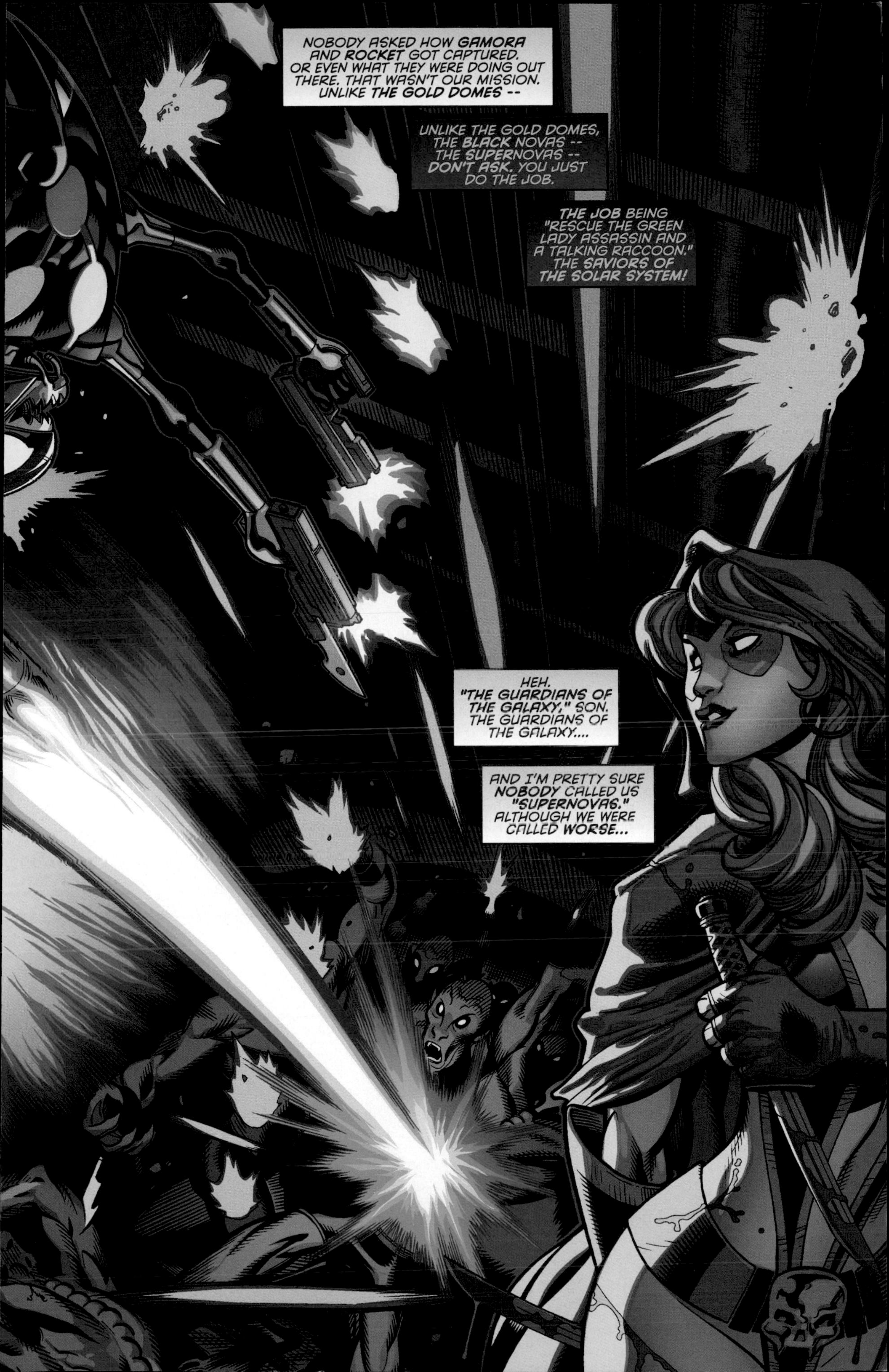
NOBODY ASKED HOW GAMORA AND ROCKET GOT CAPTURED. OR EVEN WHAT THEY WERE DOING OUT THERE. THAT WASN'T OUR MISSION. UNLIKE THE GOLD DOMES --
UNLIKE THE GOLD DOMES, THE BLACK NOVAS -- THE SUPERNOVAS -- DON'T ASK. YOU JUST DO THE JOB.
THE JOB BEING "RESCUE THE GREEN LADY ASSASSIN AND A TALKING RACCOON." THE SAVIORS OF THE SOLAR SYSTEM!
HEH. "THE GUARDIANS OF THE GALAXY," SON. THE GUARDIANS OF THE GALAXY....
AND I'M PRETTY SURE NOBODY CALLED US "SUPERNOVAS." ALTHOUGH WE WERE CALLED WORSE...

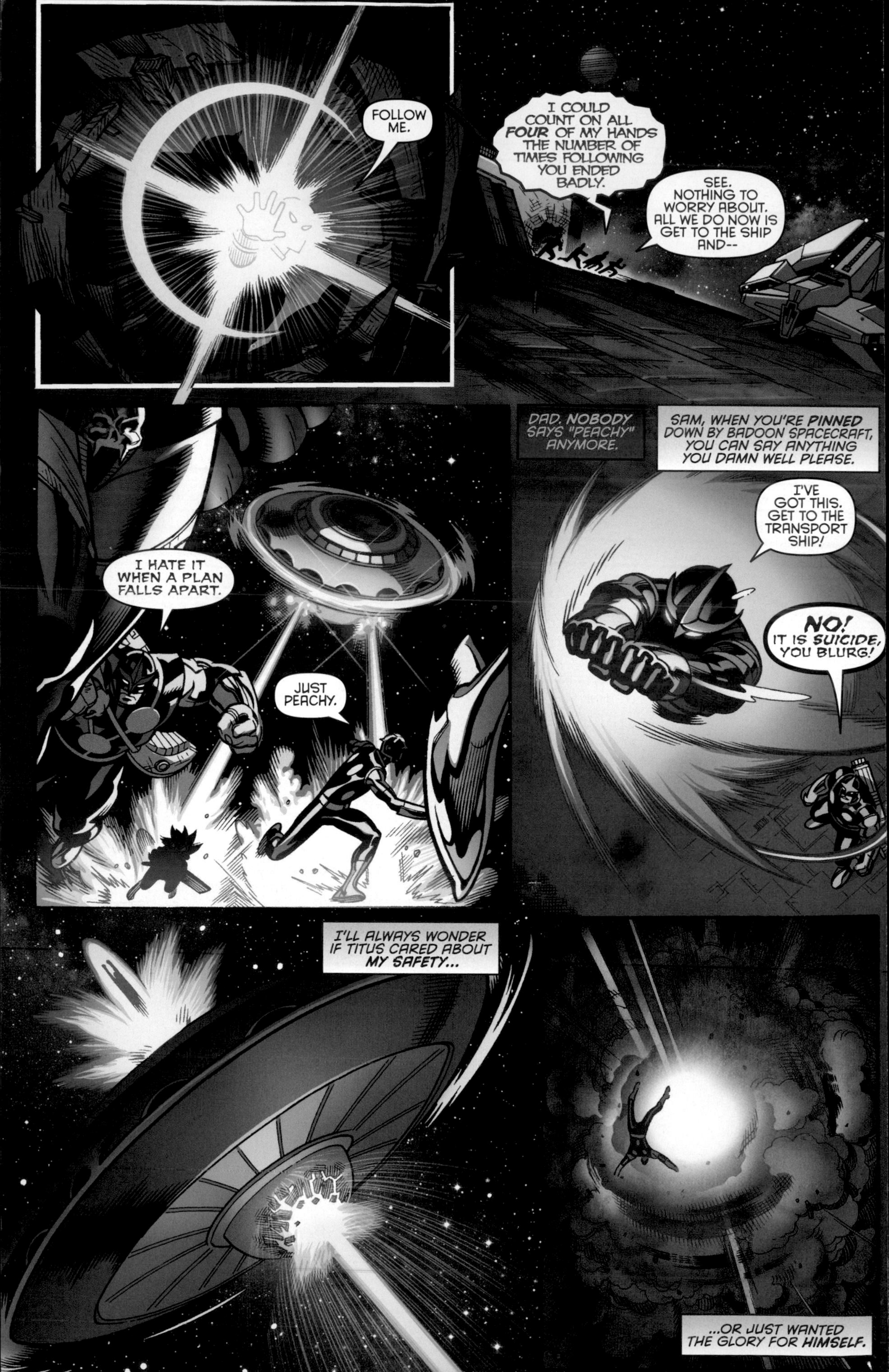
FOLLOW ME.
I COULD COUNT ON ALL FOUR OF MY HANDS THE NUMBER OF TIMES FOLLOWING YOU ENDED BADLY.
SEE. NOTHING TO WORRY ABOUT. ALL WE DO NOW IS GET TO THE SHIP AND--
I HATE IT WHEN A PLAN FALLS APART.
JUST PEACHY.
DAD. NOBODY SAYS "PEACHY" ANYMORE.
SAM, WHEN YOU'RE PINNED DOWN BY BADOON SPACECRAFT, YOU CAN SAY ANYTHING YOU DAMN WELL PLEASE.
I'VE GOT THIS. GET TO THE TRANSPORT SHIP!
NO! IT IS SUICIDE, YOU BLURG!
I'LL ALWAYS WONDER IF TITUS CARED ABOUT MY SAFETY...
...OR JUST WANTED THE GLORY FOR HIMSELF.

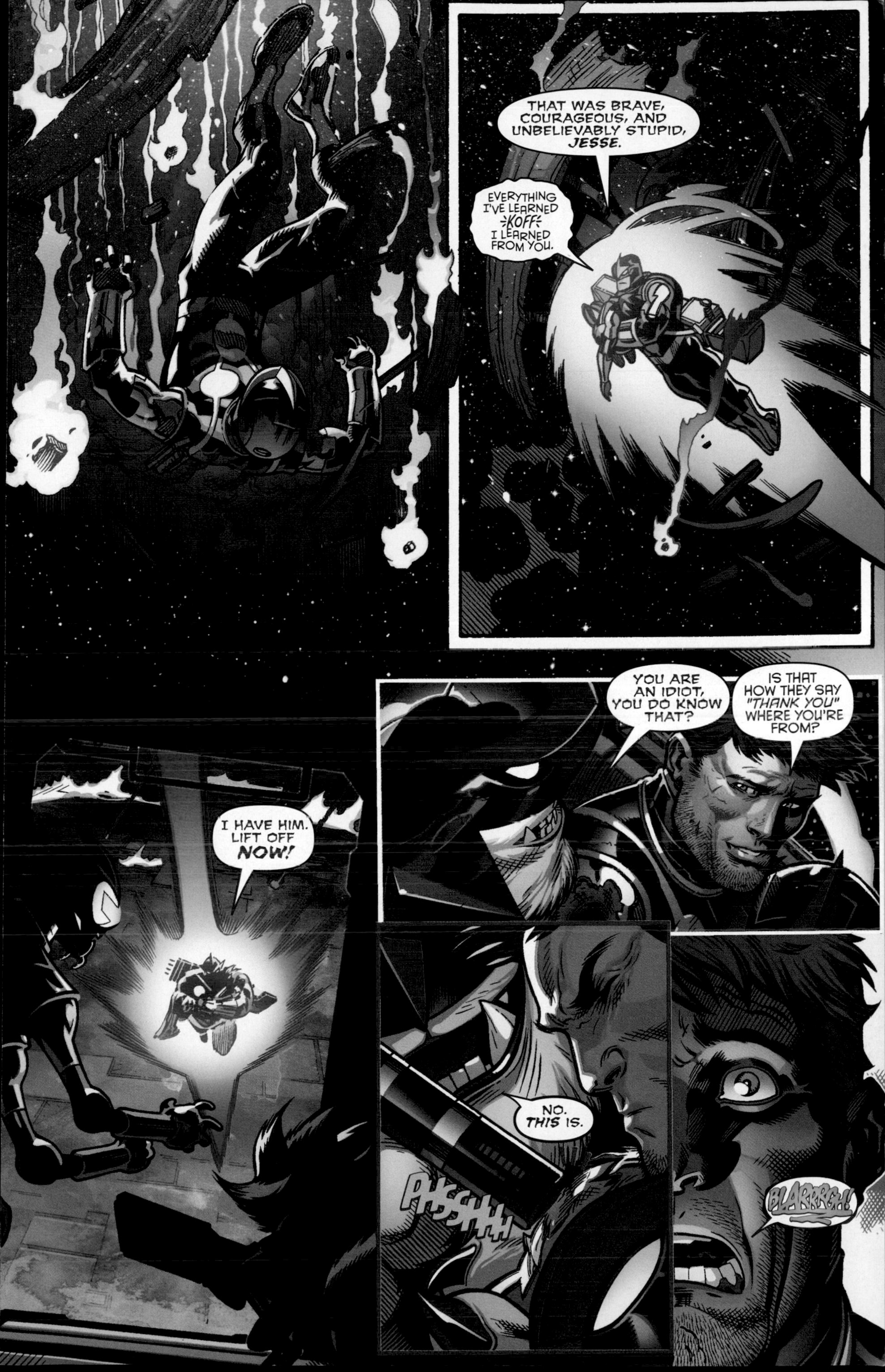
THAT WAS BRAVE, COURAGEOUS, AND UNBELIEVABLY STUPID, JESSE.
EVERYTHING I'VE LEARNED *KOFF* I LEARNED FROM YOU.
YOU ARE AN IDIOT, YOU DO KNOW THAT?
IS THAT HOW THEY SAY "THANK YOU" WHERE YOU'RE FROM?
I HAVE HIM. LIFT OFF NOW!
NO. THIS IS.
PHSSHHH
BLARRGH!

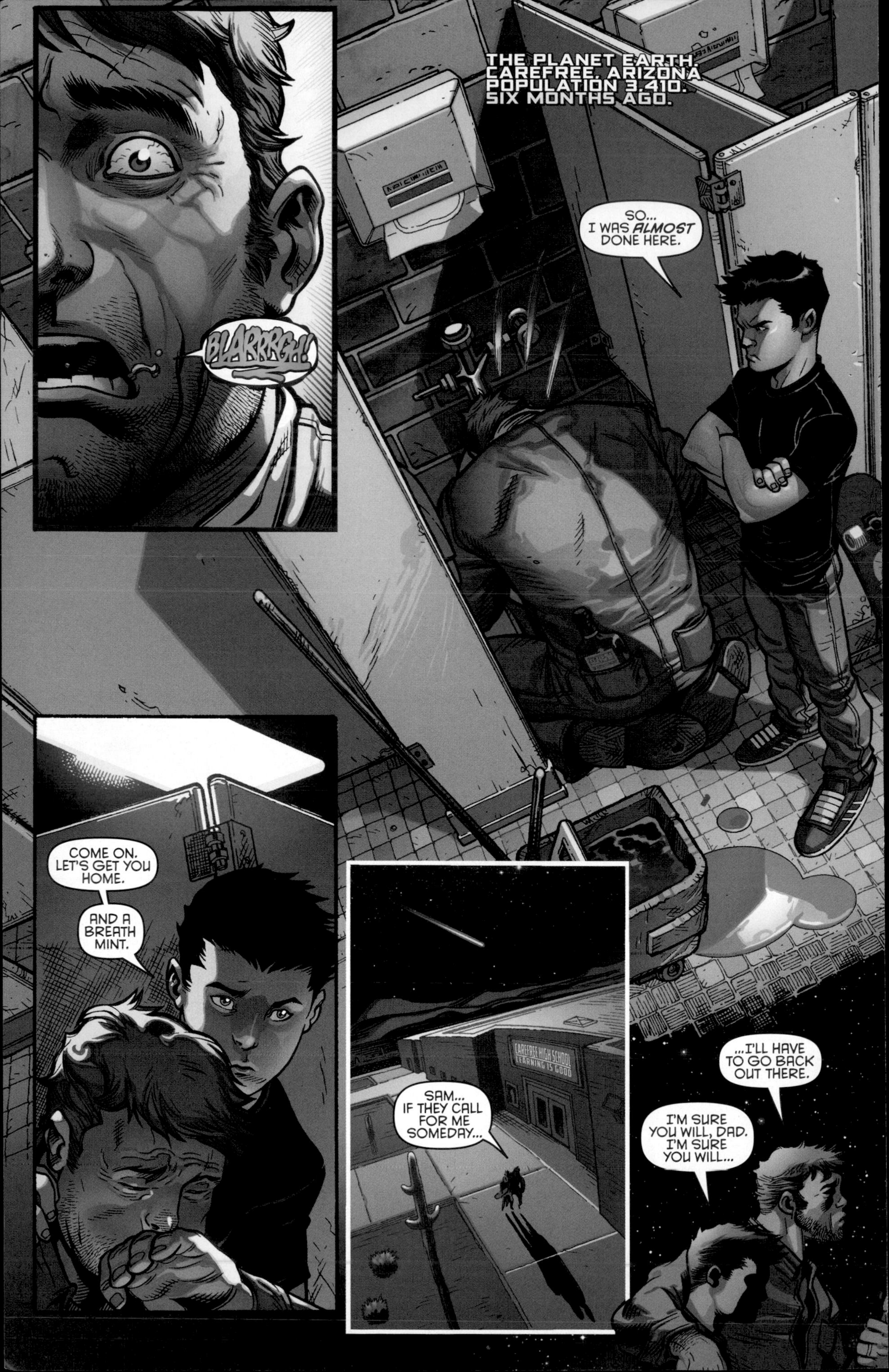
THE PLANET EARTH. CAREFREE, ARIZONA POPULATION 3,410. SIX MONTHS AGO.
BLARRRGH!
SO... I WAS ALMOST DONE HERE.
COME ON. LET'S GET YOU HOME.
AND A BREATH MINT.
CAREFREE HIGH SCHOOL LEARNING IS GOOD
SAM... IF THEY CALL FOR ME SOMEDAY...
...I'LL HAVE TO GO BACK OUT THERE.
I'M SURE YOU WILL, DAD. I'M SURE YOU WILL...

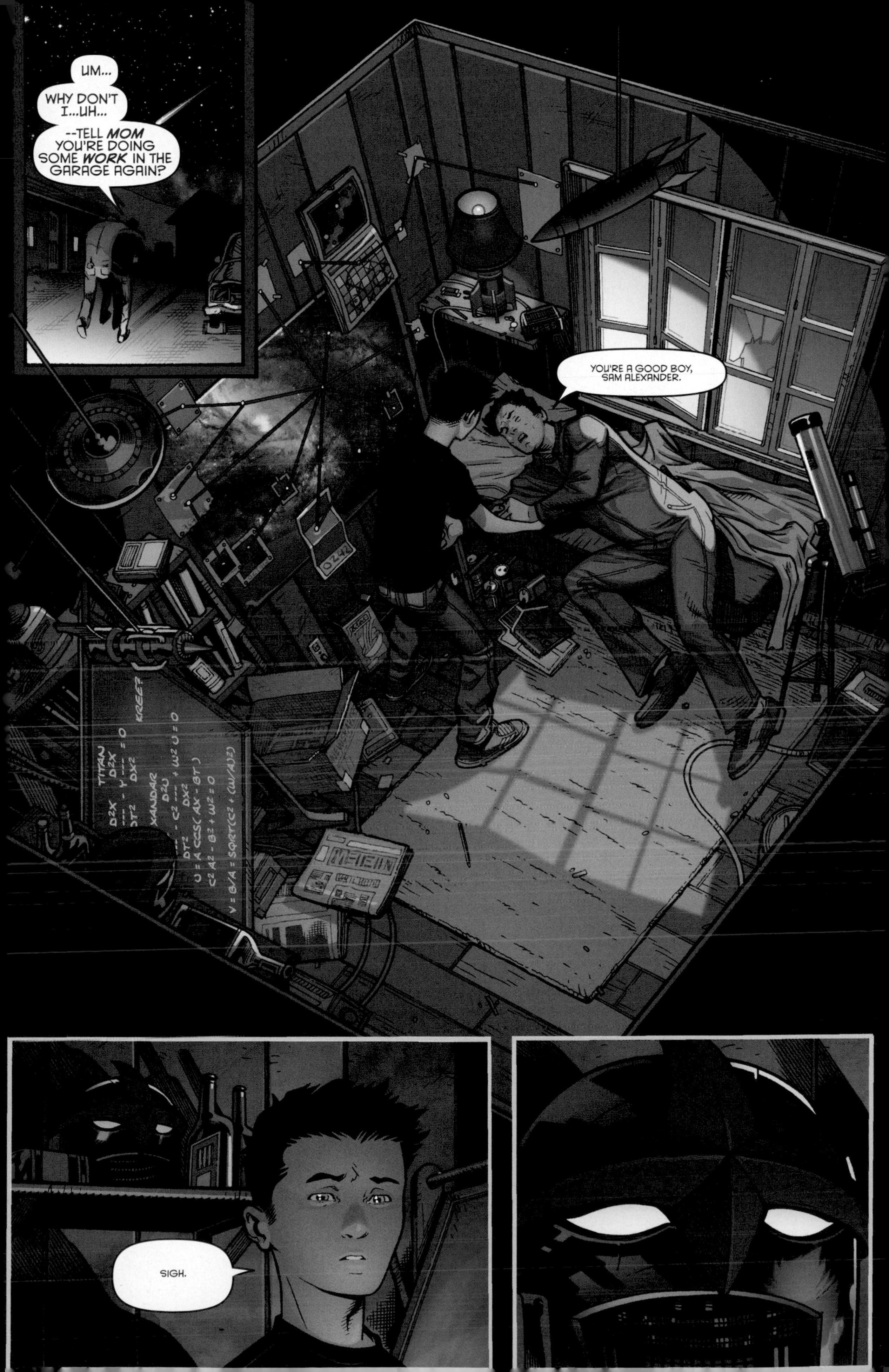
UM...
WHY DON'T I...UH...
--TELL MOM YOU'RE DOING SOME WORK IN THE GARAGE AGAIN?
YOU'RE A GOOD BOY, SAM ALEXANDER.
SIGH.

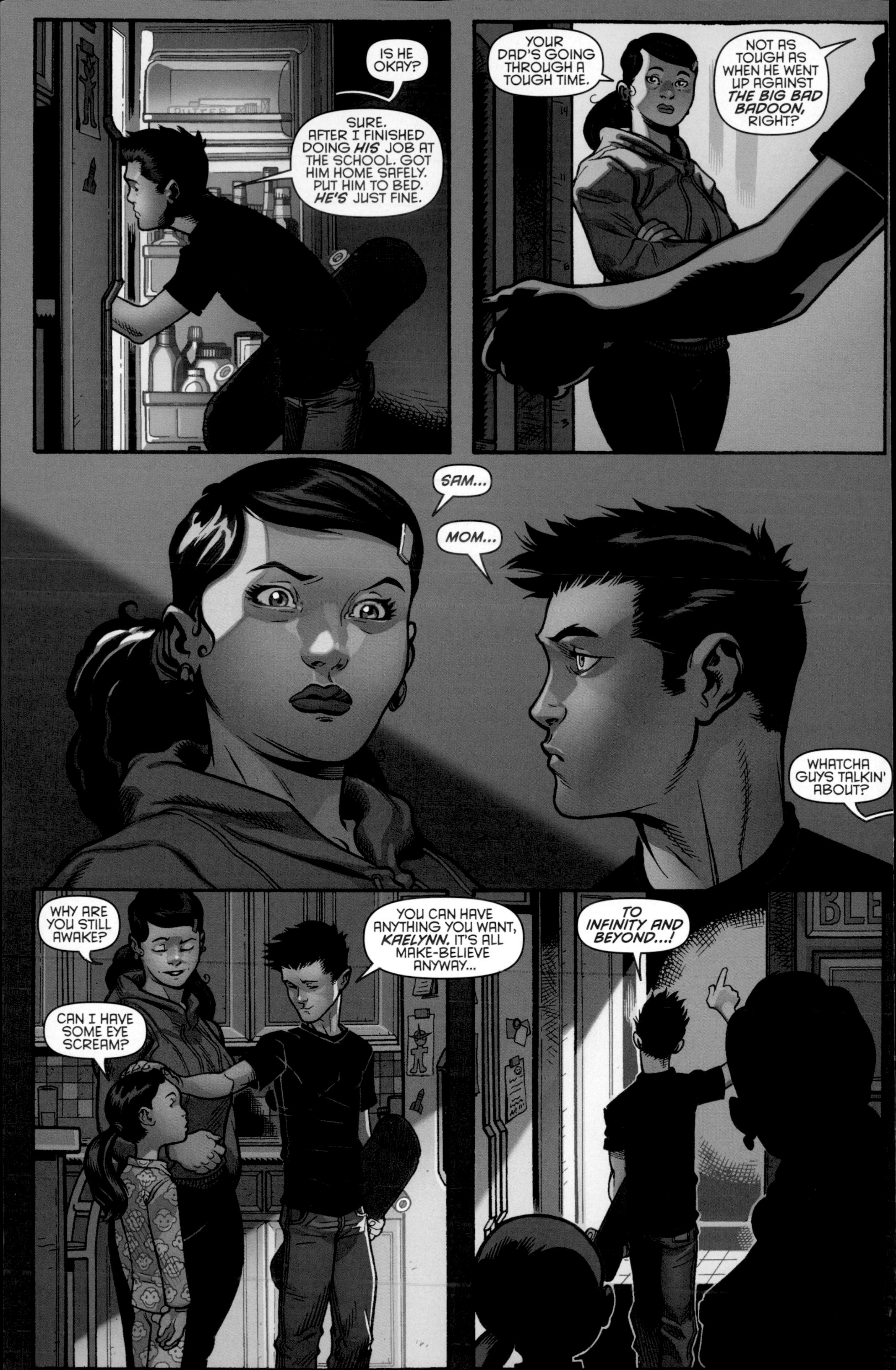
IS HE OKAY?
SURE. AFTER I FINISHED DOING HIS JOB AT THE SCHOOL. GOT HIM HOME SAFELY. PUT HIM TO BED. HE'S JUST FINE.
YOUR DAD'S GOING THROUGH A TOUGH TIME.
NOT AS TOUGH AS WHEN HE WENT UP AGAINST THE BIG BAD BADOON, RIGHT?
SAM...
MOM...
WHATCHA GUYS TALKIN' ABOUT?
WHY ARE YOU STILL AWAKE?
CAN I HAVE SOME EYE SCREAM?
YOU CAN HAVE ANYTHING YOU WANT, KAELYNN. IT'S ALL MAKE-BELIEVE ANYWAY...
TO INFINITY AND BEYOND...!

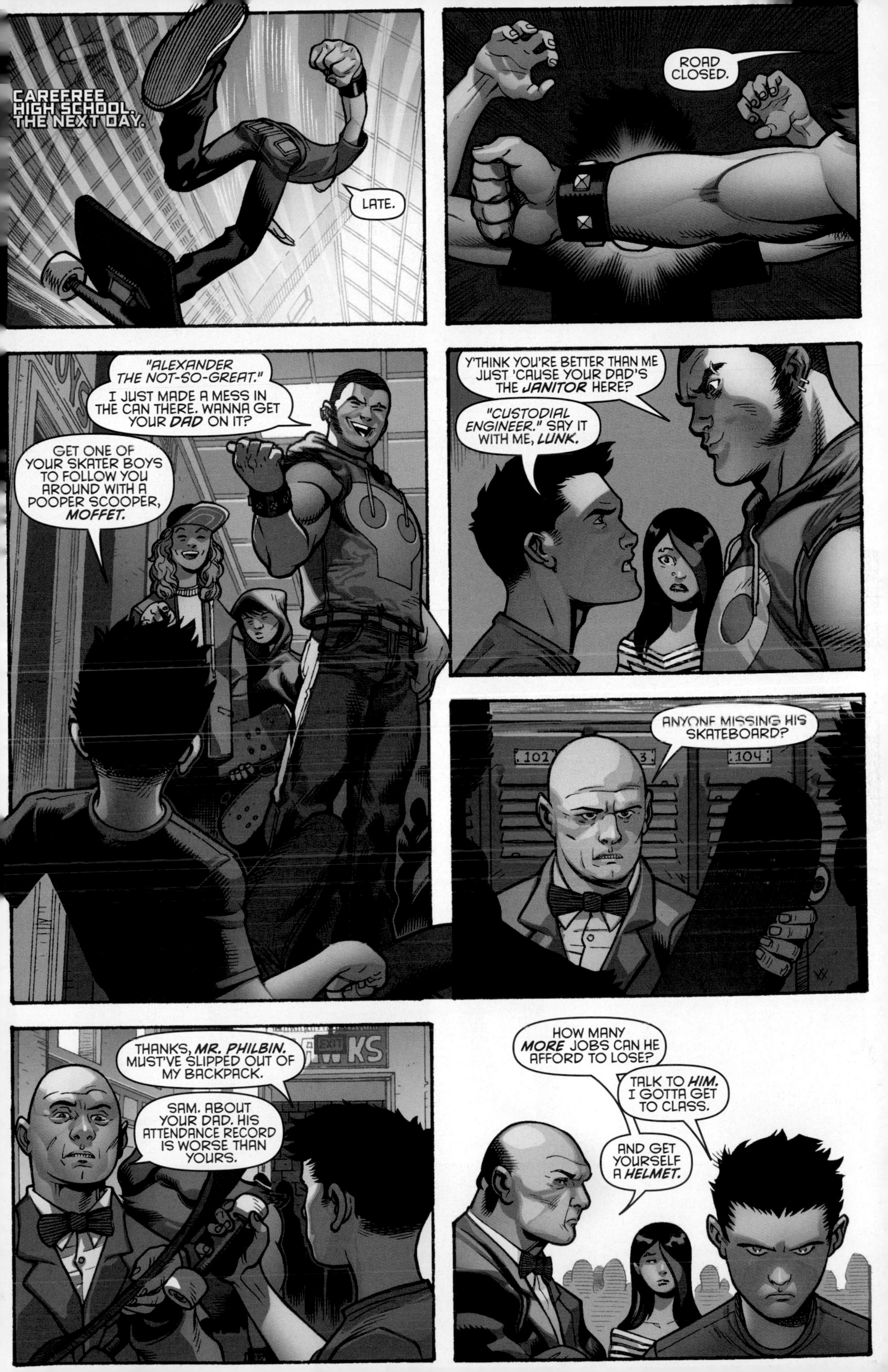
CAREFREE HIGH SCHOOL. THE NEXT DAY.
LATE.
ROAD CLOSED.
"ALEXANDER THE NOT-SO-GREAT." I JUST MADE A MESS IN THE CAN THERE. WANNA GET YOUR DAD ON IT?
GET ONE OF YOUR SKATER BOYS TO FOLLOW YOU AROUND WITH A POOPER SCOOPER, MOFFET.
Y'THINK YOU'RE BETTER THAN ME JUST 'CAUSE YOUR DAD'S THE JANITOR HERE?
"CUSTODIAL ENGINEER." SAY IT WITH ME, LUNK.
ANYONE MISSING HIS SKATEBOARD?
102
104
THANKS, MR. PHILBIN. MUST'VE SLIPPED OUT OF MY BACKPACK.
SAM. ABOUT YOUR DAD. HIS ATTENDANCE RECORD IS WORSE THAN YOURS.
HOW MANY MORE JOBS CAN HE AFFORD TO LOSE?
TALK TO HIM. I GOTTA GET TO CLASS.
AND GET YOURSELF A HELMET.

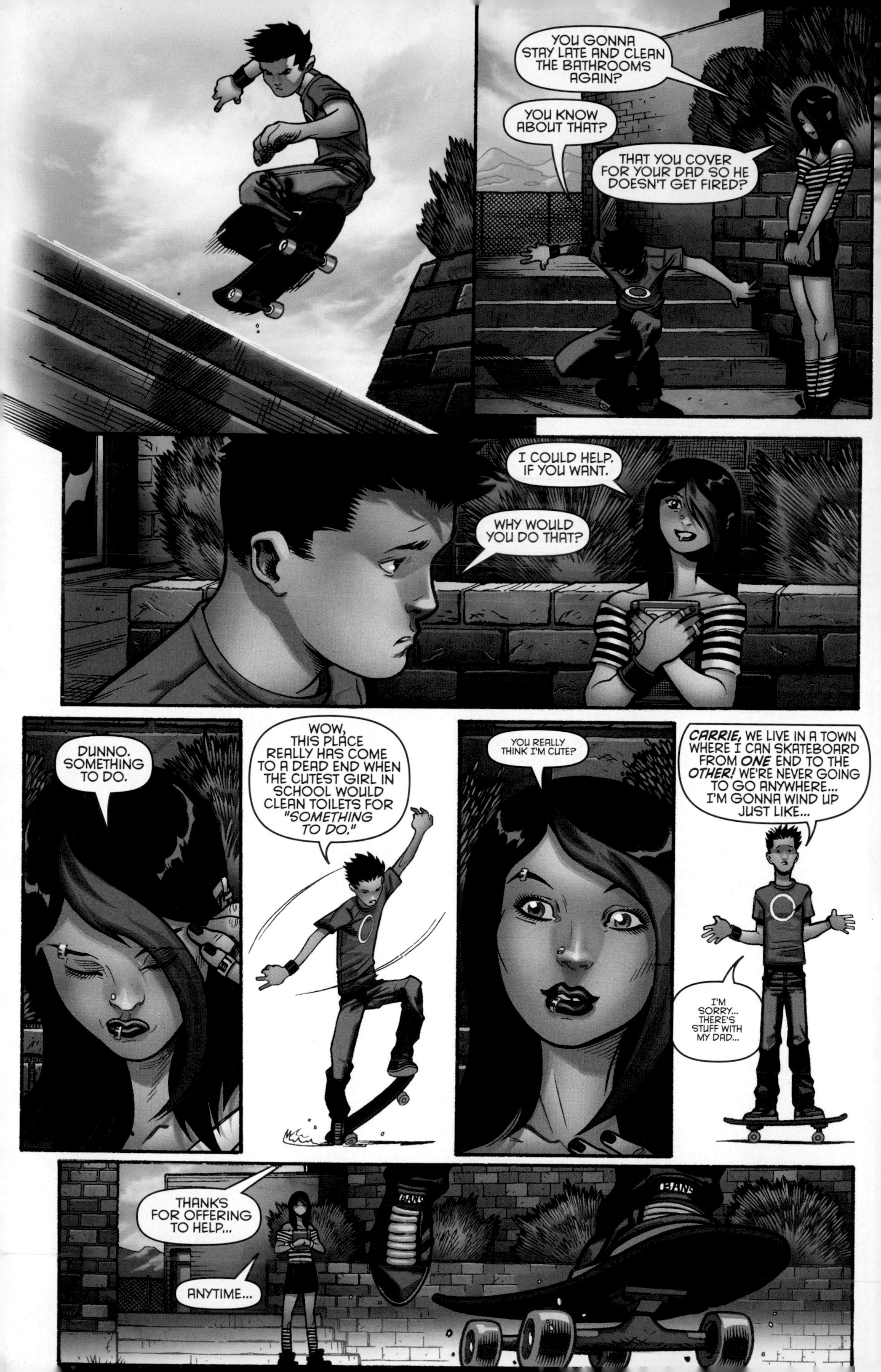
YOU GONNA STAY LATE AND CLEAN THE BATHROOMS AGAIN?
YOU KNOW ABOUT THAT?
THAT YOU COVER FOR YOUR DAD SO HE DOESN'T GET FIRED?
I COULD HELP. IF YOU WANT.
WHY WOULD YOU DO THAT?
DUNNO. SOMETHING TO DO.
WOW, THIS PLACE REALLY HAS COME TO A DEAD END WHEN THE CUTEST GIRL IN SCHOOL WOULD CLEAN TOILETS FOR "SOMETHING TO DO."
YOU REALLY THINK I'M CUTE?
CARRIE, WE LIVE IN A TOWN WHERE I CAN SKATEBOARD FROM ONE END TO THE OTHER! WE'RE NEVER GOING TO GO ANYWHERE... I'M GONNA WIND UP JUST LIKE...
I'M SORRY... THERE'S STUFF WITH MY DAD...
THANKS FOR OFFERING TO HELP...
ANYTIME...

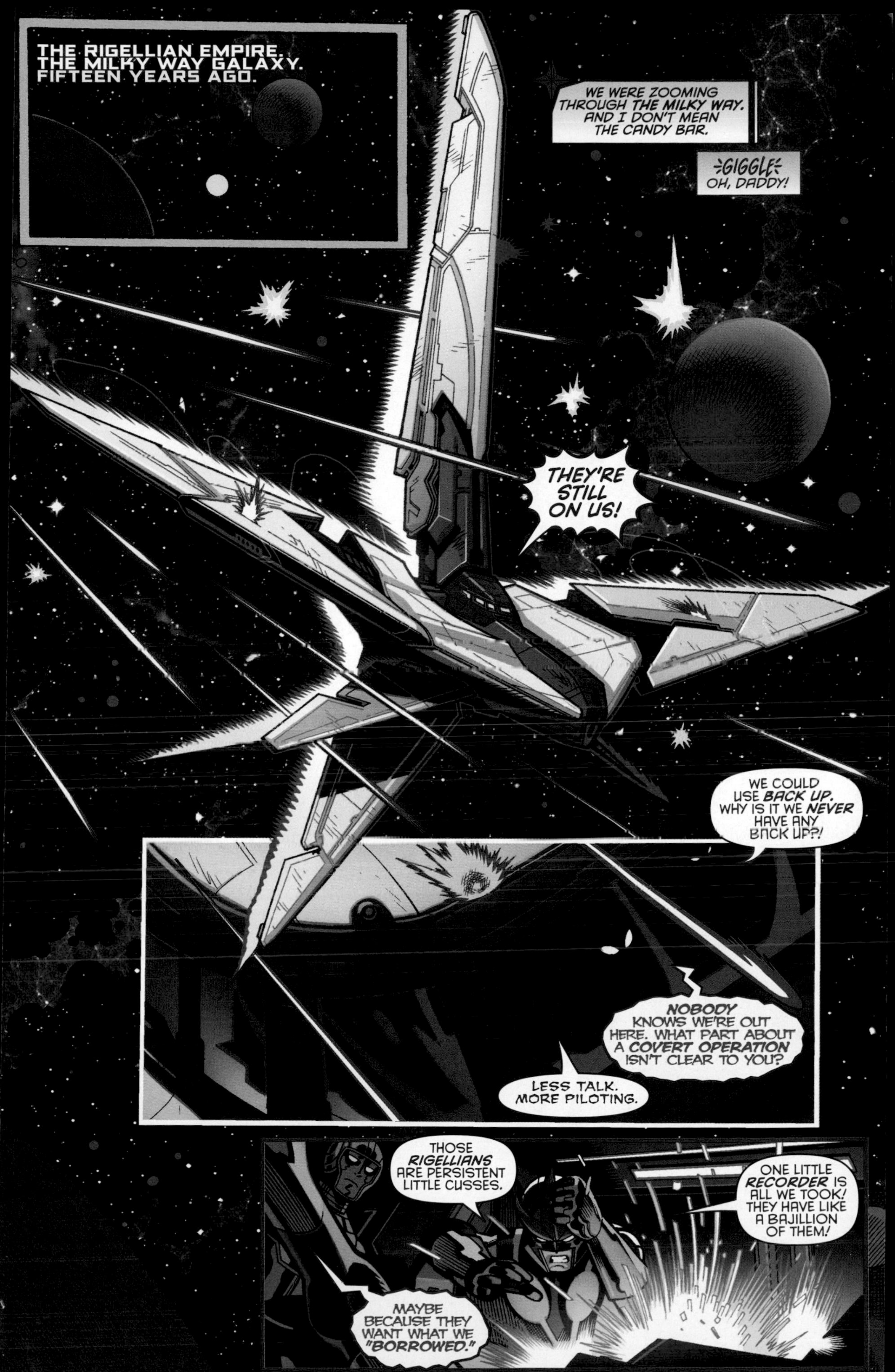
THE RIGELLIAN EMPIRE. THE MILKY WAY GALAXY. FIFTEEN YEARS AGO.
WE WERE ZOOMING THROUGH THE MILKY WAY. AND I DON'T MEAN THE CANDY BAR.
GIGGLE OH, DADDY!
THEY'RE STILL ON US!
WE COULD USE BACK UP. WHY IS IT WE NEVER HAVE ANY BACK UP?!
NOBODY KNOWS WE'RE OUT HERE. WHAT PART ABOUT A COVERT OPERATION ISN'T CLEAR TO YOU?
LESS TALK. MORE PILOTING.
THOSE RIGELLIANS ARE PERSISTENT LITTLE CUSSES.
ONE LITTLE RECORDER IS ALL WE TOOK! THEY HAVE LIKE A BAJILLION OF THEM!
MAYBE BECAUSE THEY WANT WHAT WE "BORROWED."

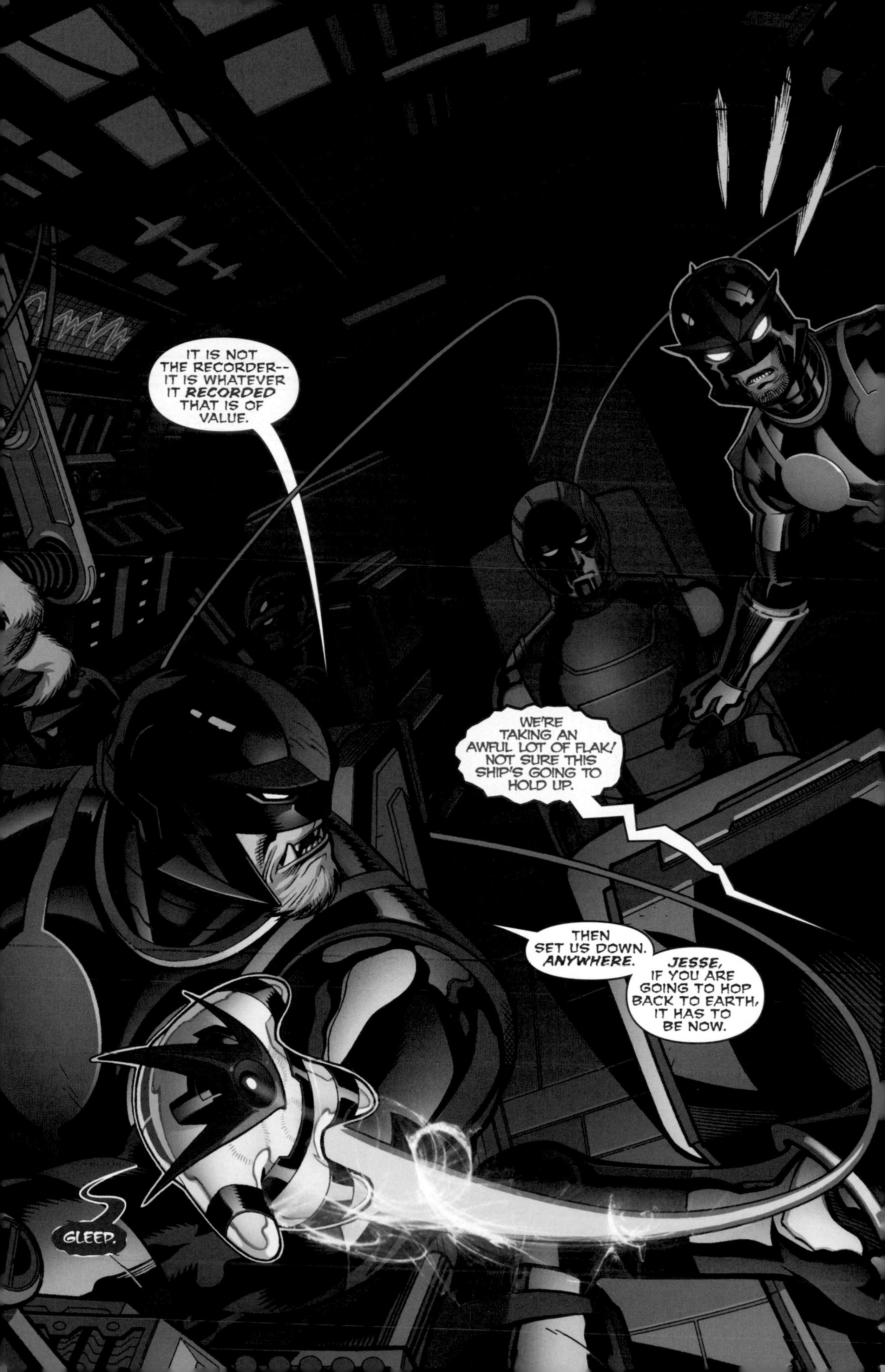
IT IS NOT THE RECORDER-- IT IS WHATEVER IT *RECORDED* THAT IS OF VALUE.
WE'RE TAKING AN AWFUL LOT OF FLAK! NOT SURE THIS SHIP'S GOING TO HOLD UP.
THEN SET US DOWN. *ANYWHERE.*
JESSE, IF YOU ARE GOING TO HOP BACK TO EARTH, IT HAS TO BE NOW.
GLEEP.

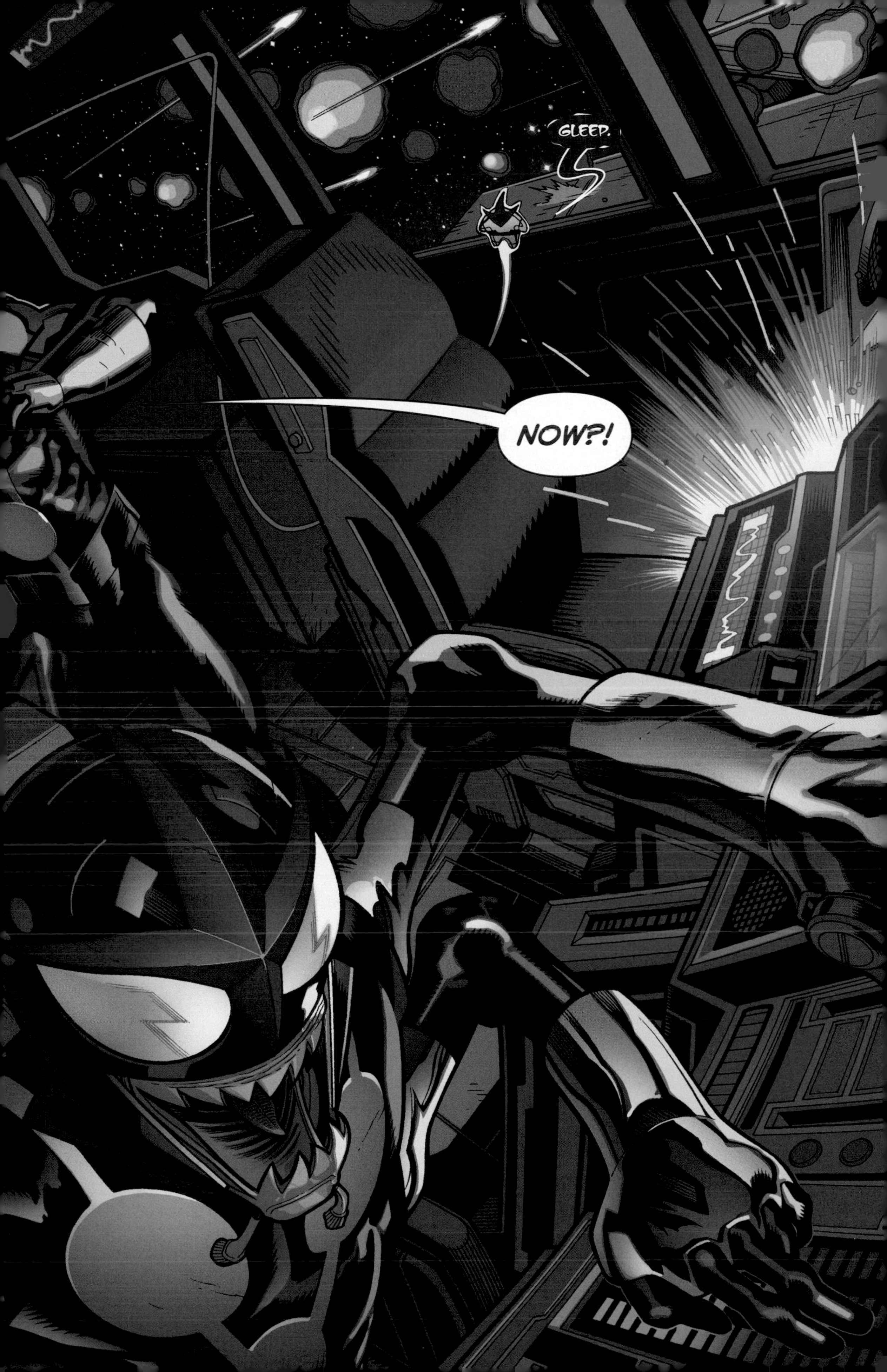
GLEEP.
NOW?!

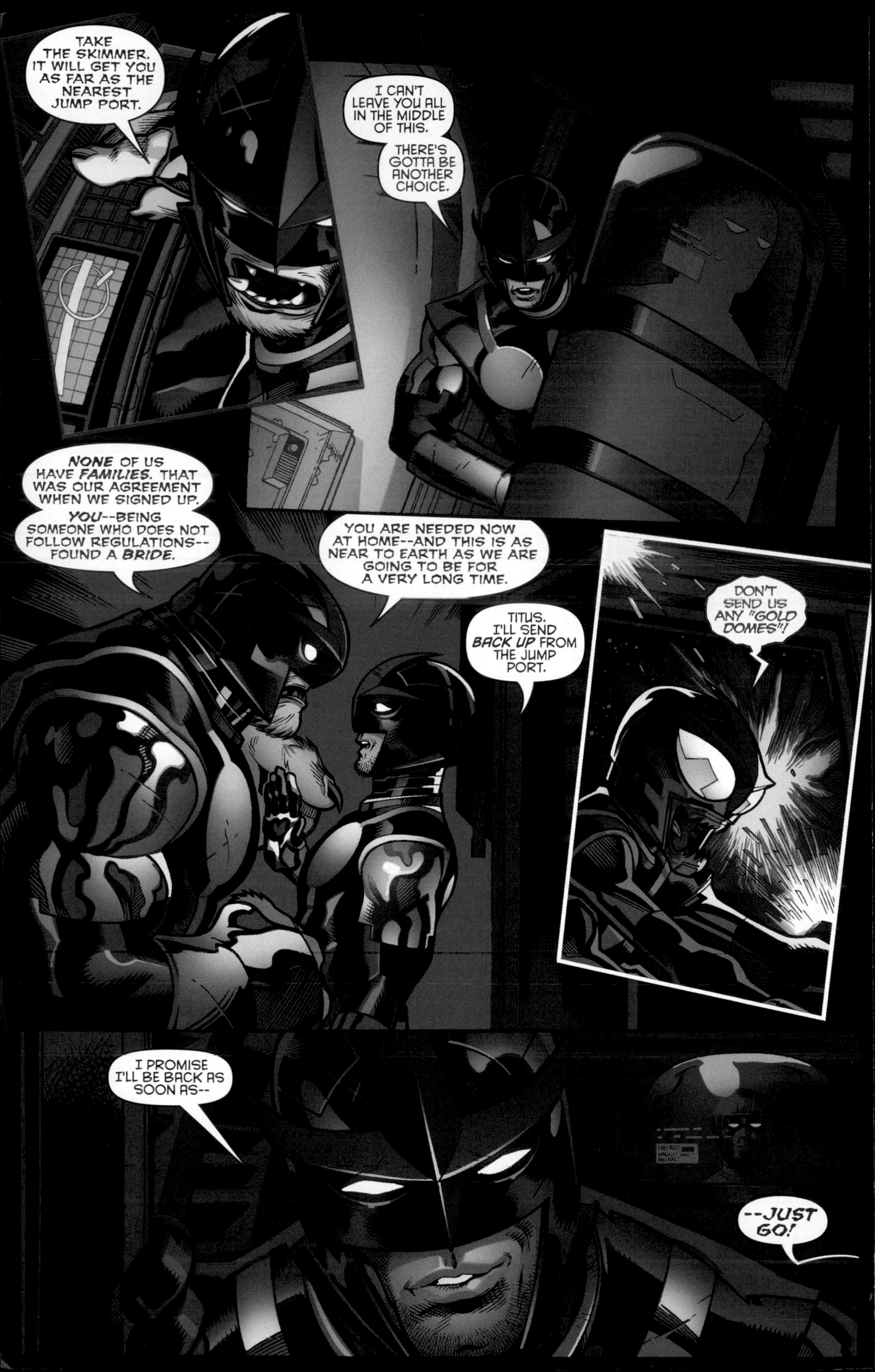
TAKE THE SKIMMER. IT WILL GET YOU AS FAR AS THE NEAREST JUMP PORT.
I CAN'T LEAVE YOU ALL IN THE MIDDLE OF THIS.
THERE'S GOTTA BE ANOTHER CHOICE.
NONE OF US HAVE FAMILIES. THAT WAS OUR AGREEMENT WHEN WE SIGNED UP.
YOU--BEING SOMEONE WHO DOES NOT FOLLOW REGULATIONS--FOUND A BRIDE.
YOU ARE NEEDED NOW AT HOME--AND THIS IS AS NEAR TO EARTH AS WE ARE GOING TO BE FOR A VERY LONG TIME.
TITUS. I'LL SEND BACK UP FROM THE JUMP PORT.
DON'T SEND US ANY "GOLD DOMES"!
I PROMISE I'LL BE BACK AS SOON AS--
--JUST GO!

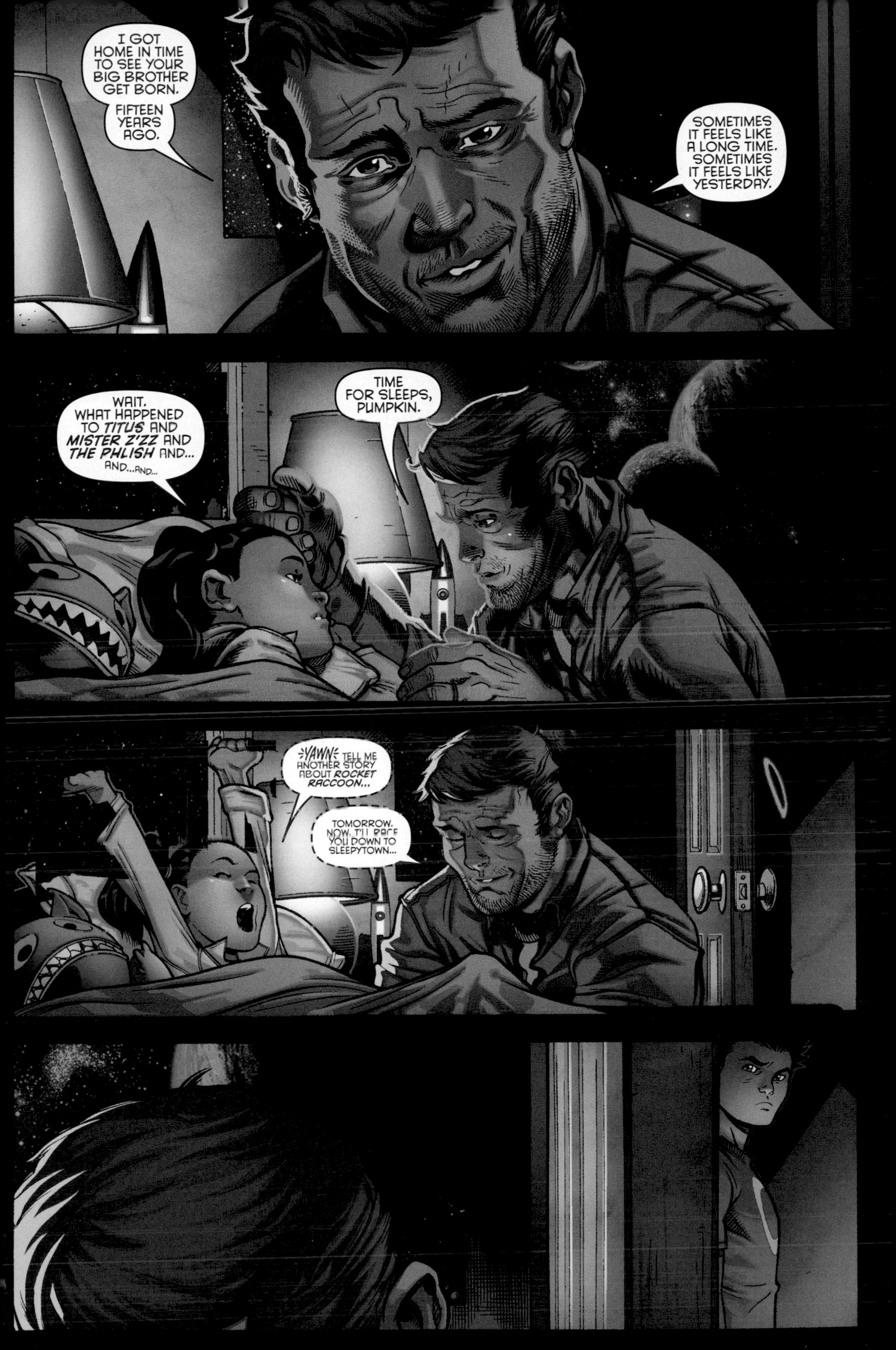
I GOT HOME IN TIME TO SEE YOUR BIG BROTHER GET BORN.
FIFTEEN YEARS AGO.
SOMETIMES IT FEELS LIKE A LONG TIME. SOMETIMES IT FEELS LIKE YESTERDAY.
WAIT. WHAT HAPPENED TO TITUS AND MISTER Z'ZZ AND THE PHLISH AND... AND...AND...
TIME FOR SLEEPS, PUMPKIN.
YAWN! TELL ME ANOTHER STORY ABOUT ROCKET RACCOON...
TOMORROW. NOW, I'LL RACE YOU DOWN TO SLEEPYTOWN...

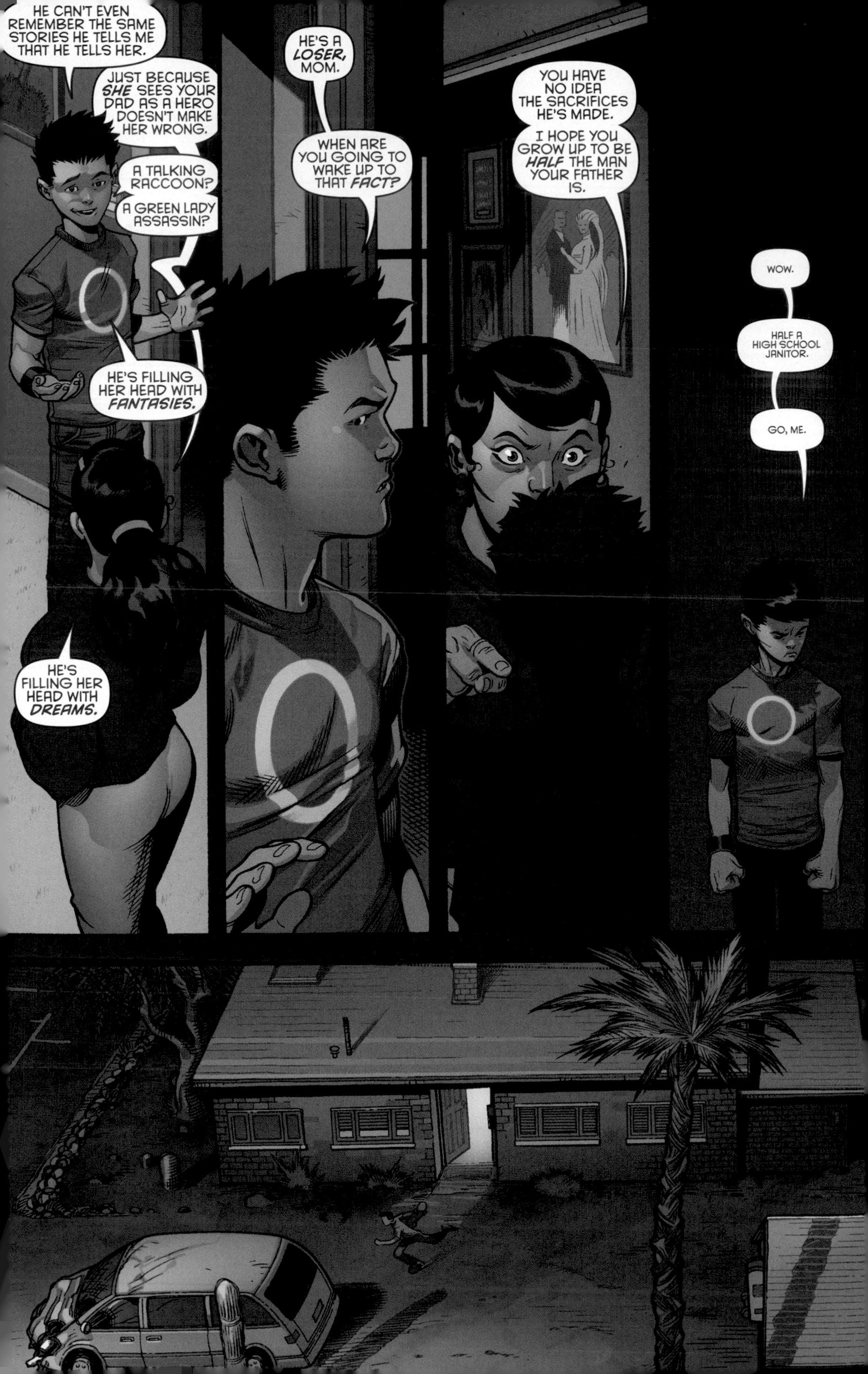
HE CAN'T EVEN REMEMBER THE SAME STORIES HE TELLS ME THAT HE TELLS HER.
JUST BECAUSE SHE SEES YOUR DAD AS A HERO DOESN'T MAKE HER WRONG.
A TALKING RACCOON?
A GREEN LADY ASSASSIN?
HE'S FILLING HER HEAD WITH FANTASIES.
HE'S FILLING HER HEAD WITH DREAMS.
HE'S A LOSER, MOM.
WHEN ARE YOU GOING TO WAKE UP TO THAT FACT?
YOU HAVE NO IDEA THE SACRIFICES HE'S MADE.
I HOPE YOU GROW UP TO BE HALF THE MAN YOUR FATHER IS.
WOW.
HALF A HIGH SCHOOL JANITOR.
GO, ME.

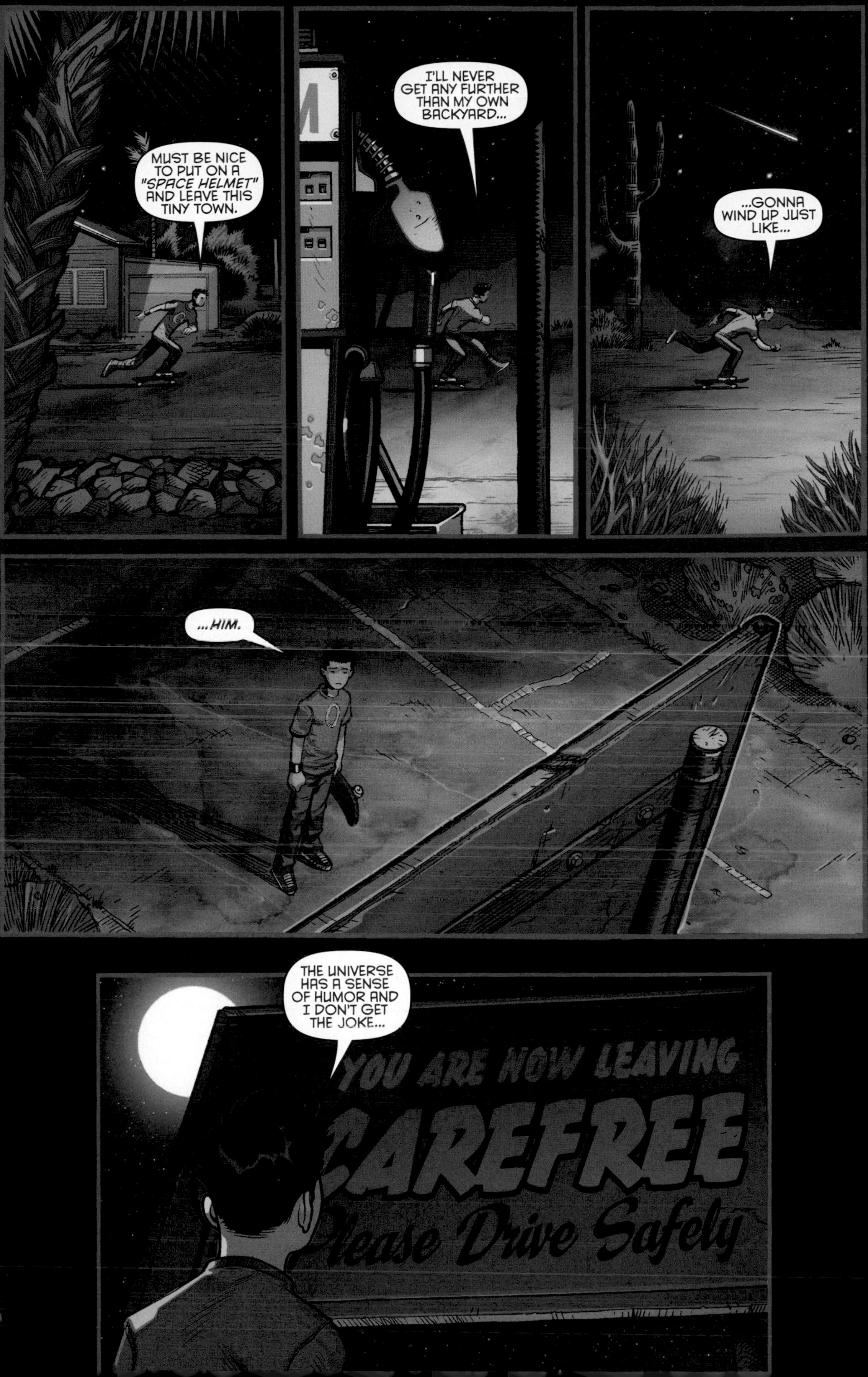
MUST BE NICE TO PUT ON A "SPACE HELMET" AND LEAVE THIS TINY TOWN.
I'LL NEVER GET ANY FURTHER THAN MY OWN BACKYARD...
...GONNA WIND UP JUST LIKE...
...HIM.
THE UNIVERSE HAS A SENSE OF HUMOR AND I DON'T GET THE JOKE...
YOU ARE NOW LEAVING
CAREFREE
Please Drive Safely

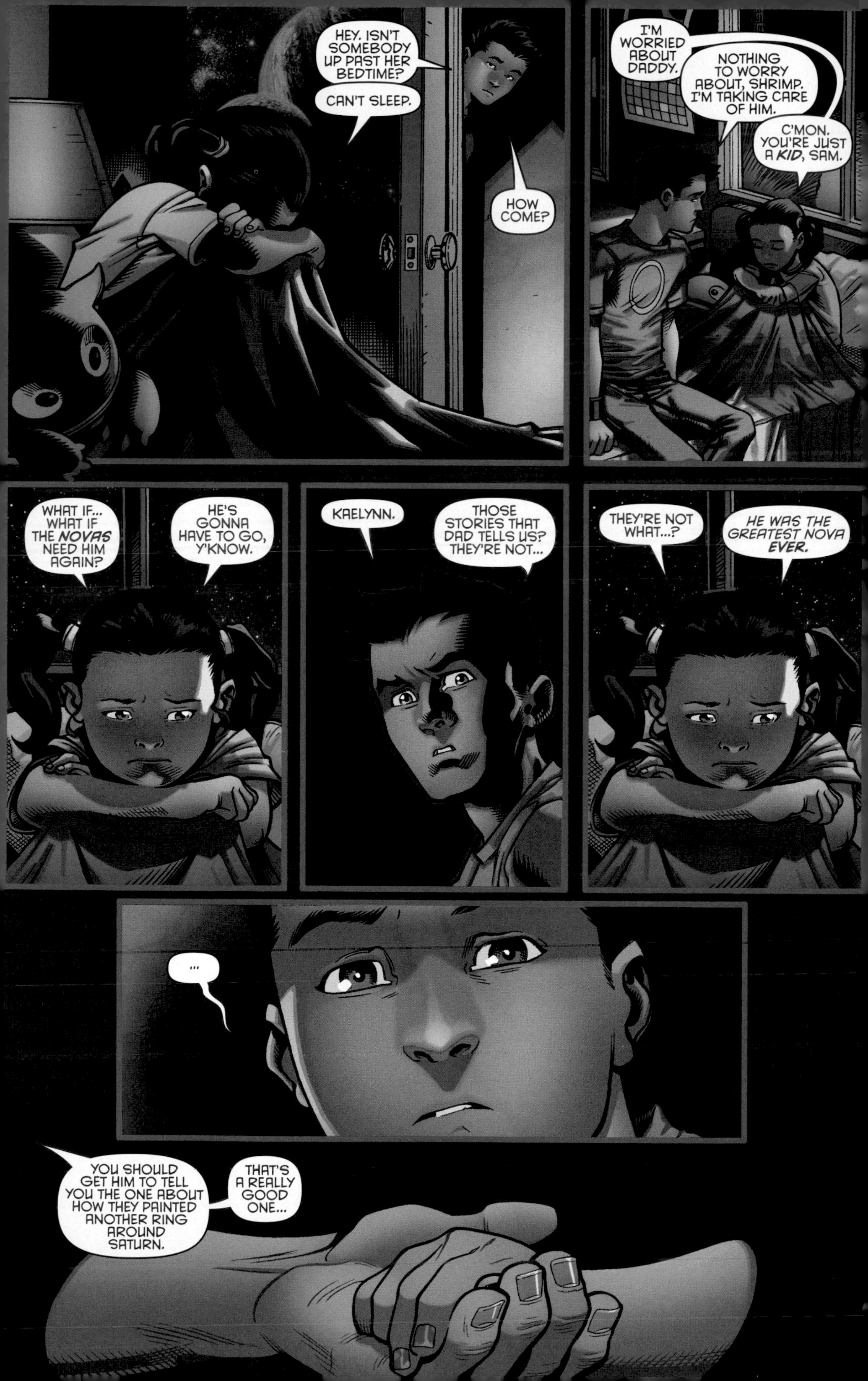
HEY. ISN'T SOMEBODY UP PAST HER BEDTIME?
CAN'T SLEEP.
HOW COME?
I'M WORRIED ABOUT DADDY.
NOTHING TO WORRY ABOUT, SHRIMP. I'M TAKING CARE OF HIM.
C'MON. YOU'RE JUST A *KID*, SAM.
WHAT IF... WHAT IF THE *NOVAS* NEED HIM AGAIN?
HE'S GONNA HAVE TO GO, Y'KNOW.
KAELYNN.
THOSE STORIES THAT DAD TELLS US? THEY'RE NOT...
THEY'RE NOT WHAT...?
*HE WAS THE GREATEST NOVA **EVER.***
...
YOU SHOULD GET HIM TO TELL YOU THE ONE ABOUT HOW THEY PAINTED ANOTHER RING AROUND SATURN.
THAT'S A REALLY GOOD ONE...

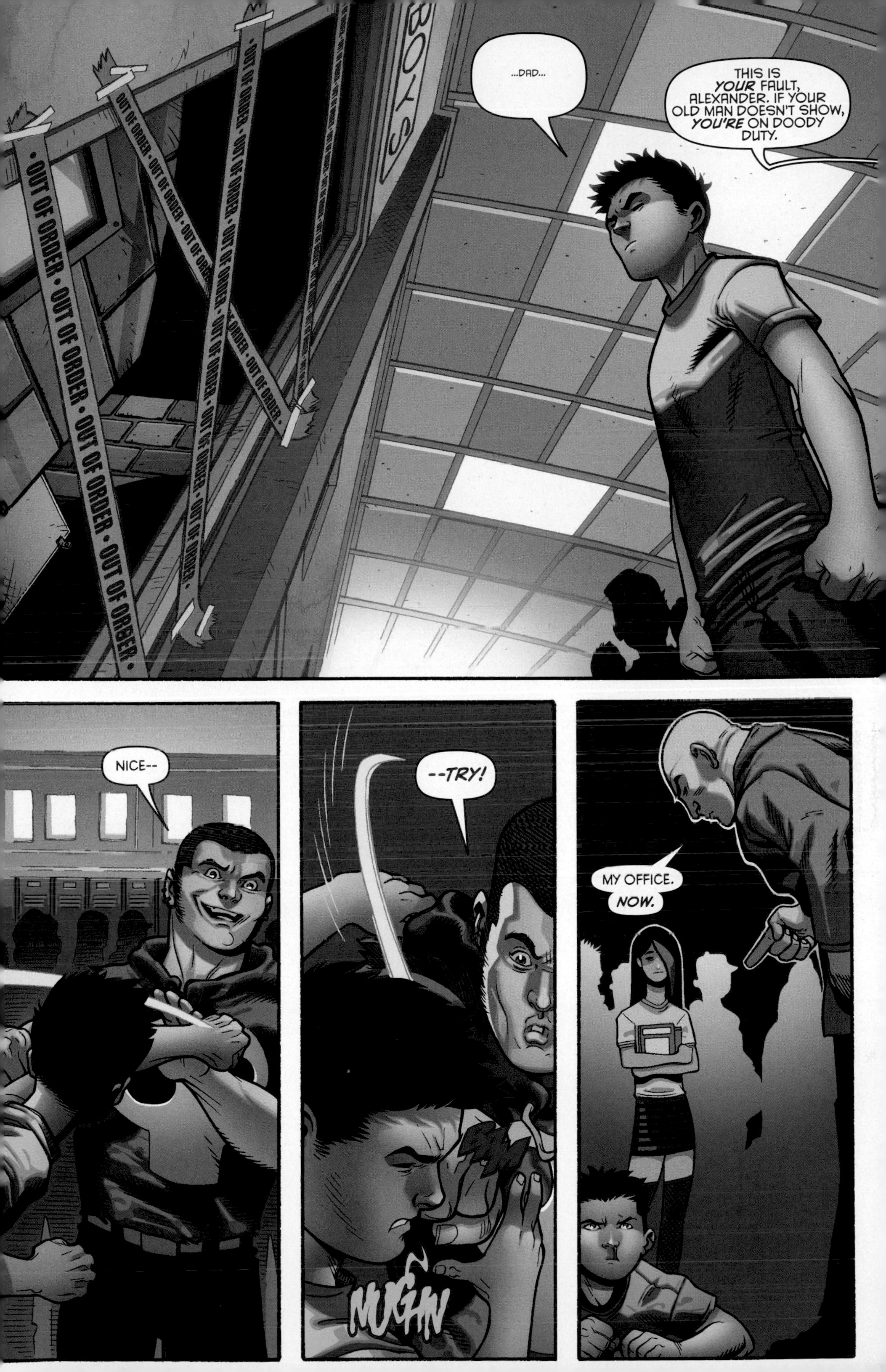
BOYS
OUT OF ORDER
...DAD...
THIS IS YOUR FAULT, ALEXANDER. IF YOUR OLD MAN DOESN'T SHOW, YOU'RE ON DOODY DUTY.
NICE--
--TRY!
MUGHN
MY OFFICE. NOW.

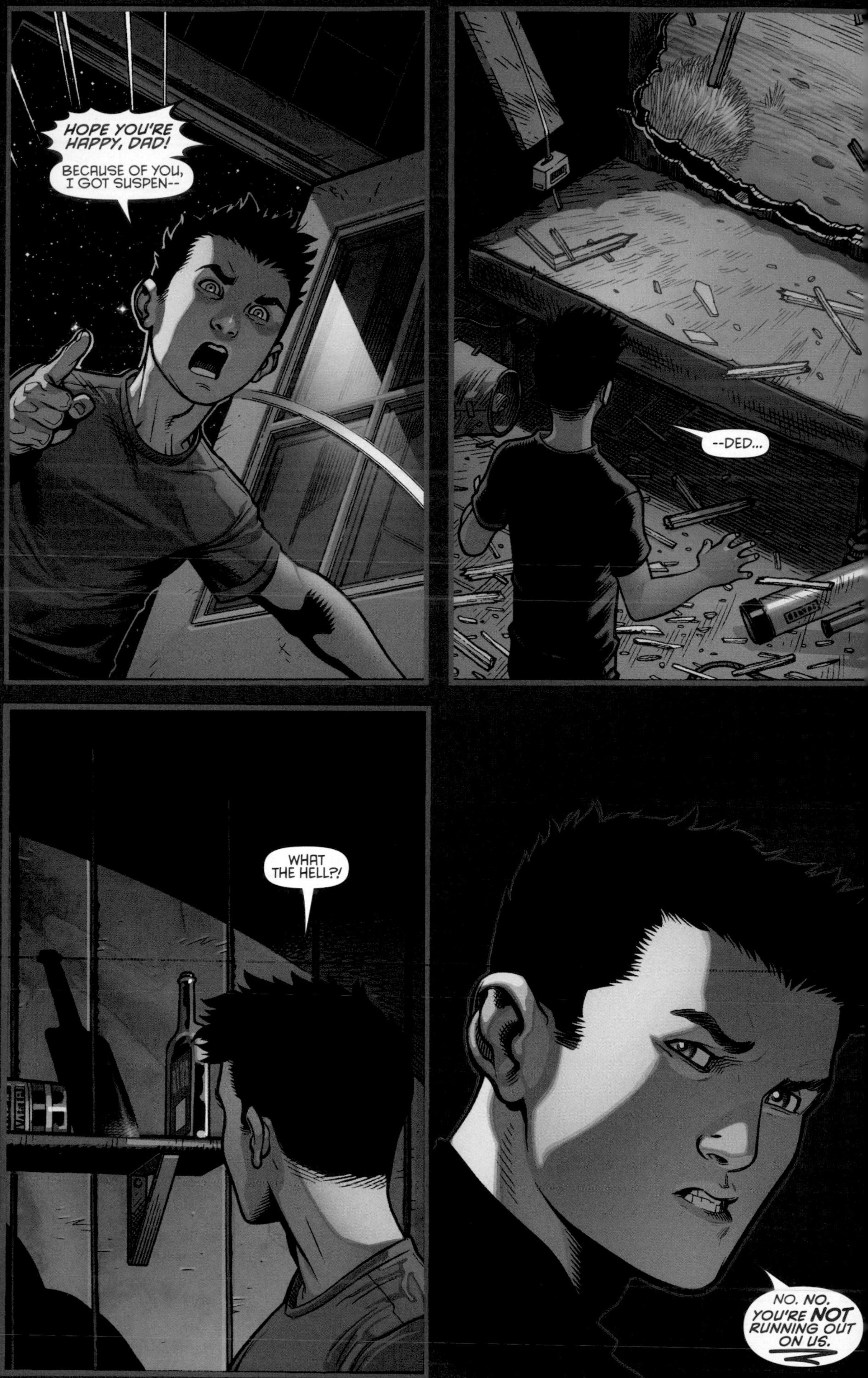
HOPE YOU'RE HAPPY, DAD!
BECAUSE OF YOU, I GOT SUSPEN--
--DED...
WHAT THE HELL?!
NO. NO. YOU'RE **NOT** RUNNING OUT ON US.

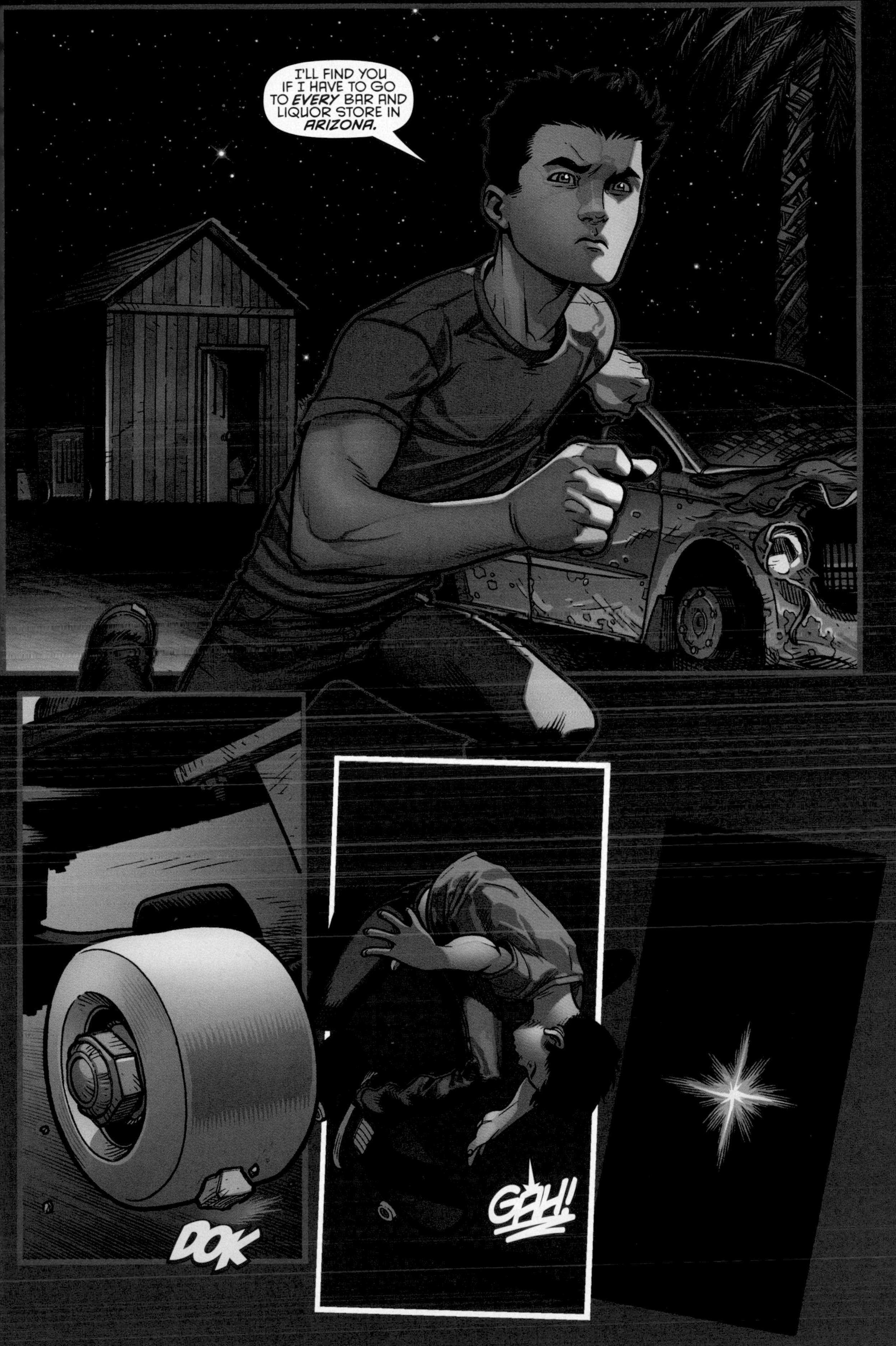
I'LL FIND YOU IF I HAVE TO GO TO *EVERY* BAR AND LIQUOR STORE IN *ARIZONA.*
DOK
GAH!

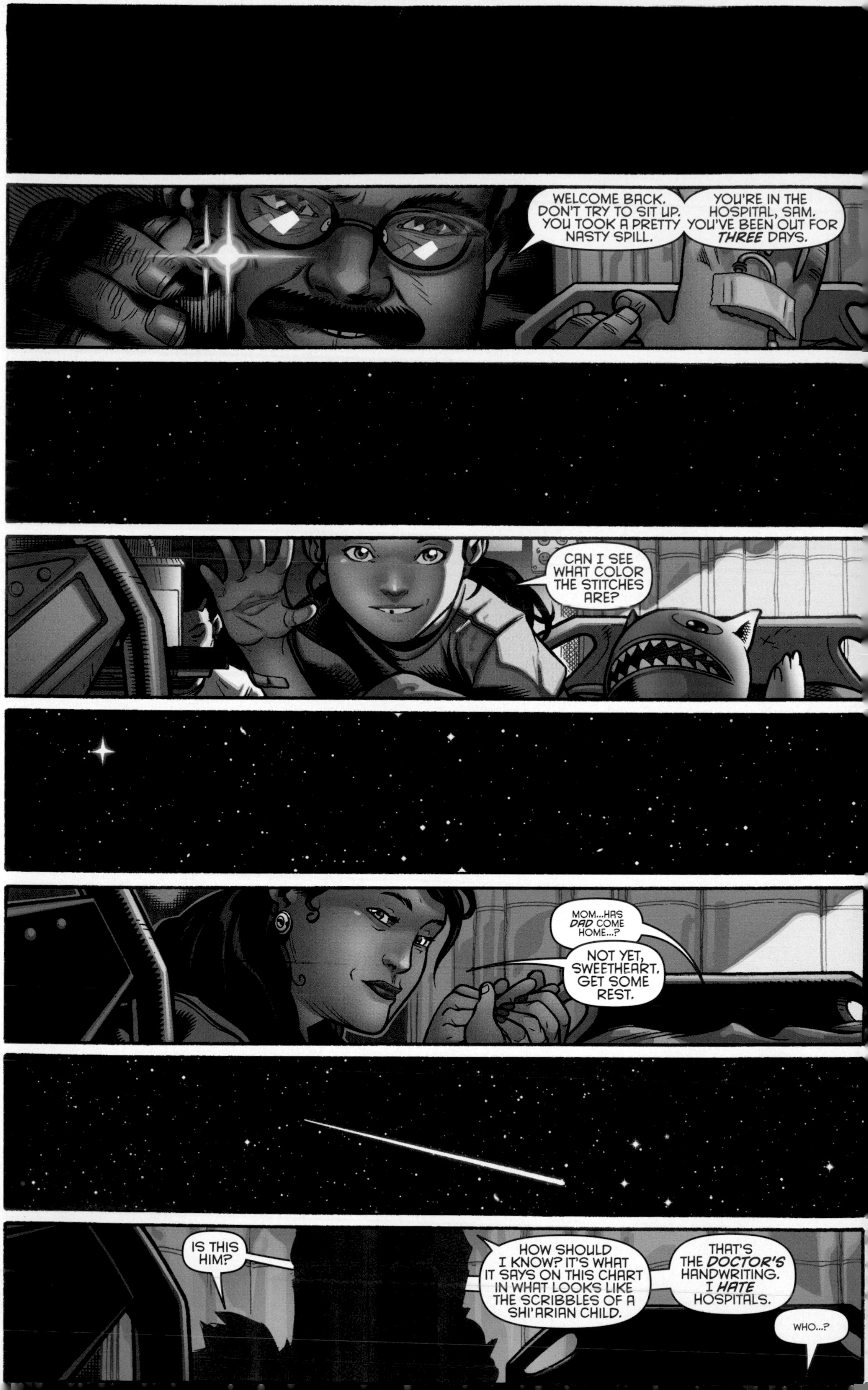
WELCOME BACK. DON'T TRY TO SIT UP. YOU TOOK A PRETTY NASTY SPILL.
YOU'RE IN THE HOSPITAL, SAM. YOU'VE BEEN OUT FOR THREE DAYS.
CAN I SEE WHAT COLOR THE STITCHES ARE?
MOM...HAS DAD COME HOME...?
NOT YET, SWEETHEART. GET SOME REST.
IS THIS HIM?
HOW SHOULD I KNOW? IT'S WHAT IT SAYS ON THIS CHART IN WHAT LOOKS LIKE THE SCRIBBLES OF A SHI'ARIAN CHILD.
THAT'S THE DOCTOR'S HANDWRITING. I HATE HOSPITALS.
WHO...?

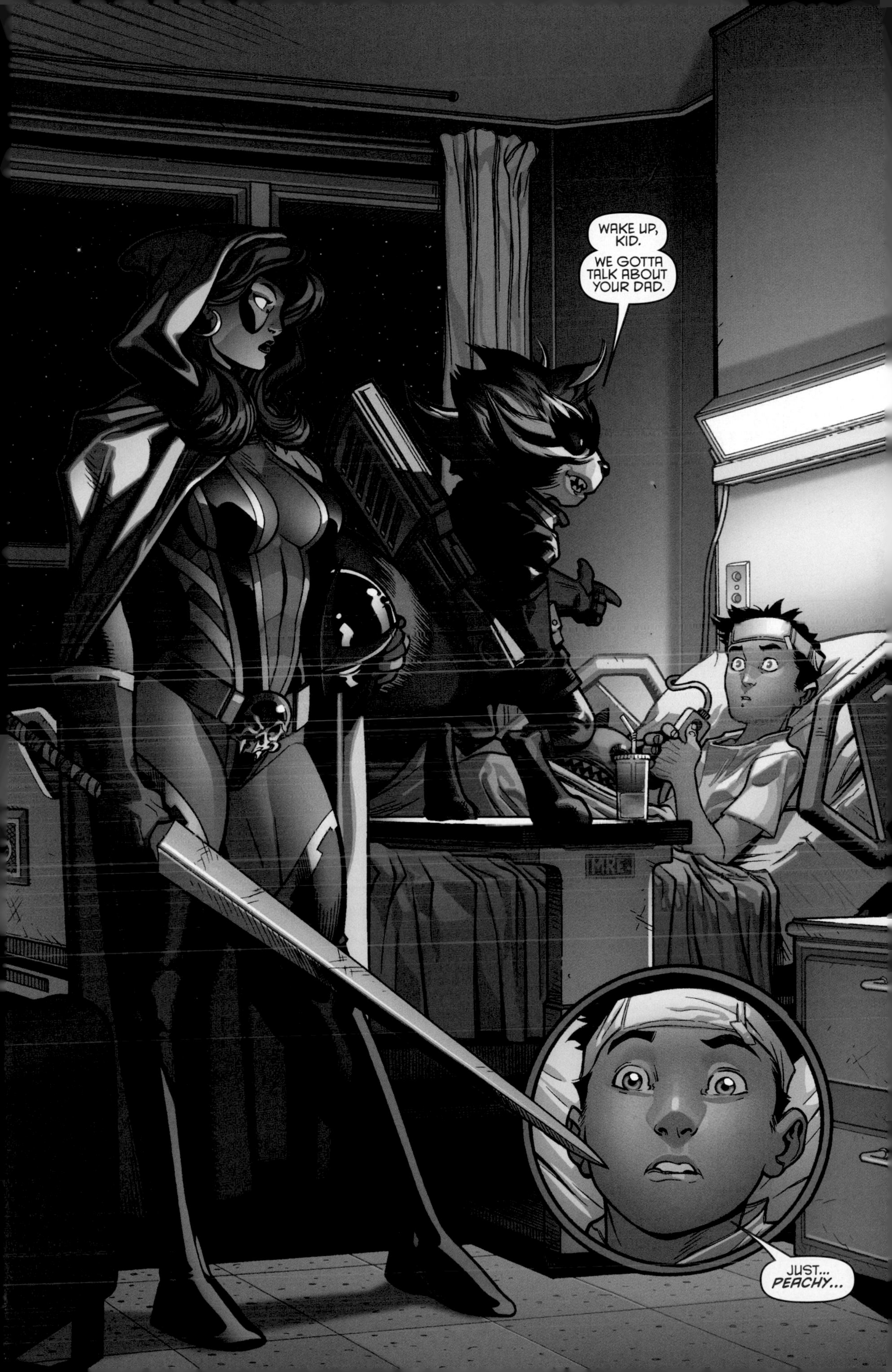
WAKE UP, KID.
WE GOTTA TALK ABOUT YOUR DAD.
JUST... *PEACHY*...

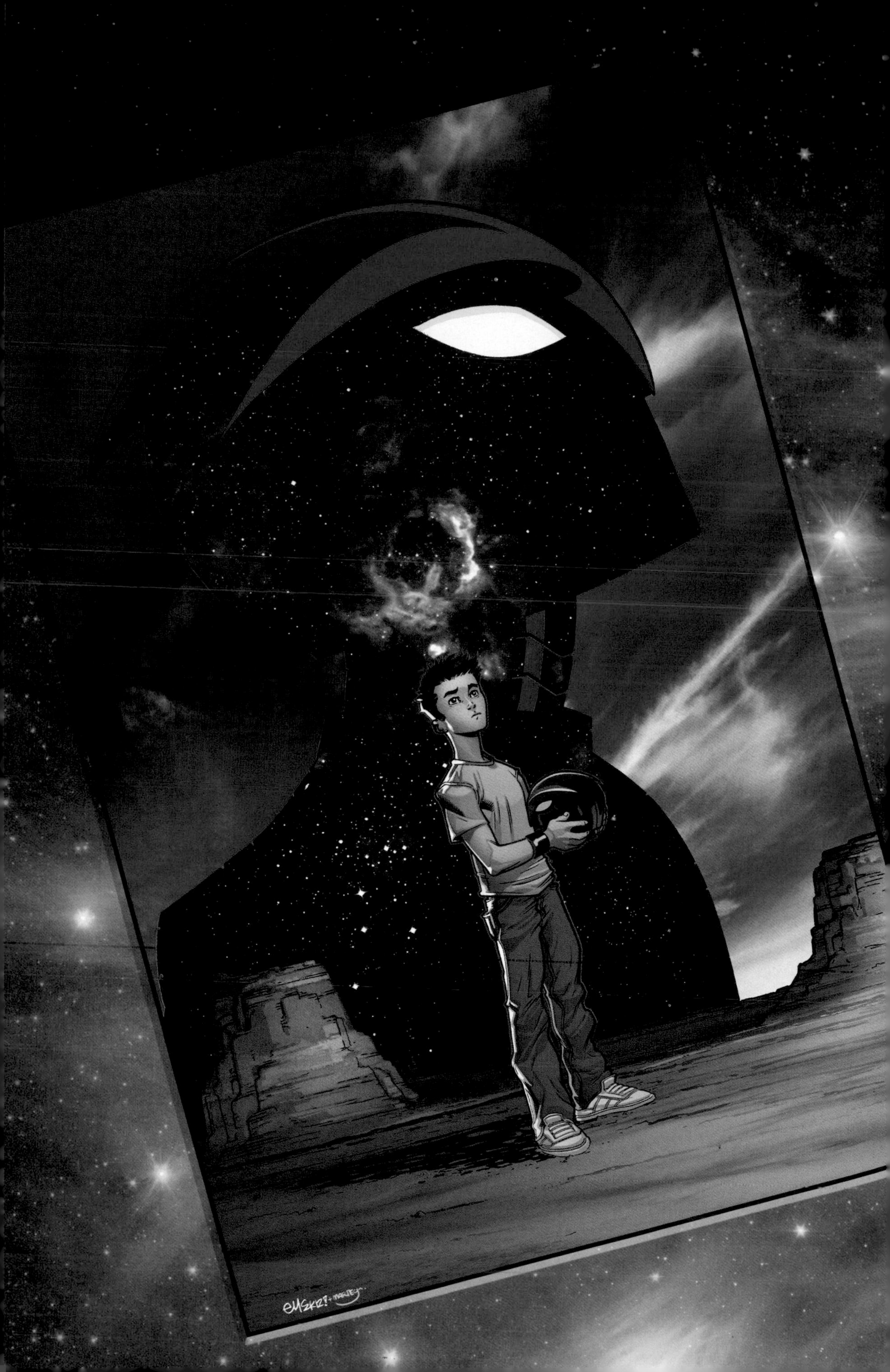

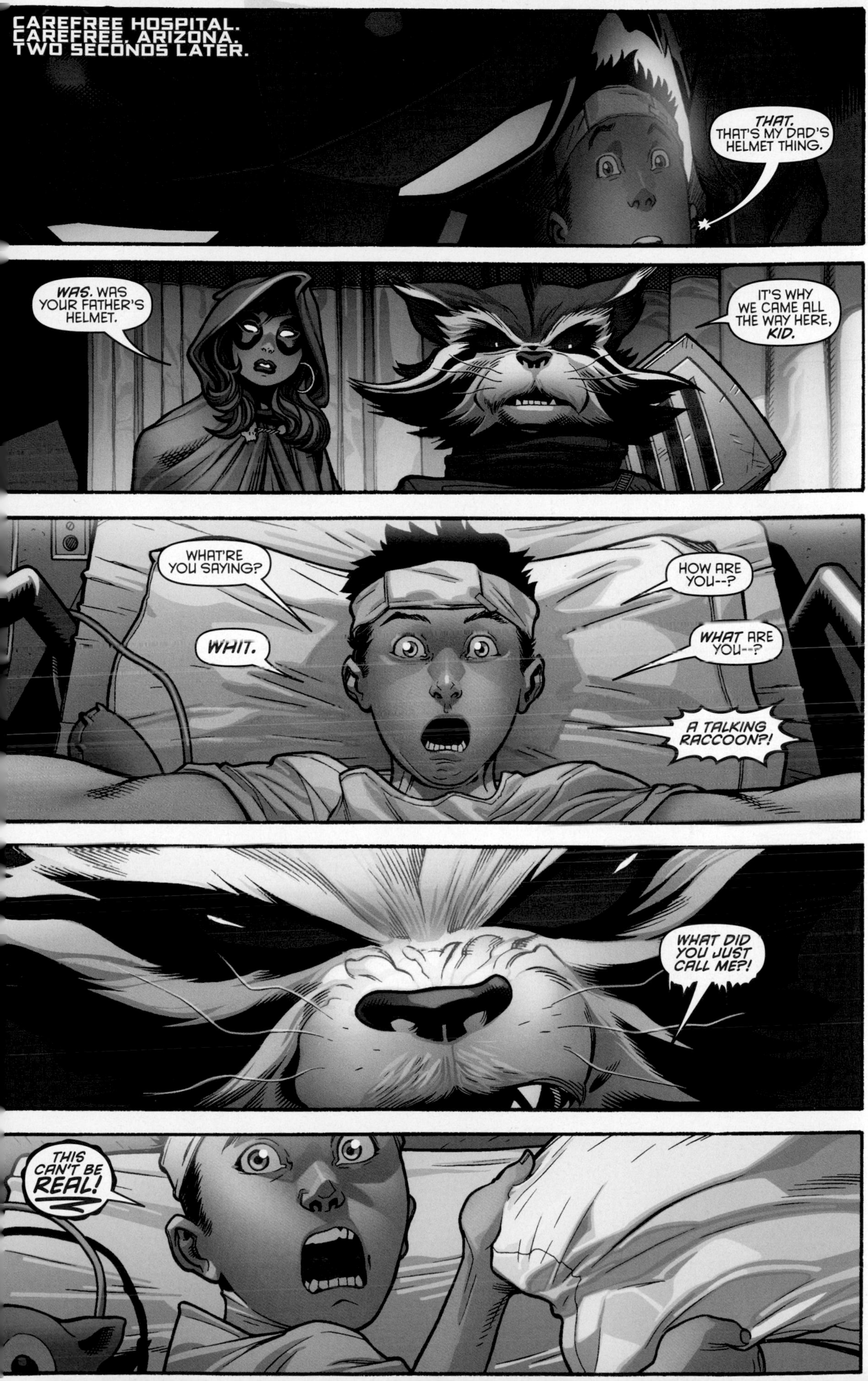
CAREFREE HOSPITAL. CAREFREE, ARIZONA. TWO SECONDS LATER.
THAT. THAT'S MY DAD'S HELMET THING.
WAS. WAS YOUR FATHER'S HELMET.
IT'S WHY WE CAME ALL THE WAY HERE, KID.
WHAT'RE YOU SAYING?
HOW ARE YOU--?
WHIT.
WHAT ARE YOU--?
A TALKING RACCOON?!
WHAT DID YOU JUST CALL ME?!
THIS CAN'T BE REAL!

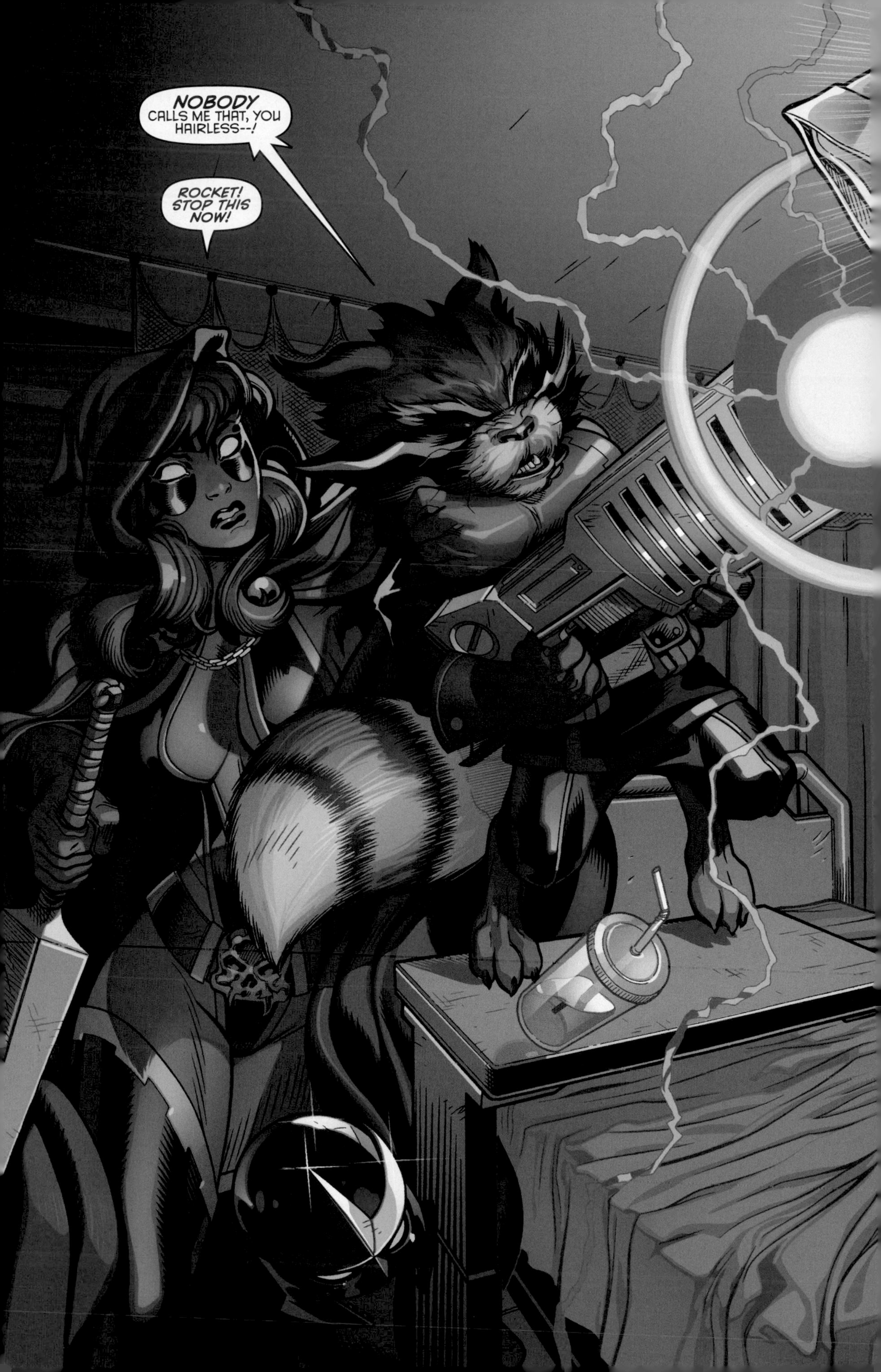
NOBODY CALLS ME THAT, YOU HAIRLESS--!
ROCKET! STOP THIS NOW!

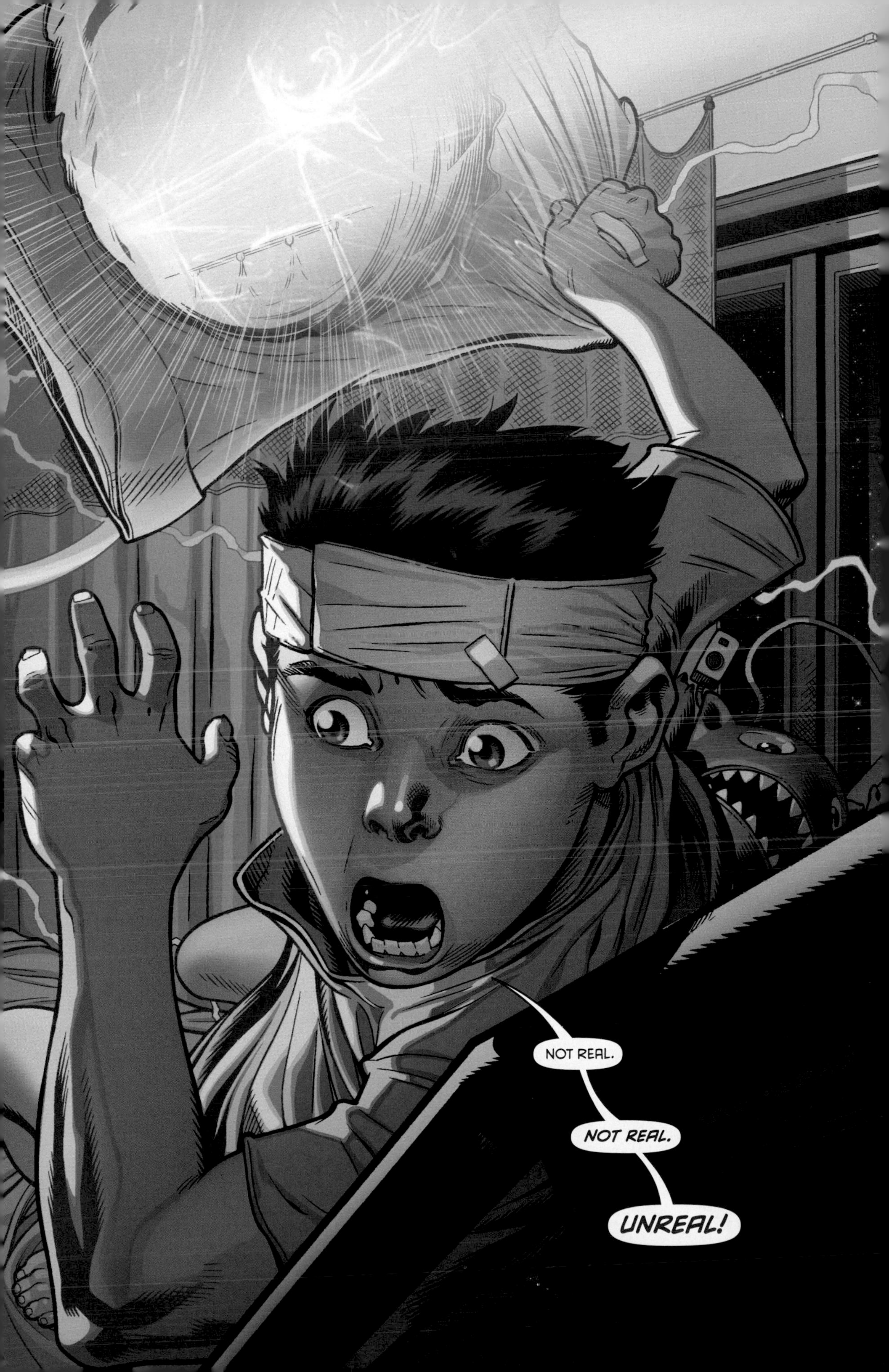
NOT REAL.
NOT REAL.
UNREAL!

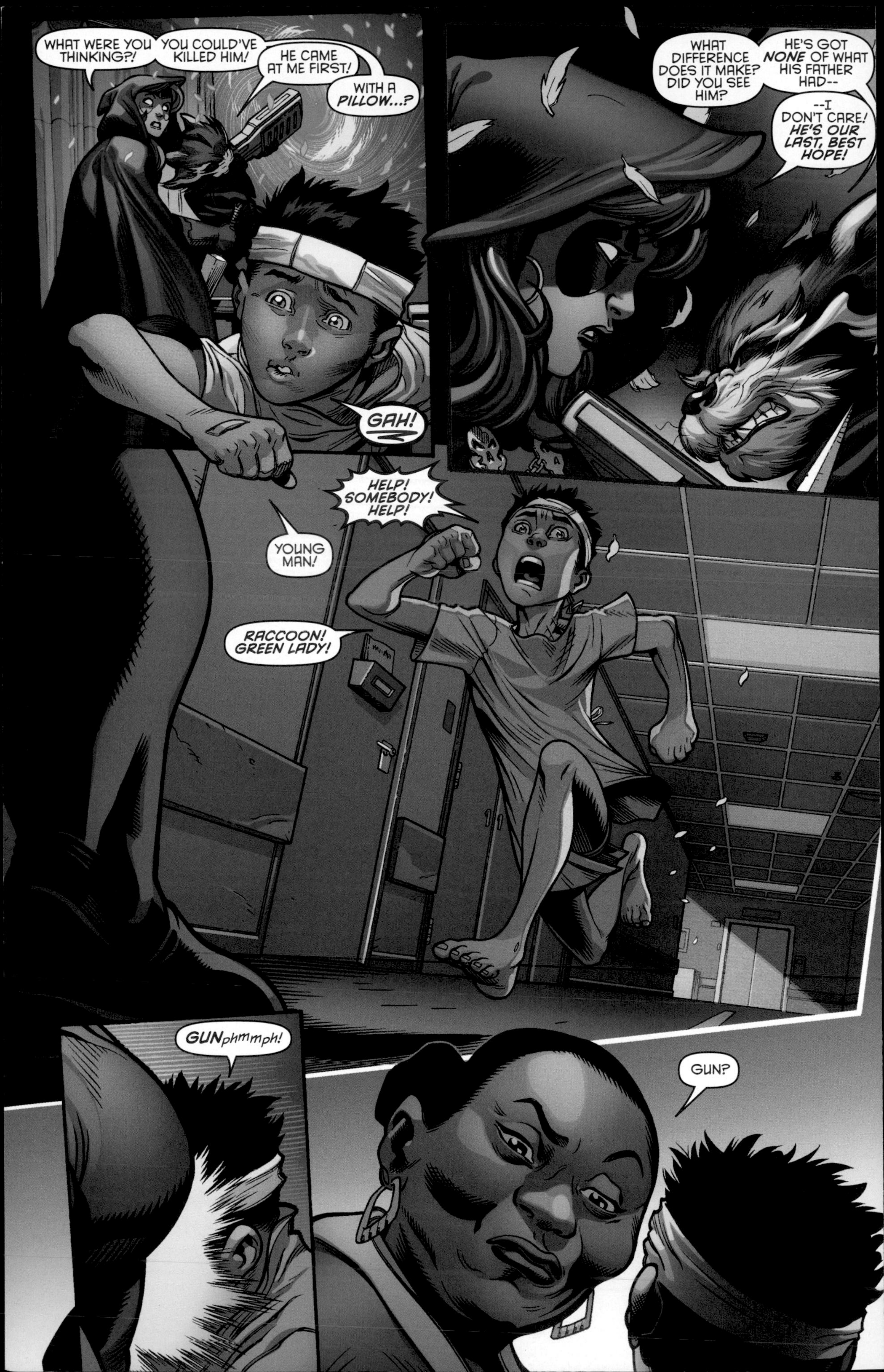
WHAT WERE YOU THINKING?!
YOU COULD'VE KILLED HIM!
HE CAME AT ME FIRST!
WITH A *PILLOW...?*
WHAT DIFFERENCE DOES IT MAKE? DID YOU SEE HIM?
HE'S GOT *NONE* OF WHAT HIS FATHER HAD--
--I DON'T CARE! *HE'S OUR LAST, BEST HOPE!*
GAH!
HELP! SOMEBODY! HELP!
YOUNG MAN!
RACCOON! GREEN LADY!
GUNphmmph!
GUN?

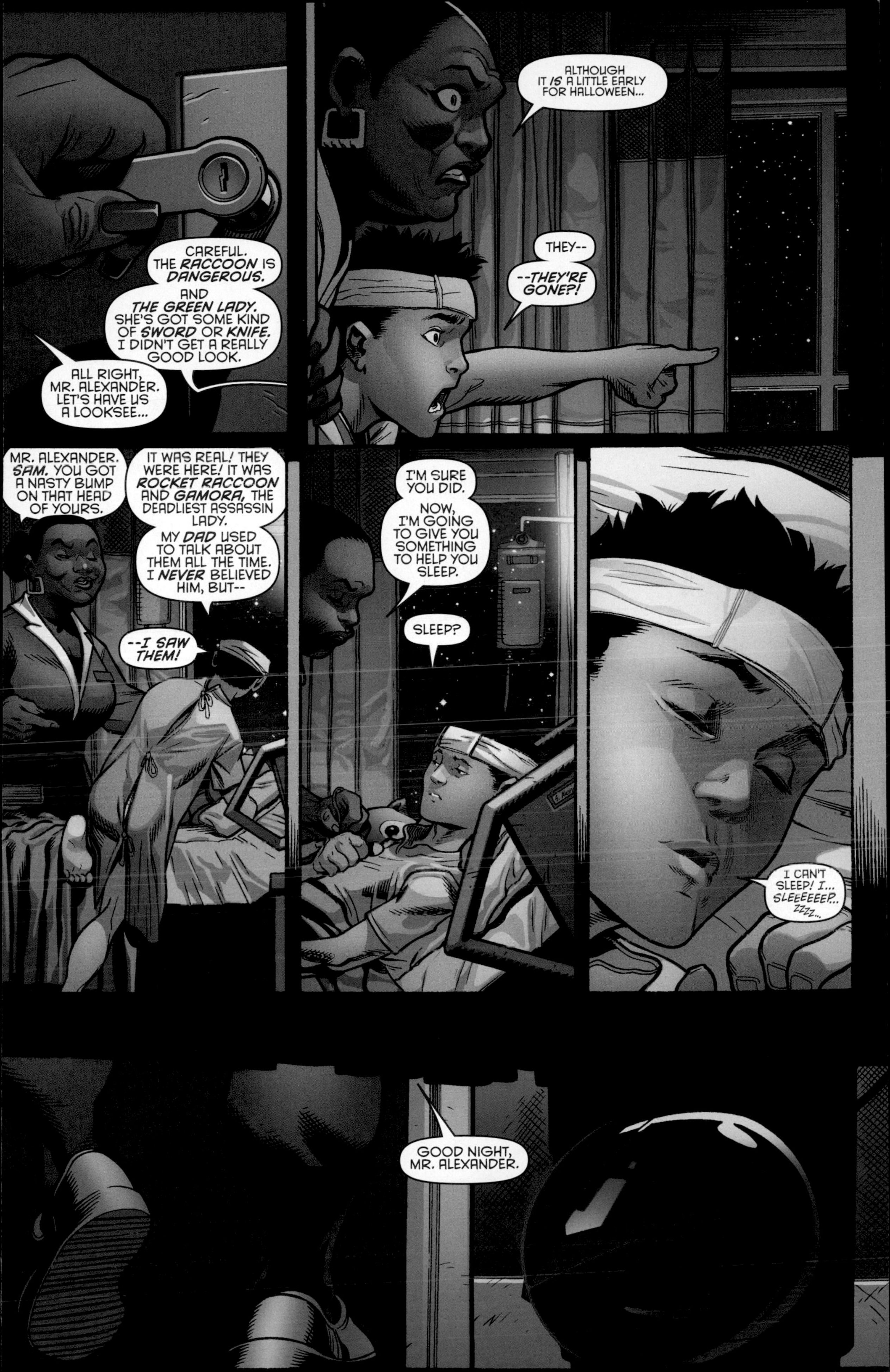
CAREFUL. THE RACCOON IS DANGEROUS.
AND THE GREEN LADY. SHE'S GOT SOME KIND OF SWORD OR KNIFE. I DIDN'T GET A REALLY GOOD LOOK.
ALL RIGHT, MR. ALEXANDER. LET'S HAVE US A LOOKSEE...
ALTHOUGH IT IS A LITTLE EARLY FOR HALLOWEEN...
THEY--
--THEY'RE GONE?!
MR. ALEXANDER. SAM. YOU GOT A NASTY BUMP ON THAT HEAD OF YOURS.
IT WAS REAL! THEY WERE HERE! IT WAS ROCKET RACCOON AND GAMORA, THE DEADLIEST ASSASSIN LADY.
MY DAD USED TO TALK ABOUT THEM ALL THE TIME. I NEVER BELIEVED HIM, BUT--
--I SAW THEM!
I'M SURE YOU DID.
NOW, I'M GOING TO GIVE YOU SOMETHING TO HELP YOU SLEEP.
SLEEP?
I CAN'T SLEEP! I... SLEEEEEEP... ZZZZ...
GOOD NIGHT, MR. ALEXANDER.

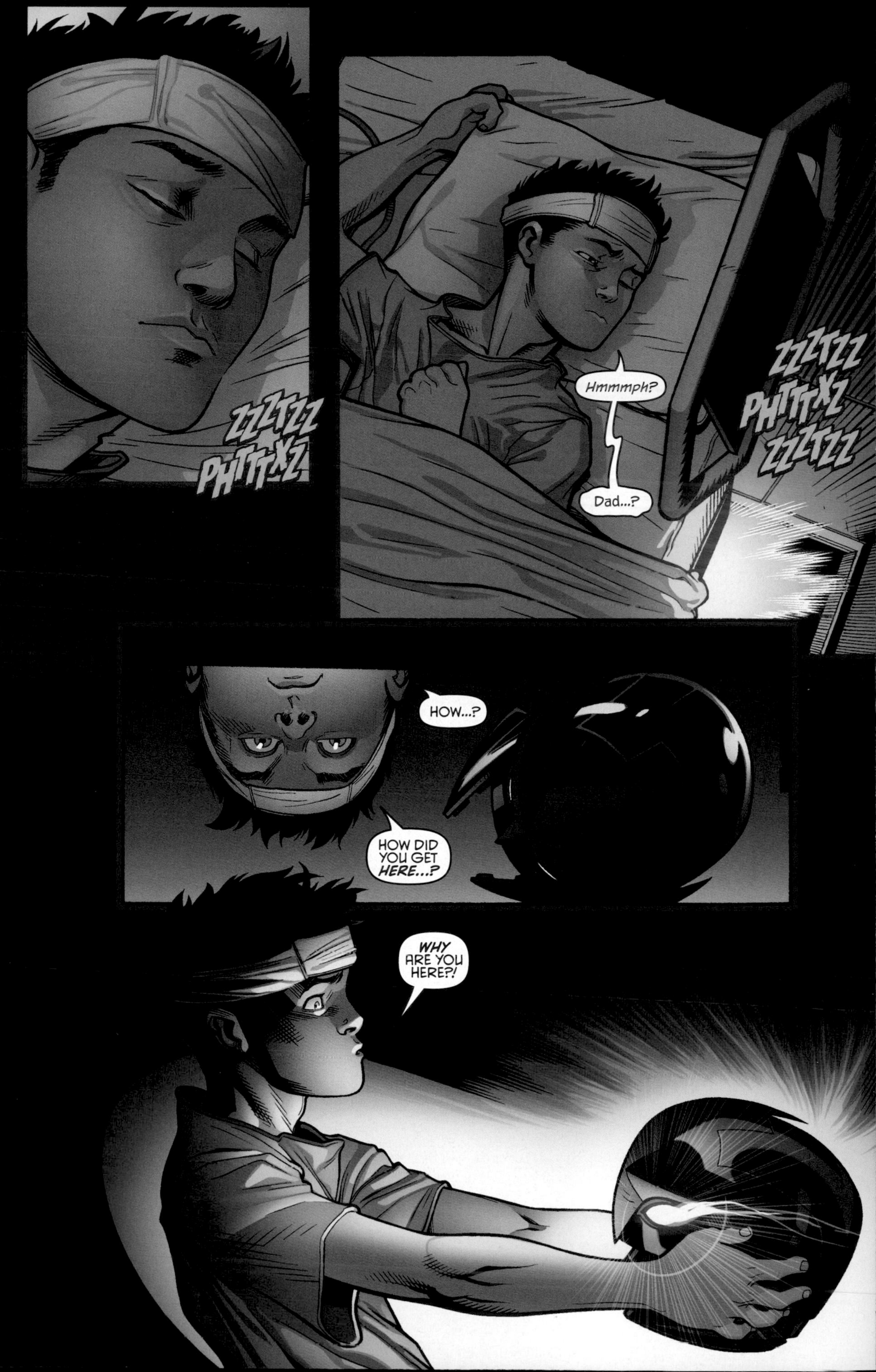
ZZZTZZ
PHTTTXZ
Hmmmph?
Dad...?
ZZZTZZ
PHTTTXZ
ZZZTZZ
HOW...?
HOW DID YOU GET HERE...?
WHY ARE YOU HERE?!

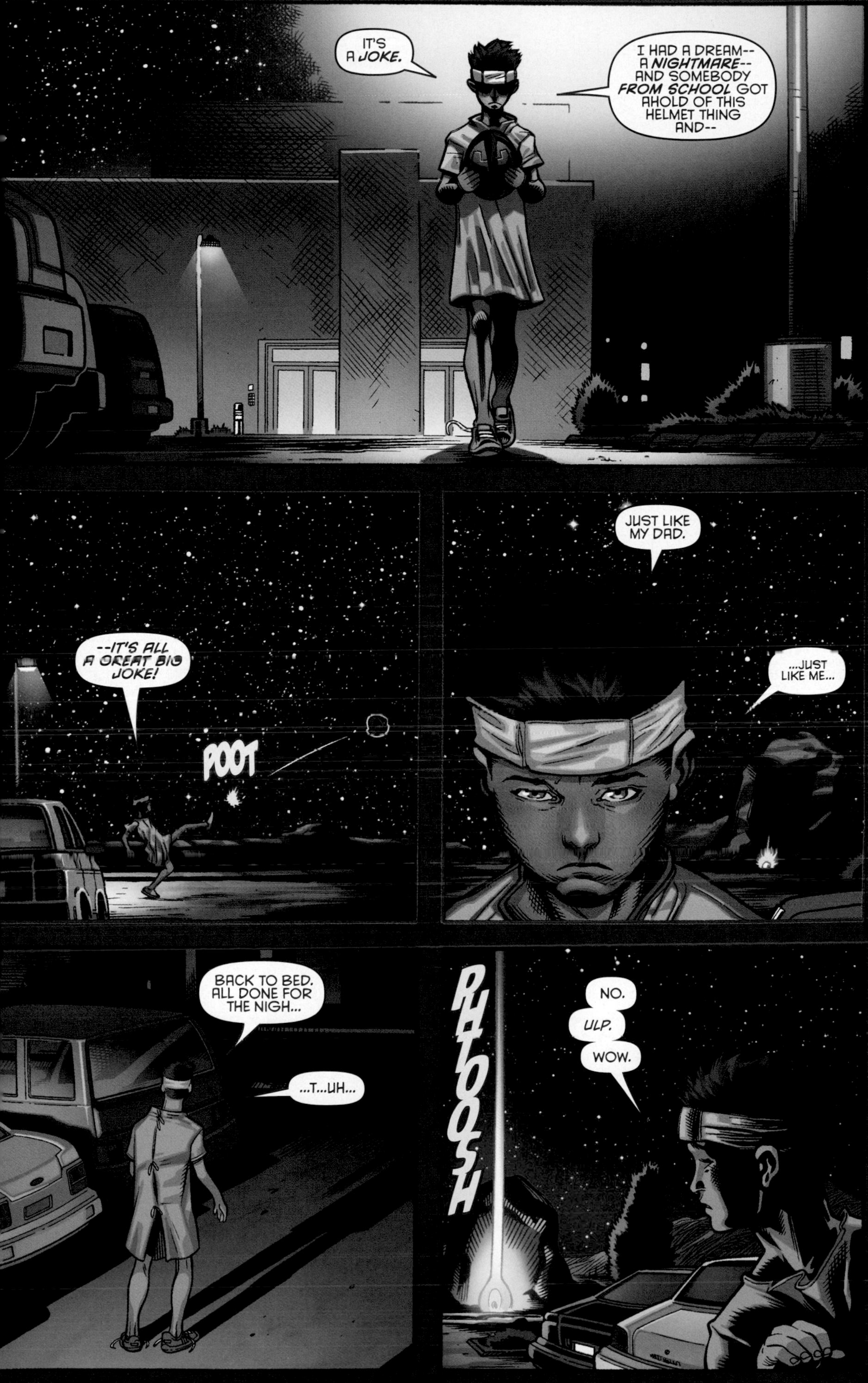
IT'S A JOKE.
I HAD A DREAM-- A NIGHTMARE-- AND SOMEBODY FROM SCHOOL GOT AHOLD OF THIS HELMET THING AND--
--IT'S ALL A GREAT BIG JOKE!
POOT
JUST LIKE MY DAD.
...JUST LIKE ME...
BACK TO BED. ALL DONE FOR THE NIGH...
...T...UH...
RHOOSH
NO.
ULP.
WOW.

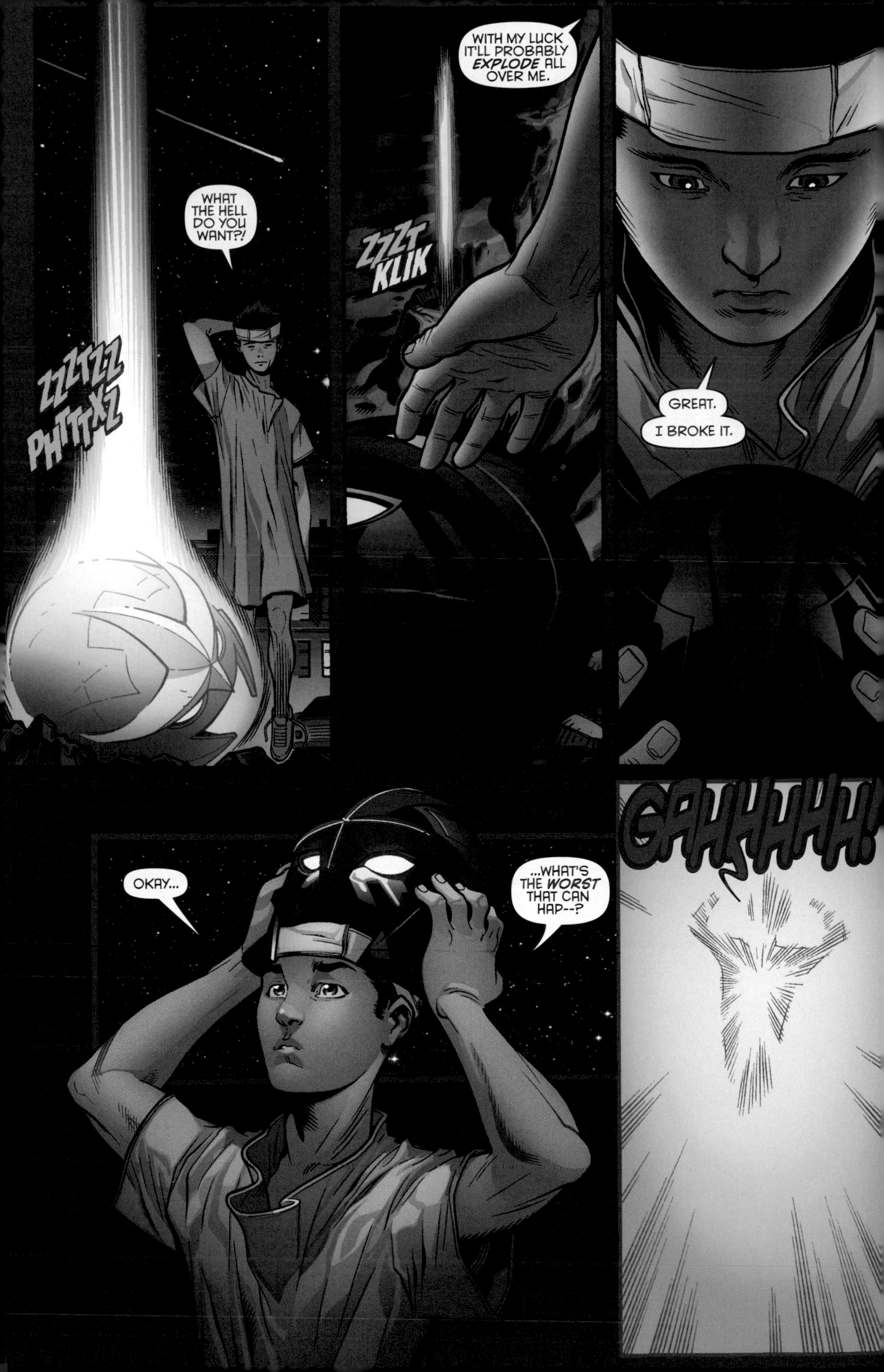
WHAT THE HELL DO YOU WANT?!
ZZZTZZ PHTTTXZ
WITH MY LUCK IT'LL PROBABLY EXPLODE ALL OVER ME.
ZZZT KLIK
GREAT.
I BROKE IT.
OKAY...
...WHAT'S THE WORST THAT CAN HAP--?
GAHHHHH!

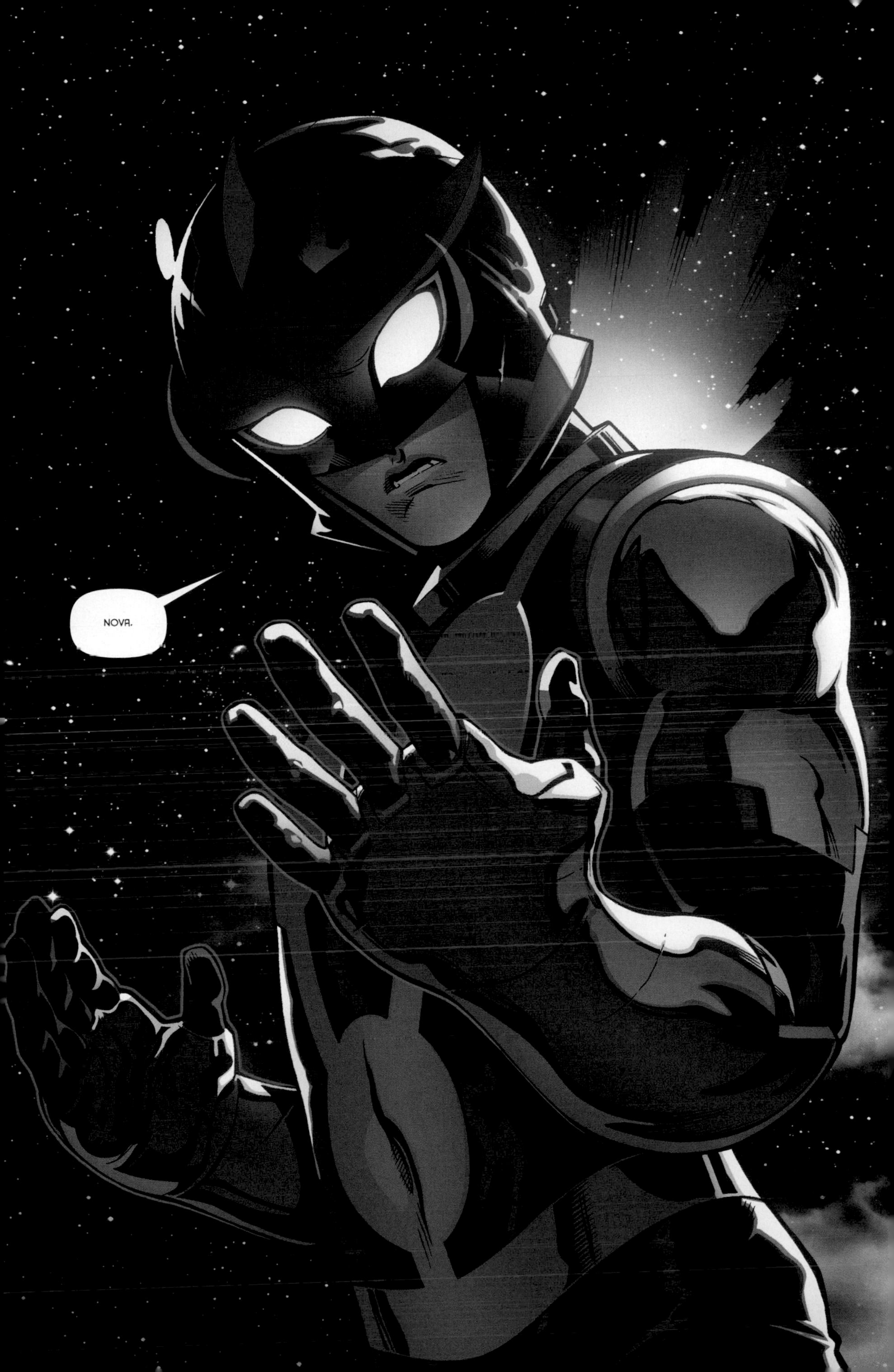
NOVA.

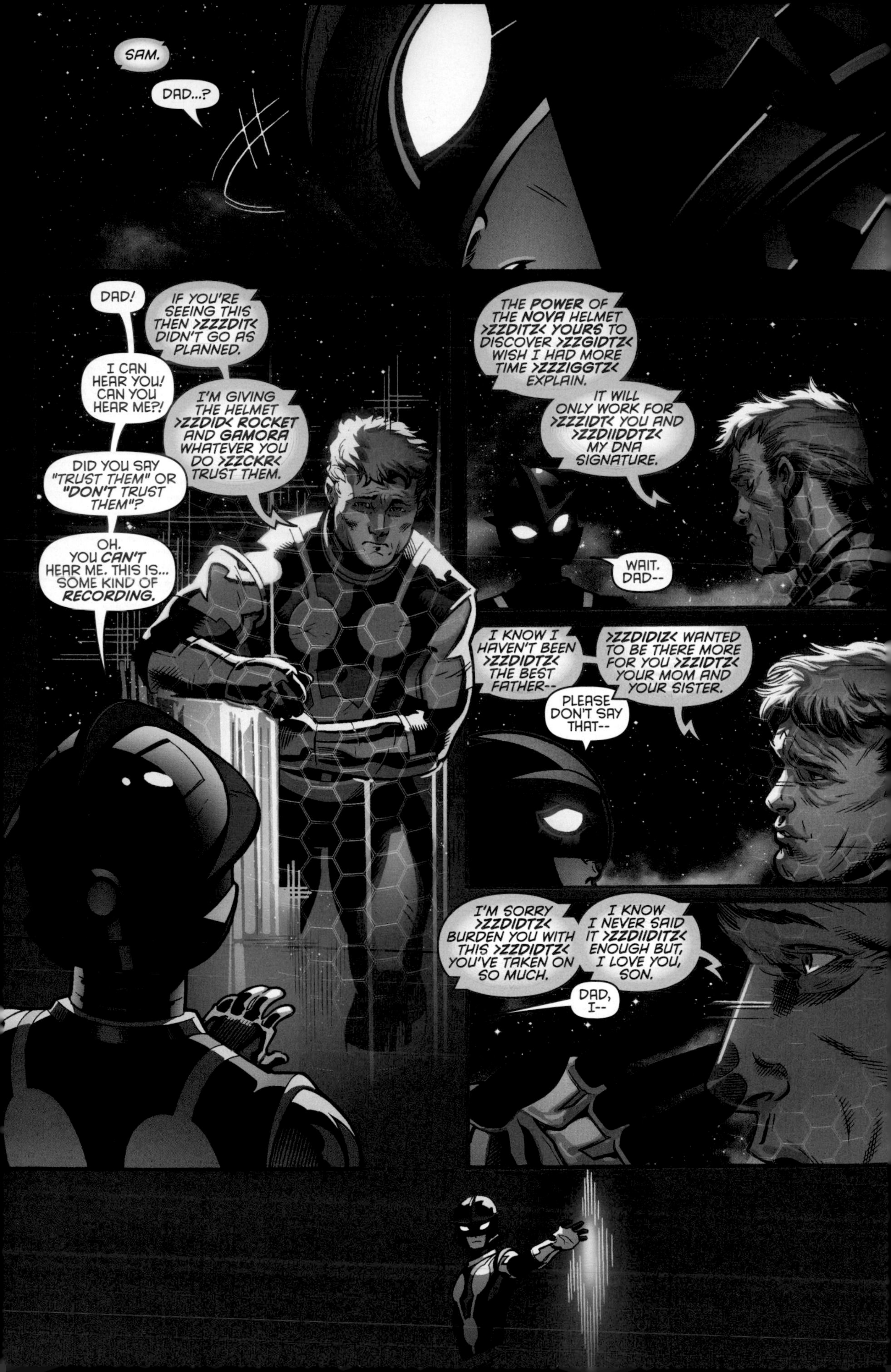
SAM.
DAD...?
DAD!
IF YOU'RE SEEING THIS THEN >ZZZDIT< DIDN'T GO AS PLANNED.
I CAN HEAR YOU! CAN YOU HEAR ME?!
I'M GIVING THE HELMET >ZZDID< ROCKET AND GAMORA WHATEVER YOU DO >ZZCKR< TRUST THEM.
DID YOU SAY "TRUST THEM" OR "DON'T TRUST THEM"?
OH. YOU CAN'T HEAR ME. THIS IS... SOME KIND OF RECORDING.
THE POWER OF THE NOVA HELMET >ZZDITZ< YOURS TO DISCOVER >ZZGIDTZ< WISH I HAD MORE TIME >ZZZIGGTZ< EXPLAIN.
IT WILL ONLY WORK FOR >ZZZIDT< YOU AND >ZZDIIDDTZ< MY DNA SIGNATURE.
WAIT. DAD--
I KNOW I HAVEN'T BEEN >ZZDIDTZ< THE BEST FATHER--
>ZZDIDIZ< WANTED TO BE THERE MORE FOR YOU >ZZIDTZ< YOUR MOM AND YOUR SISTER.
PLEASE DON'T SAY THAT--
I'M SORRY >ZZDIDTZ< BURDEN YOU WITH THIS >ZZDIDTZ< YOU'VE TAKEN ON SO MUCH.
I KNOW I NEVER SAID IT >ZZDIIDITZ< ENOUGH BUT, I LOVE YOU, SON.
DAD, I--

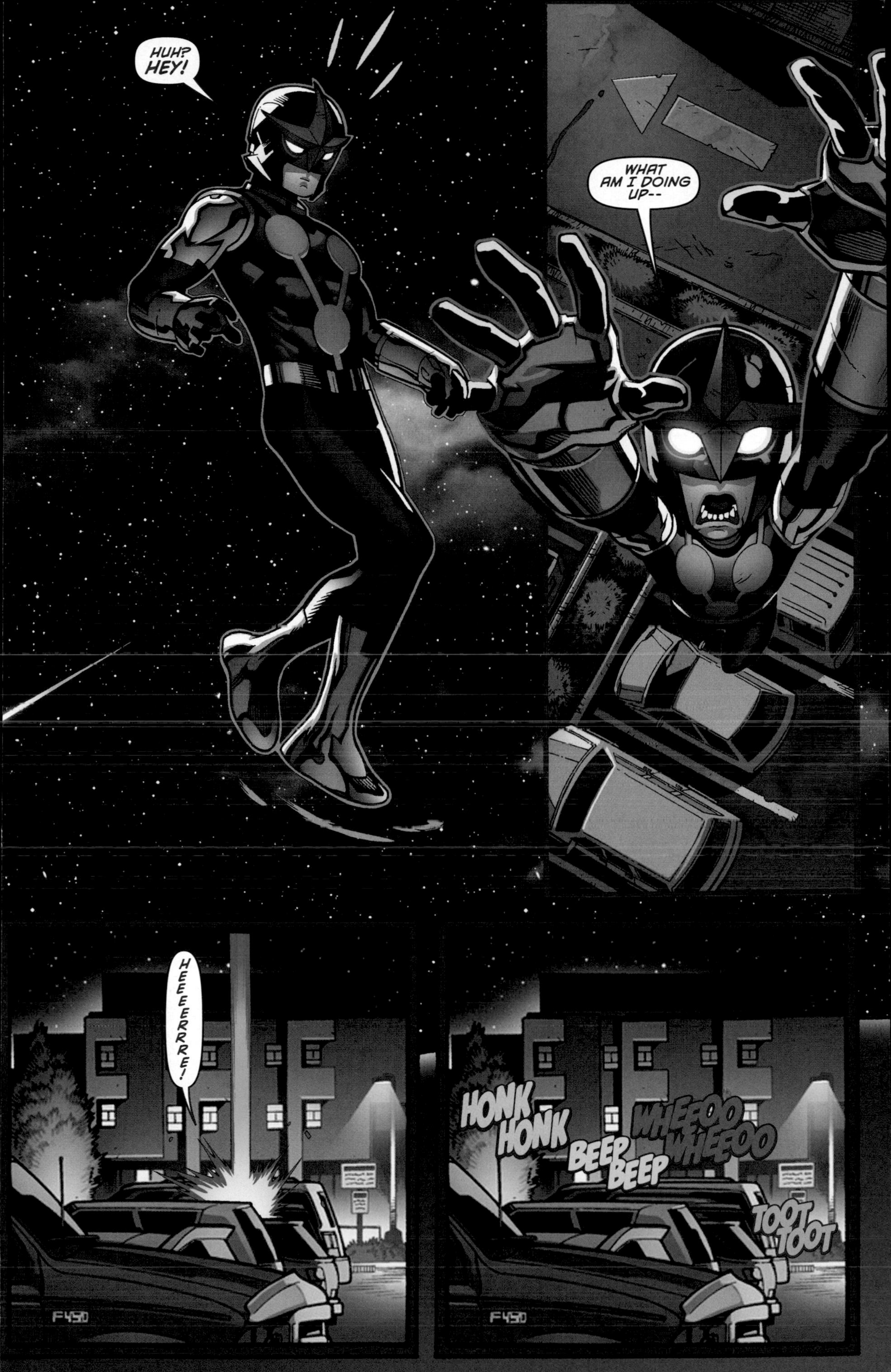
HUH? HEY!
WHAT AM I DOING UP--
HEEEEERRRE!
HONK HONK
BEEP BEEP
WHEEOO WHEEOO
TOOT TOOT
F450
F450

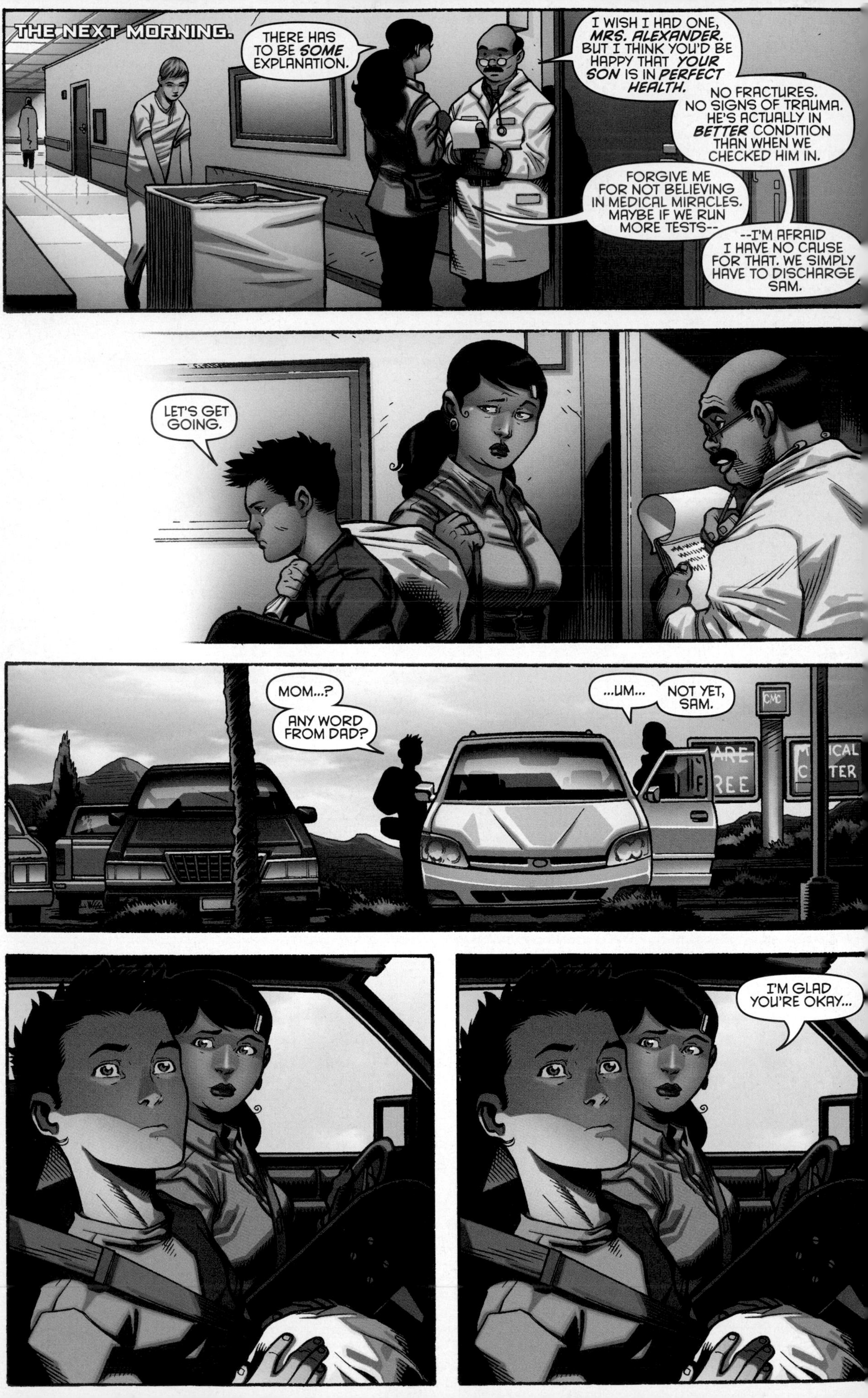
THE NEXT MORNING.
THERE HAS TO BE SOME EXPLANATION.
I WISH I HAD ONE, MRS. ALEXANDER. BUT I THINK YOU'D BE HAPPY THAT YOUR SON IS IN PERFECT HEALTH.
NO FRACTURES. NO SIGNS OF TRAUMA. HE'S ACTUALLY IN BETTER CONDITION THAN WHEN WE CHECKED HIM IN.
FORGIVE ME FOR NOT BELIEVING IN MEDICAL MIRACLES. MAYBE IF WE RUN MORE TESTS--
--I'M AFRAID I HAVE NO CAUSE FOR THAT. WE SIMPLY HAVE TO DISCHARGE SAM.
LET'S GET GOING.
MOM...?
ANY WORD FROM DAD?
...UM...
NOT YET, SAM.
CMC
I'M GLAD YOU'RE OKAY...

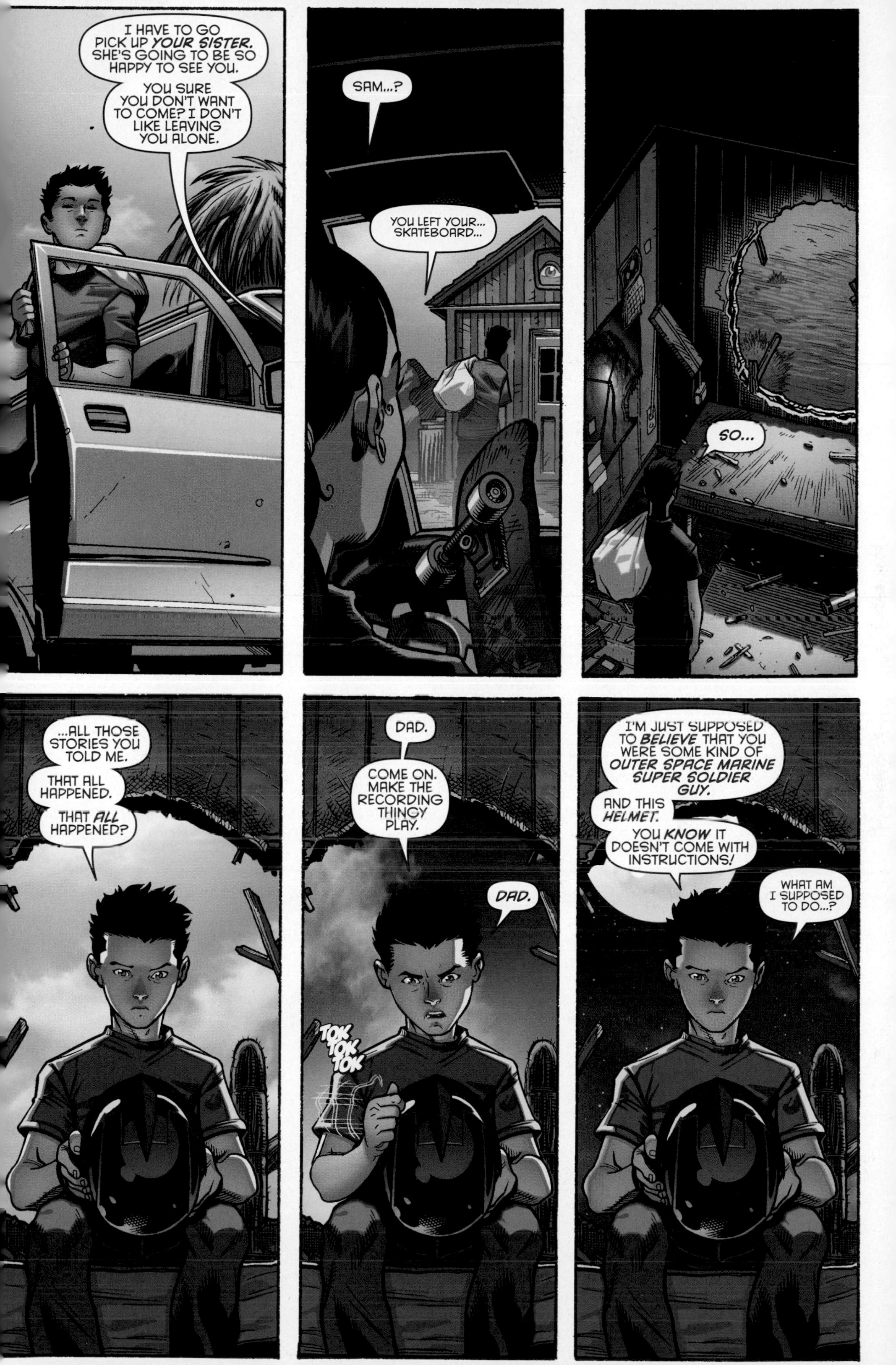

I HAVE TO GO PICK UP YOUR SISTER. SHE'S GOING TO BE SO HAPPY TO SEE YOU.
YOU SURE YOU DON'T WANT TO COME? I DON'T LIKE LEAVING YOU ALONE.
SAM...?
YOU LEFT YOUR... SKATEBOARD...
SO...
...ALL THOSE STORIES YOU TOLD ME.
THAT ALL HAPPENED.
THAT ALL HAPPENED?
DAD.
COME ON. MAKE THE RECORDING THINGY PLAY.
DAD.
TOK TOK TOK
I'M JUST SUPPOSED TO BELIEVE THAT YOU WERE SOME KIND OF OUTER SPACE MARINE SUPER SOLDIER GUY.
AND THIS HELMET.
YOU KNOW IT DOESN'T COME WITH INSTRUCTIONS!
WHAT AM I SUPPOSED TO DO...?

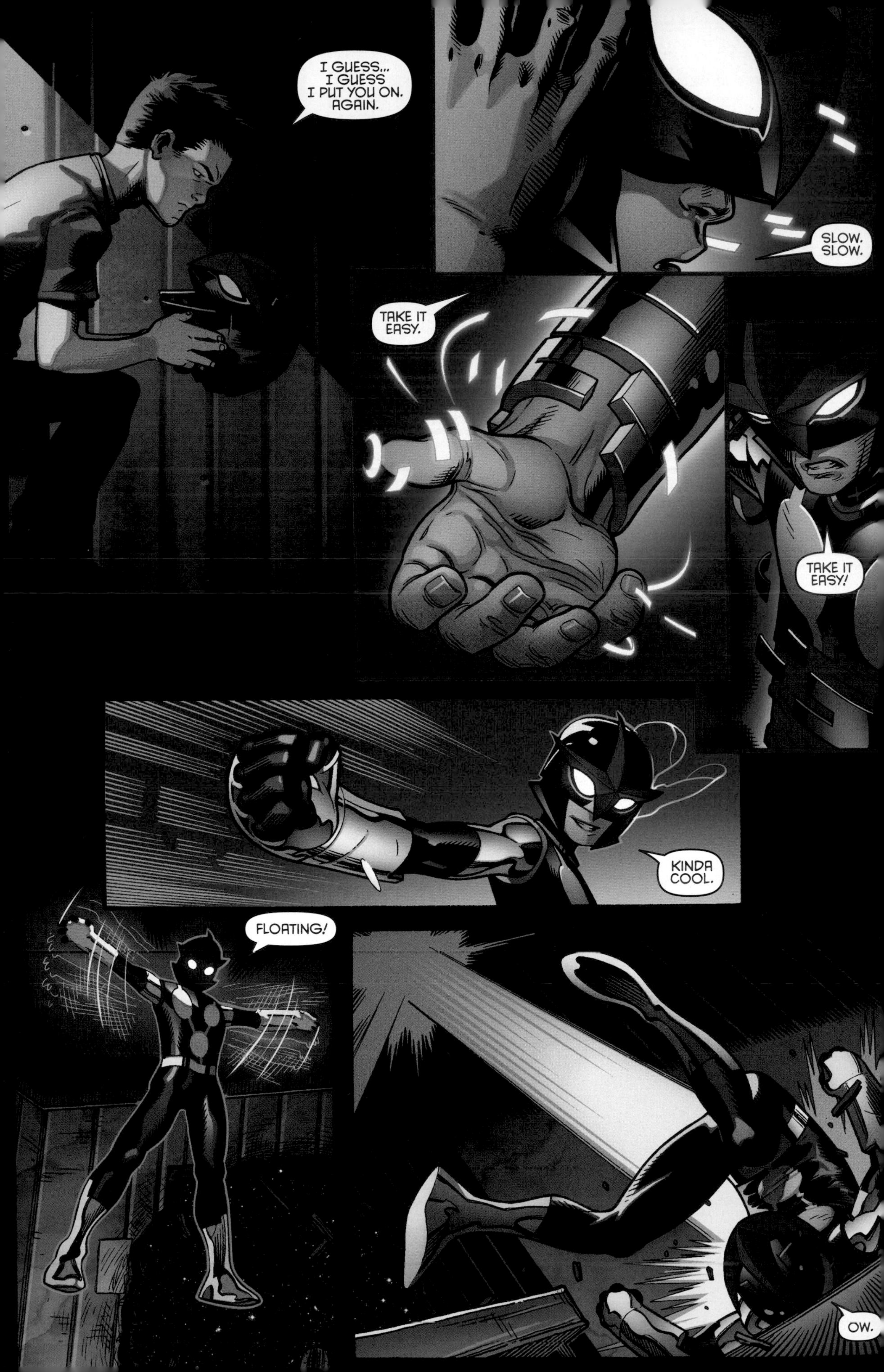
I GUESS... I GUESS I PUT YOU ON. AGAIN.
SLOW. SLOW.
TAKE IT EASY.
TAKE IT EASY!
KINDA COOL.
FLOATING!
OW.

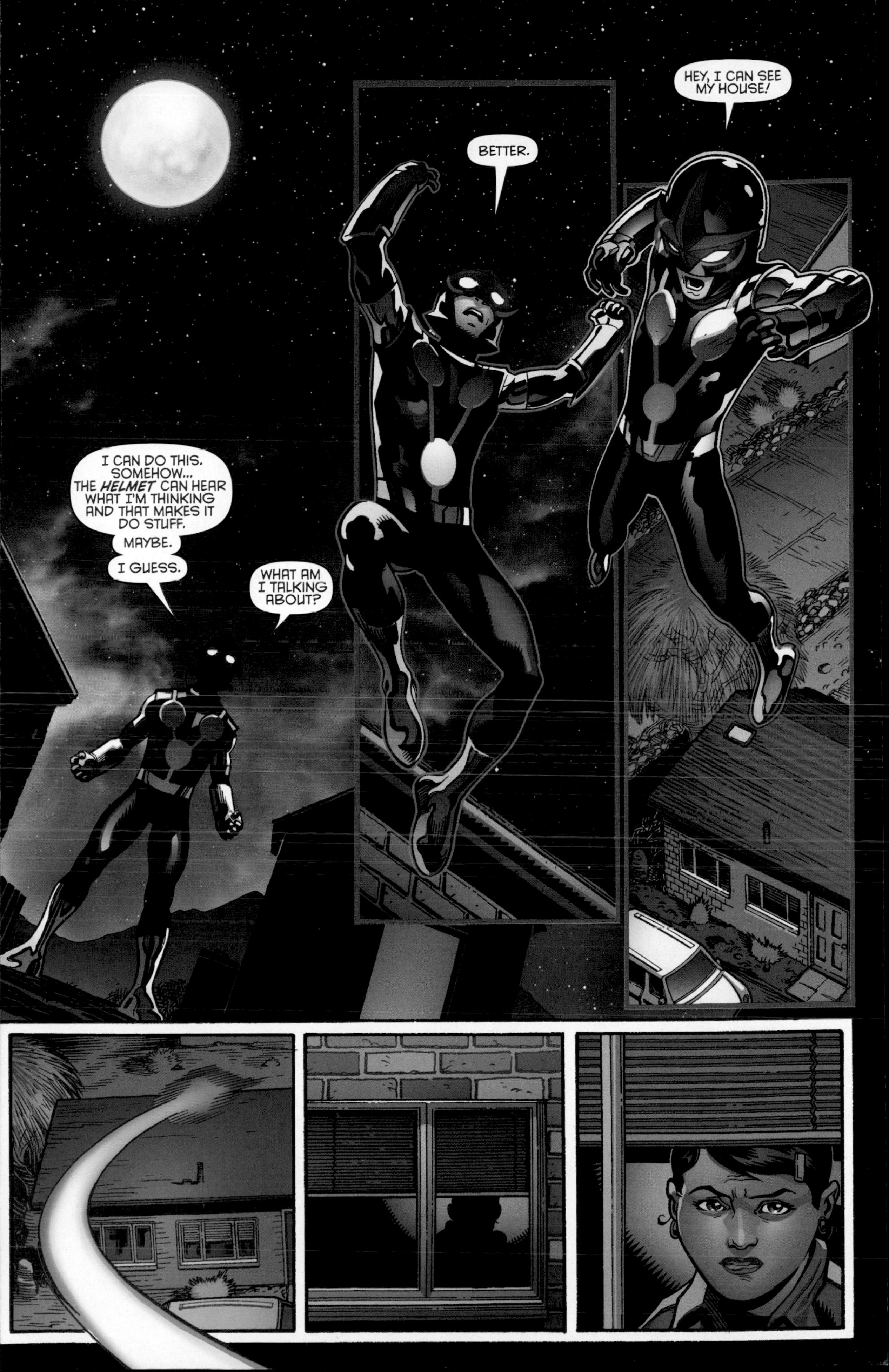
I CAN DO THIS. SOMEHOW... THE *HELMET* CAN HEAR WHAT I'M THINKING AND THAT MAKES IT DO STUFF.
MAYBE.
I GUESS.
WHAT AM I TALKING ABOUT?
BETTER.
HEY, I CAN SEE MY HOUSE!

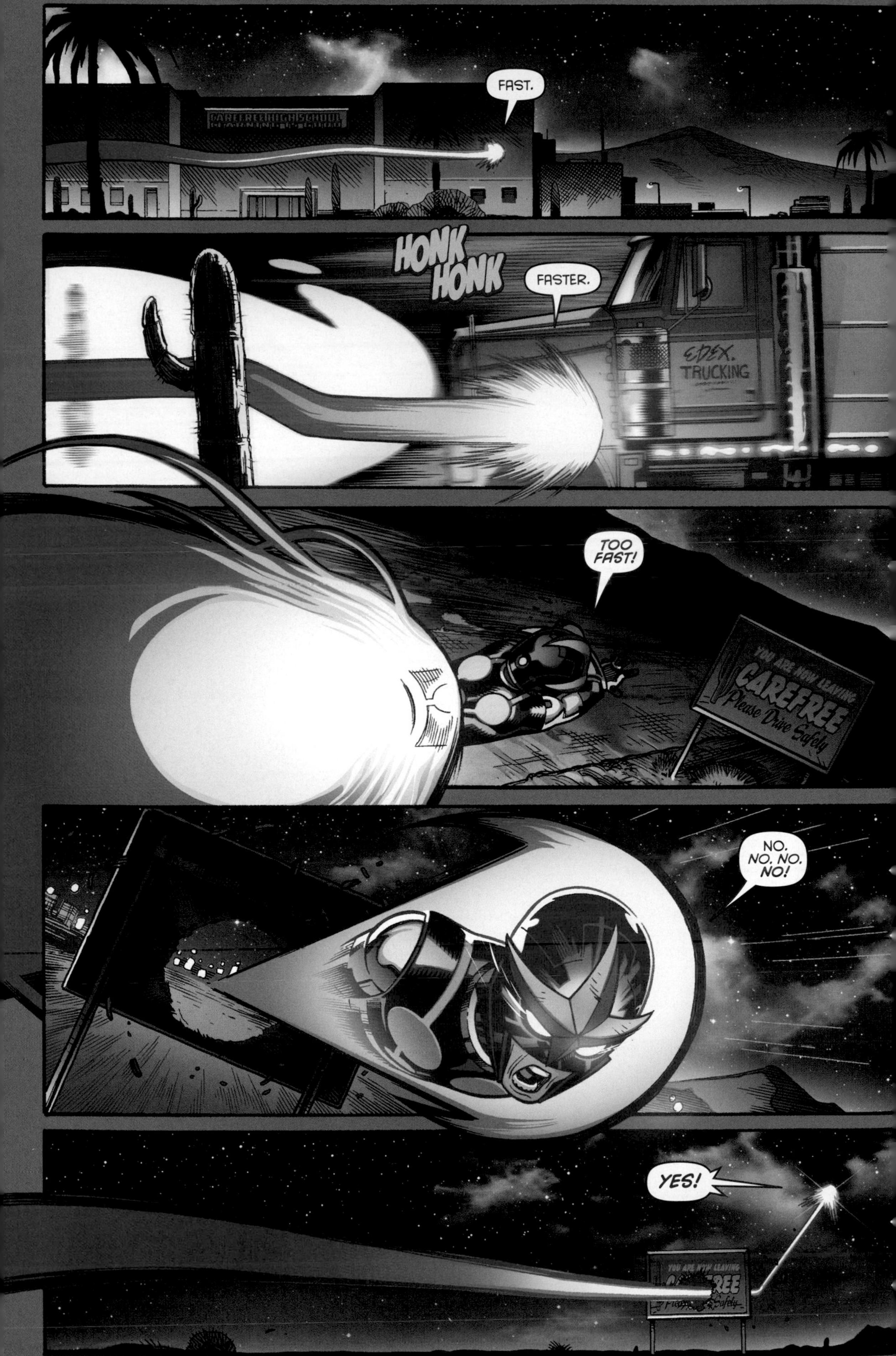
CAREFREE HIGH SCHOOL
FAST.
HONK HONK
FASTER.
EDEX. TRUCKING
TOO FAST!
YOU ARE NOW LEAVING CAREFREE Please Drive Safely
NO. NO. NO. NO!
YES!

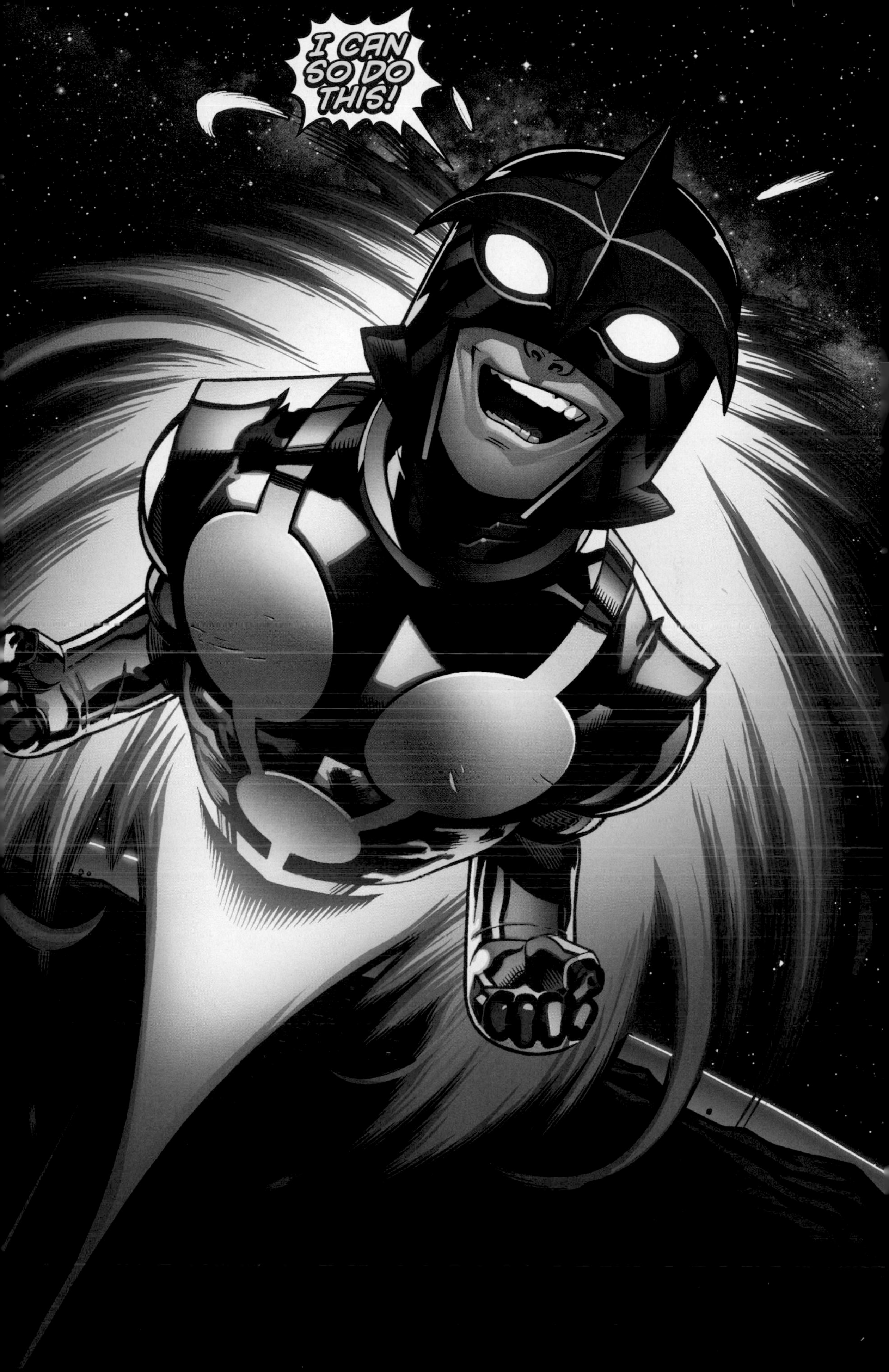
I CAN SO DO THIS!

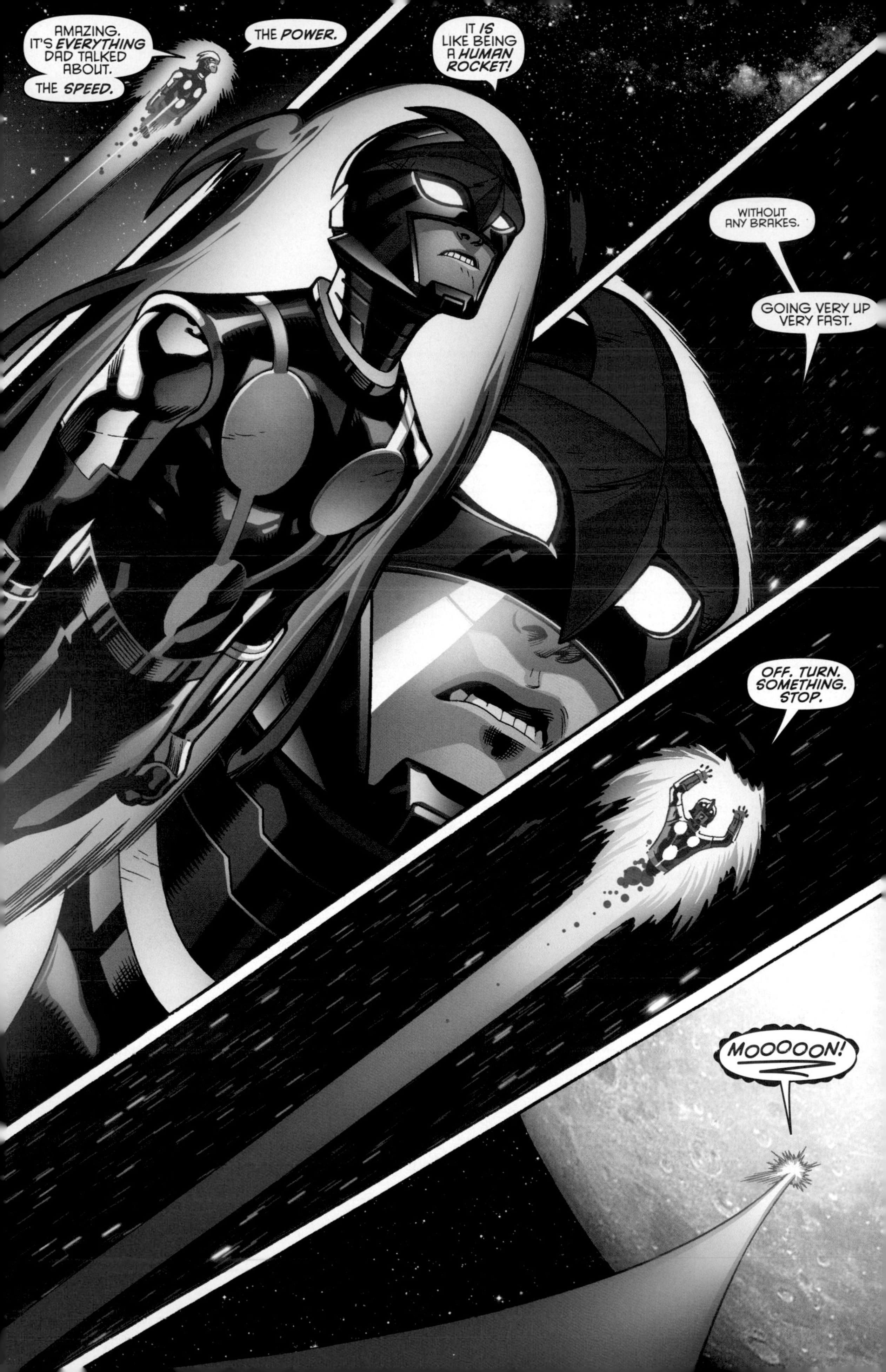
AMAZING. IT'S *EVERYTHING* DAD TALKED ABOUT.
THE *SPEED*.
THE *POWER*.
IT *IS* LIKE BEING A *HUMAN ROCKET!*
WITHOUT ANY BRAKES.
GOING VERY UP VERY FAST.
OFF. TURN. SOMETHING. STOP.
MOOOOON!

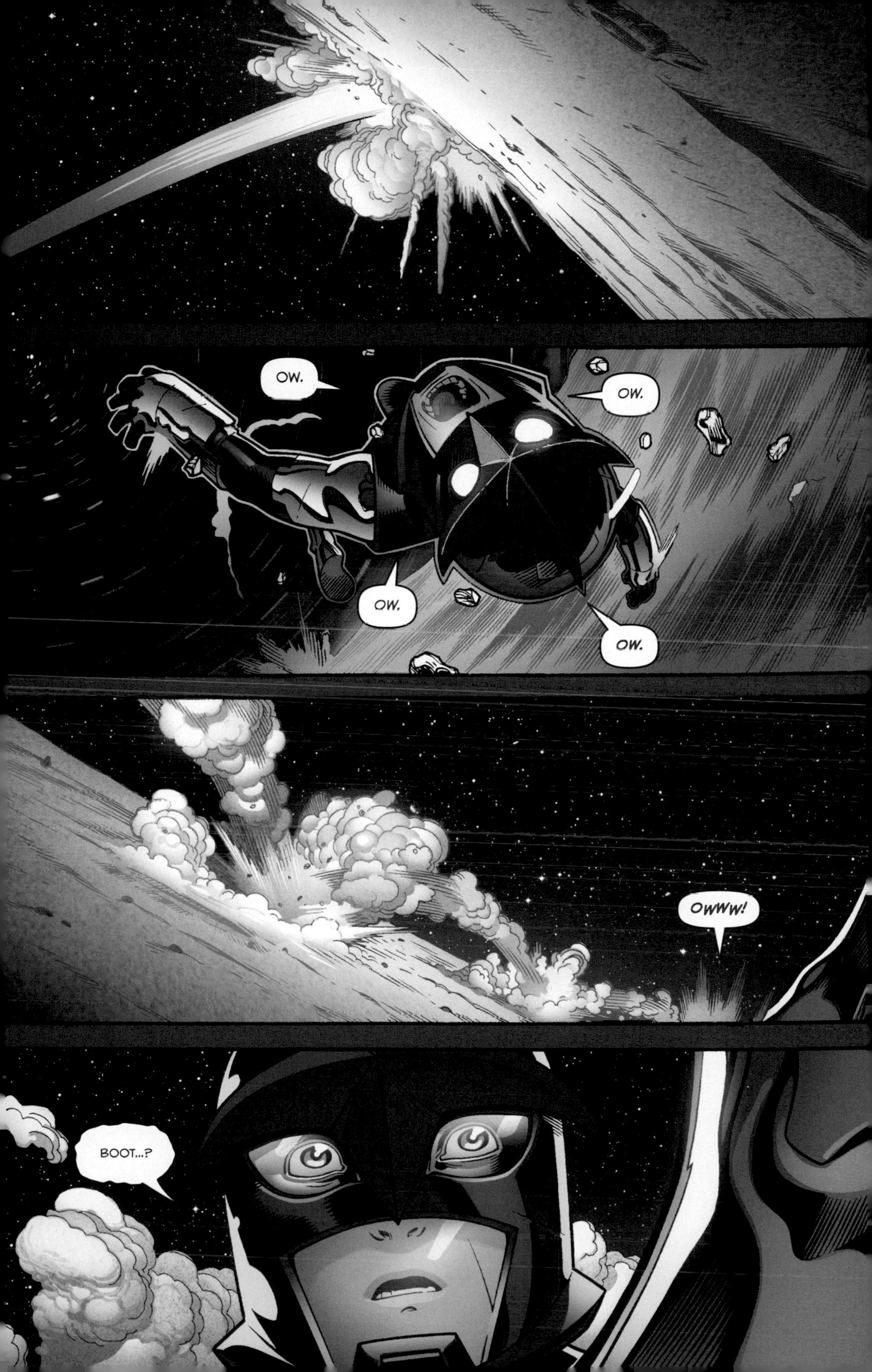
OW.
OW.
OW.
OW.
OWWW!
BOOT...?

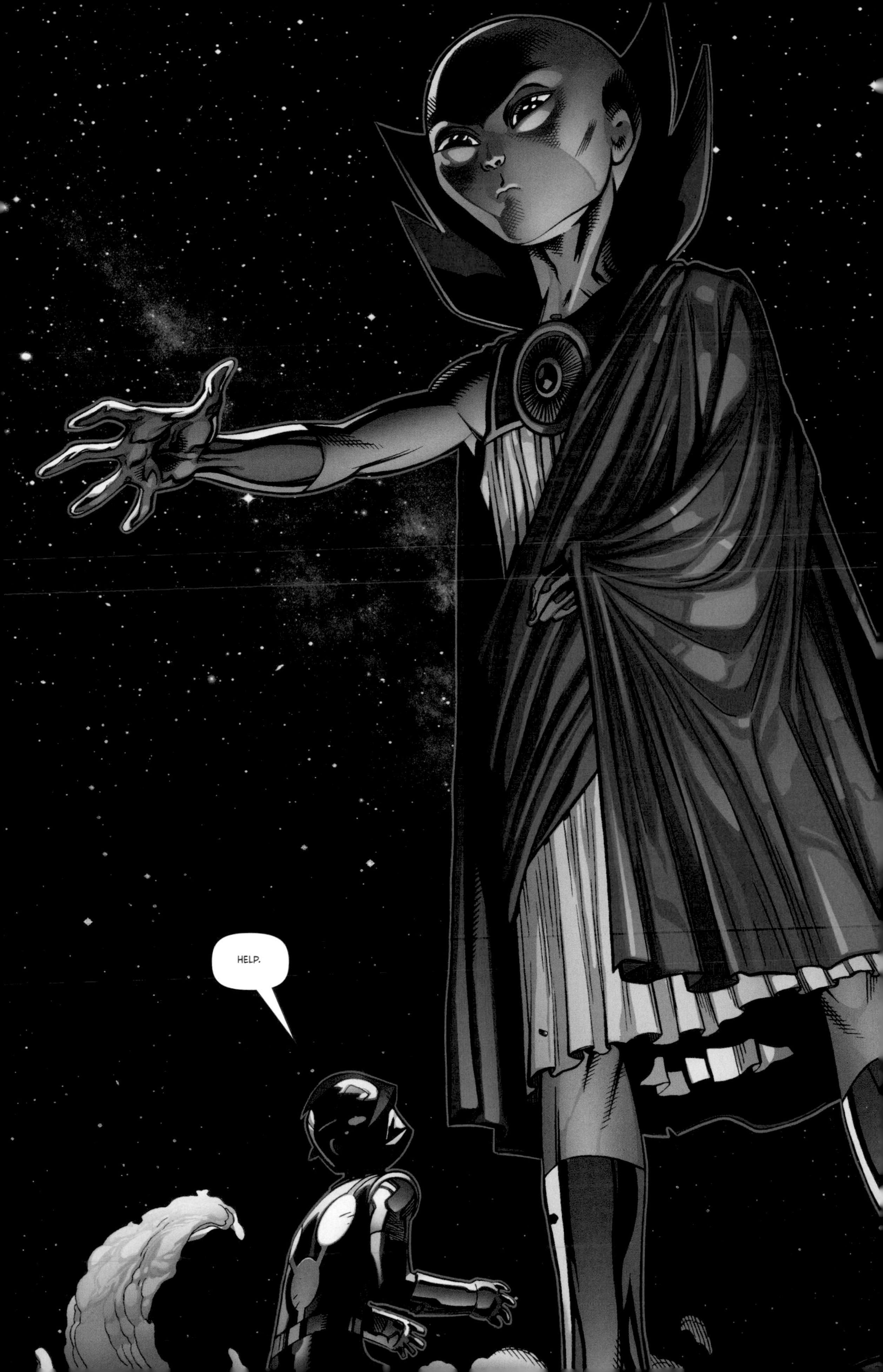
HELP.

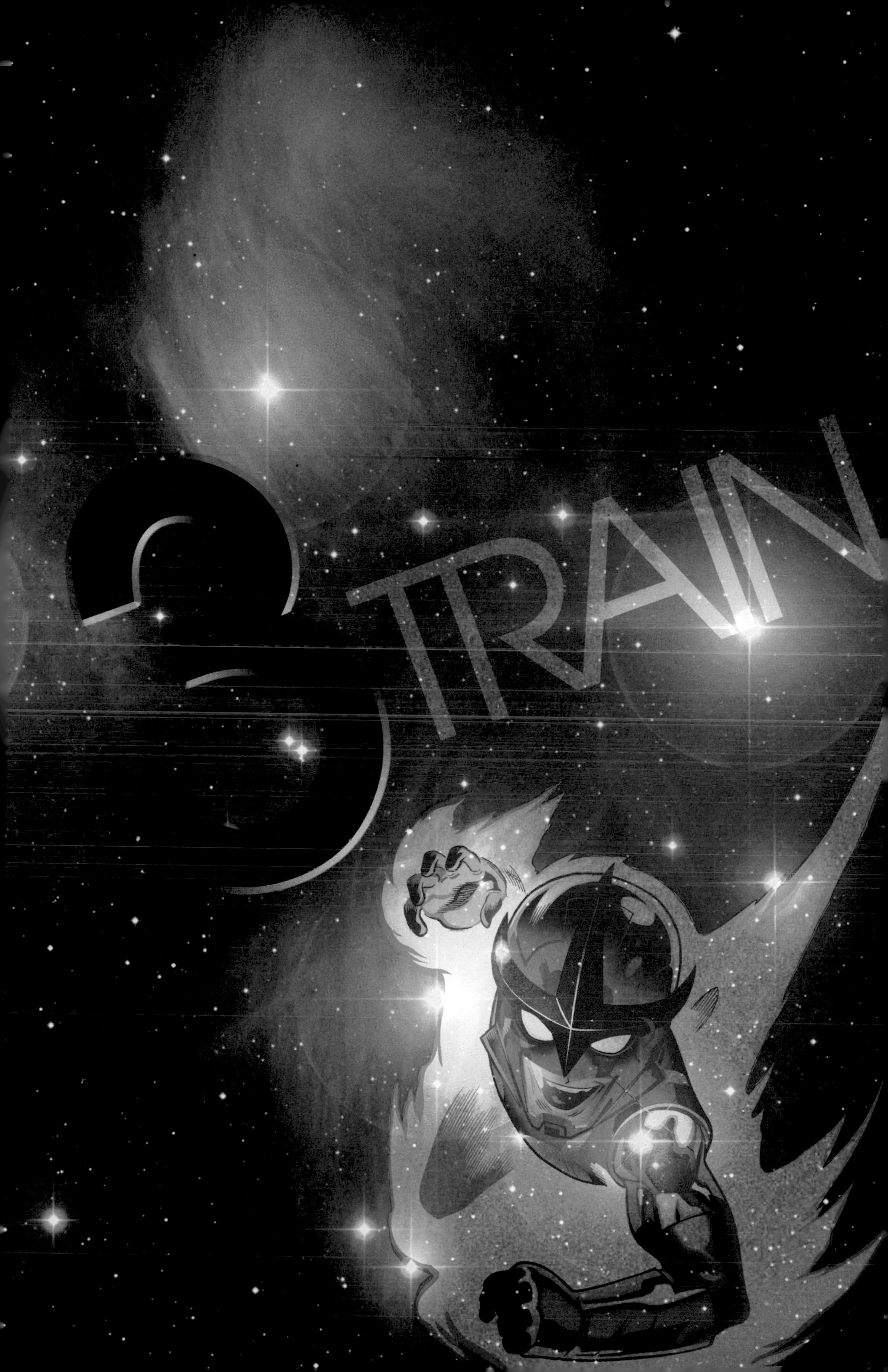
TRAN

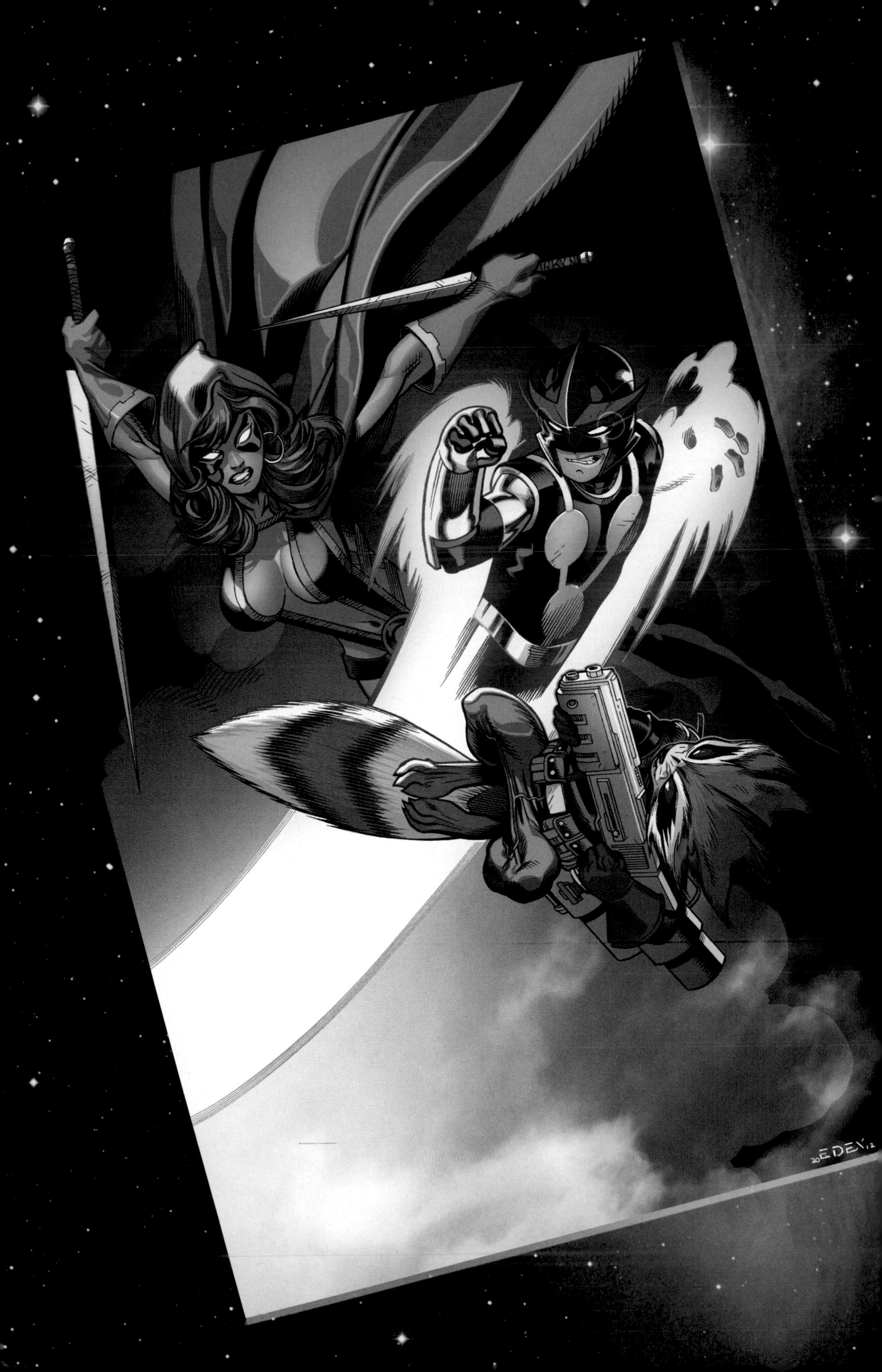

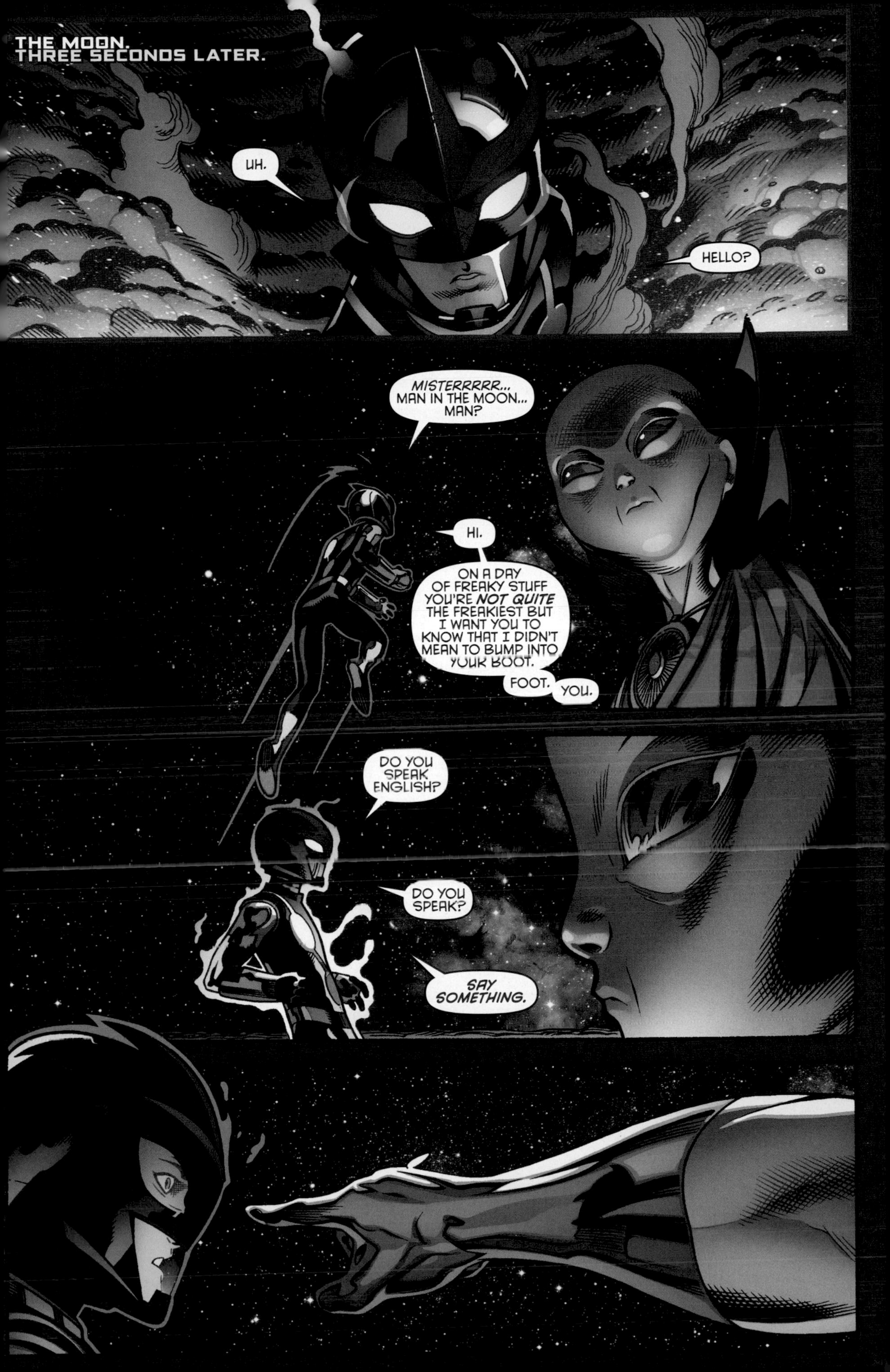
THE MOON. THREE SECONDS LATER.
UH.
HELLO?
MISTERRRRR... MAN IN THE MOON... MAN?
HI.
ON A DAY OF FREAKY STUFF YOU'RE *NOT QUITE* THE FREAKIEST BUT I WANT YOU TO KNOW THAT I DIDN'T MEAN TO BUMP INTO YOUR BOOT.
FOOT.
YOU.
DO YOU SPEAK ENGLISH?
DO YOU SPEAK?
SAY SOMETHING.

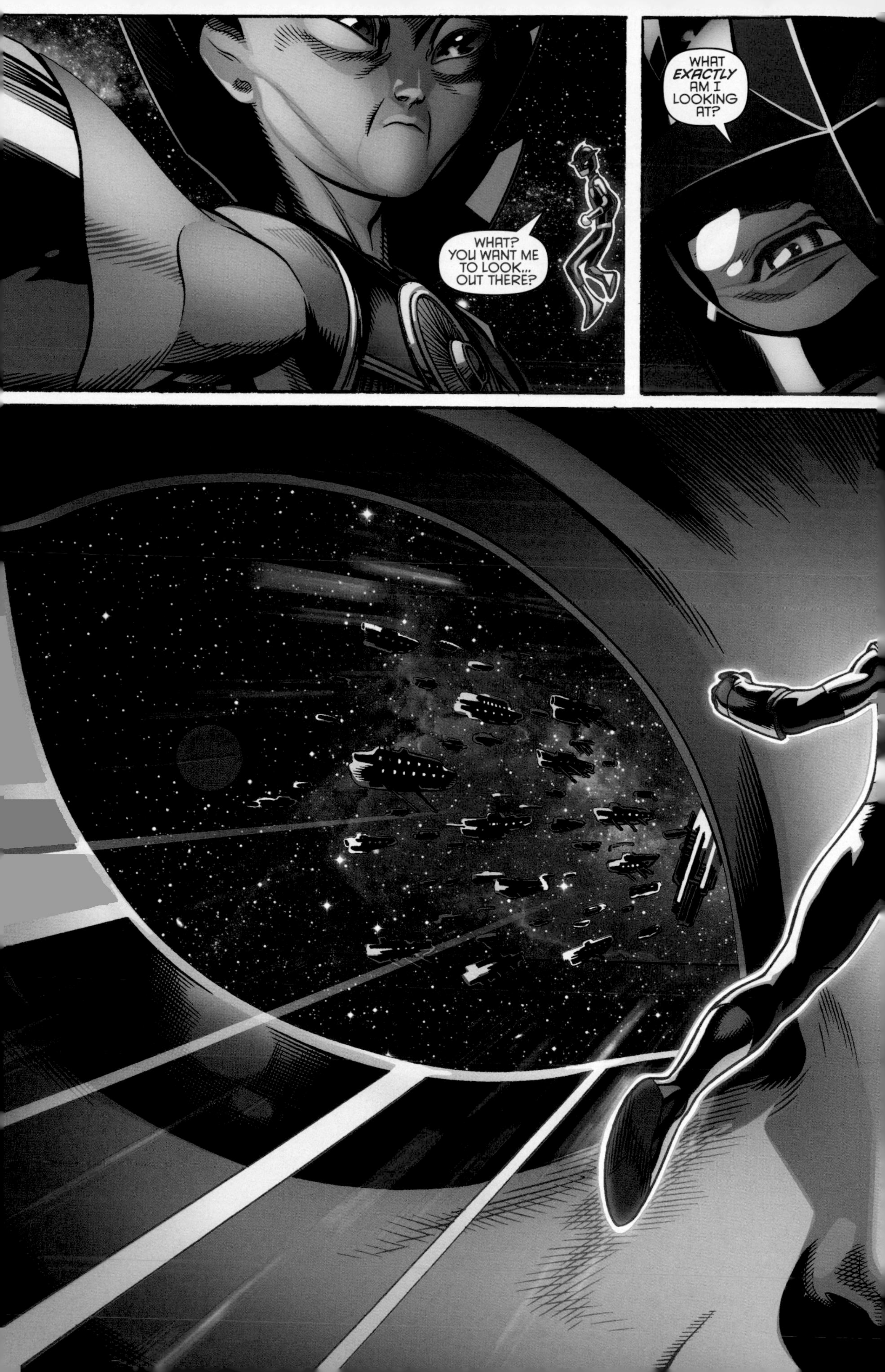
WHAT? YOU WANT ME TO LOOK... OUT THERE?
WHAT *EXACTLY* AM I LOOKING AT?

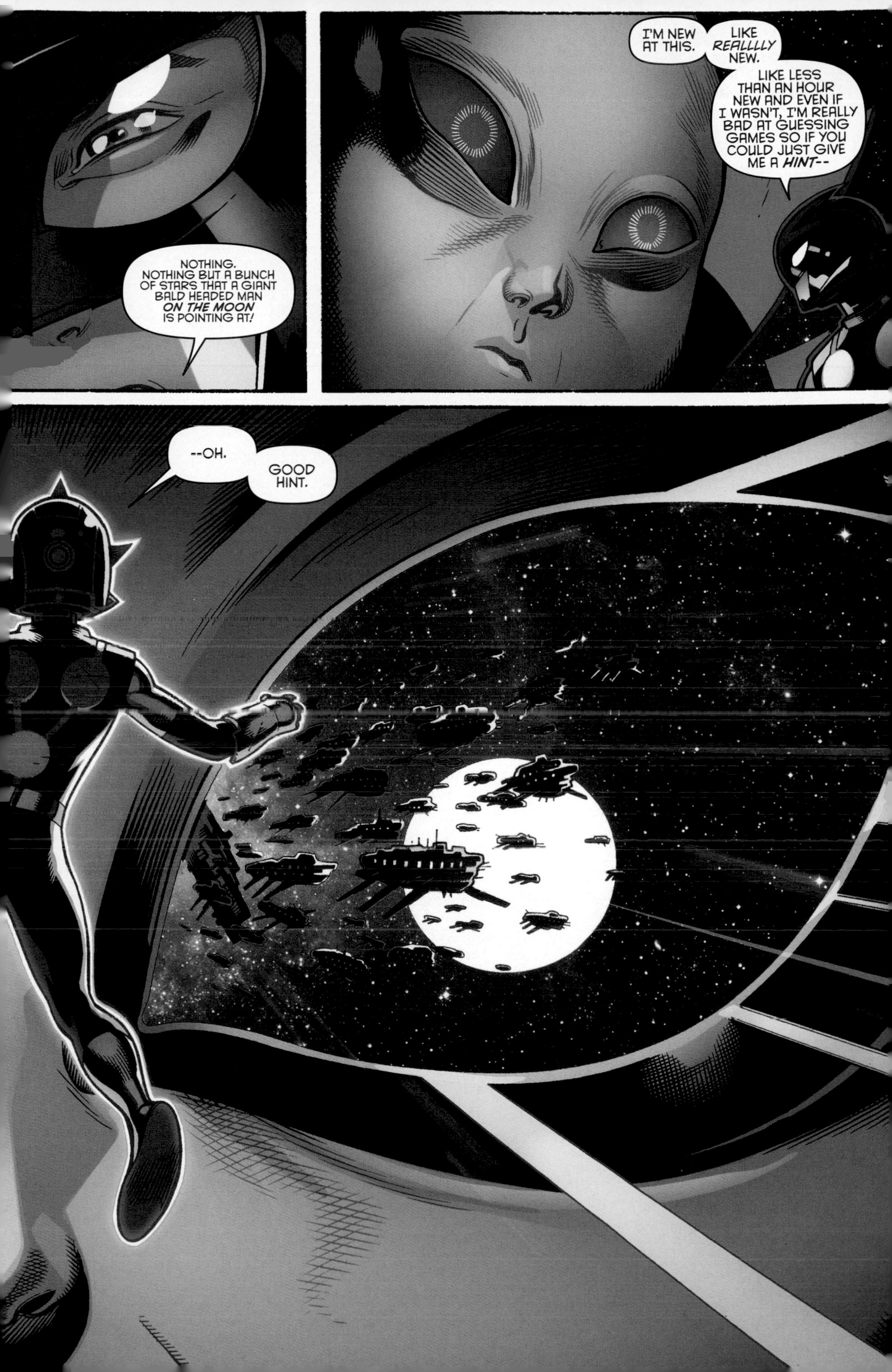
NOTHING. NOTHING BUT A BUNCH OF STARS THAT A GIANT BALD HEADED MAN *ON THE MOON* IS POINTING AT!
I'M NEW AT THIS.
LIKE *REALLLLY* NEW.
LIKE LESS THAN AN HOUR NEW AND EVEN IF I WASN'T, I'M REALLY BAD AT GUESSING GAMES SO IF YOU COULD JUST GIVE ME A *HINT*--
--OH.
GOOD HINT.

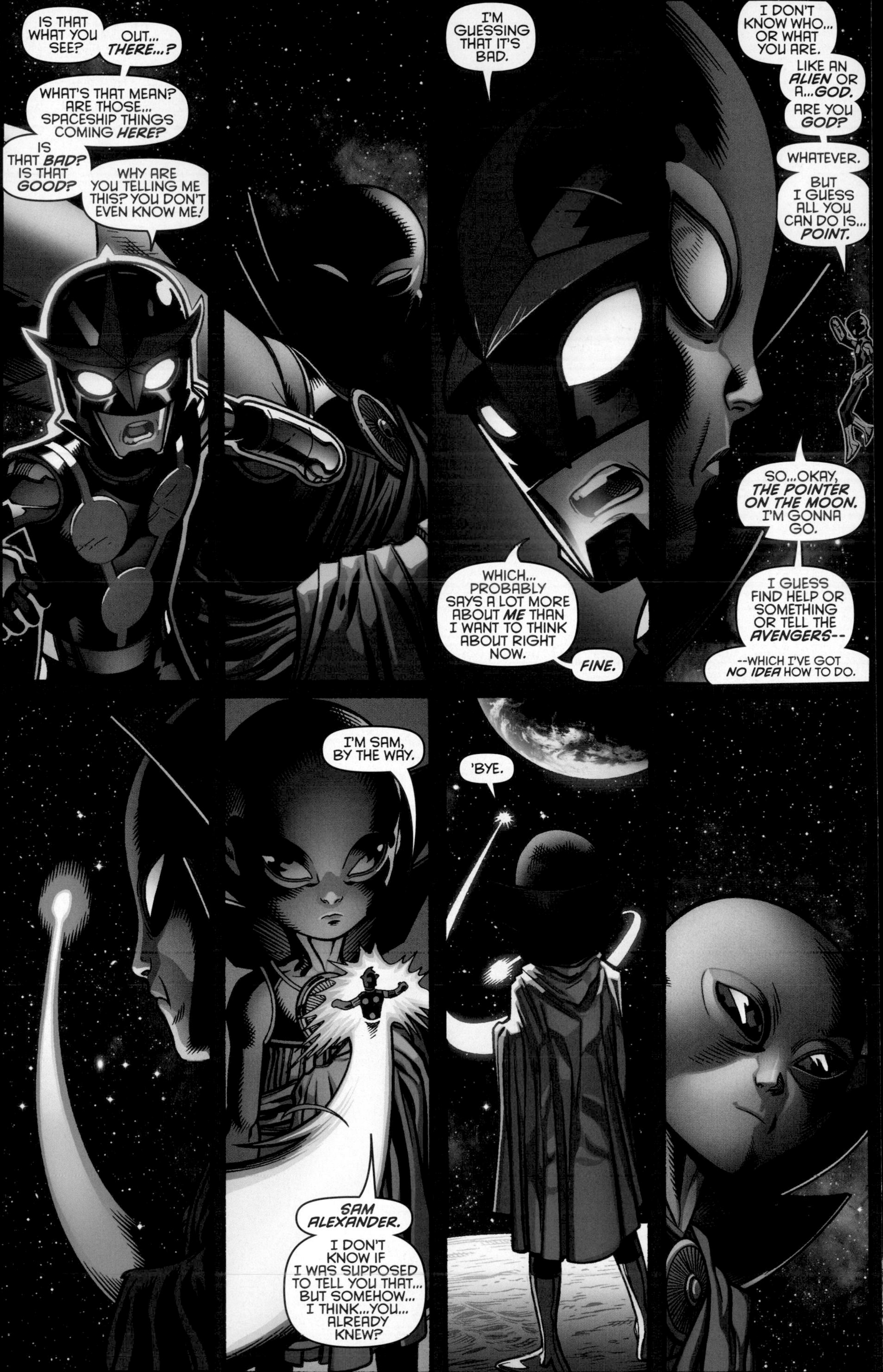

IS THAT WHAT YOU SEE?
OUT... THERE...?
WHAT'S THAT MEAN? ARE THOSE... SPACESHIP THINGS COMING HERE?
IS THAT BAD? IS THAT GOOD?
WHY ARE YOU TELLING ME THIS? YOU DON'T EVEN KNOW ME!
I'M GUESSING THAT IT'S BAD.
WHICH... PROBABLY SAYS A LOT MORE ABOUT ME THAN I WANT TO THINK ABOUT RIGHT NOW.
FINE.
I DON'T KNOW WHO... OR WHAT YOU ARE.
LIKE AN ALIEN OR A...GOD.
ARE YOU GOD?
WHATEVER.
BUT I GUESS ALL YOU CAN DO IS... POINT.
SO...OKAY, THE POINTER ON THE MOON. I'M GONNA GO.
I GUESS FIND HELP OR SOMETHING OR TELL THE AVENGERS--
--WHICH I'VE GOT NO IDEA HOW TO DO.
I'M SAM, BY THE WAY.
SAM ALEXANDER.
I DON'T KNOW IF I WAS SUPPOSED TO TELL YOU THAT... BUT SOMEHOW... I THINK...YOU... ALREADY KNEW?
'BYE.

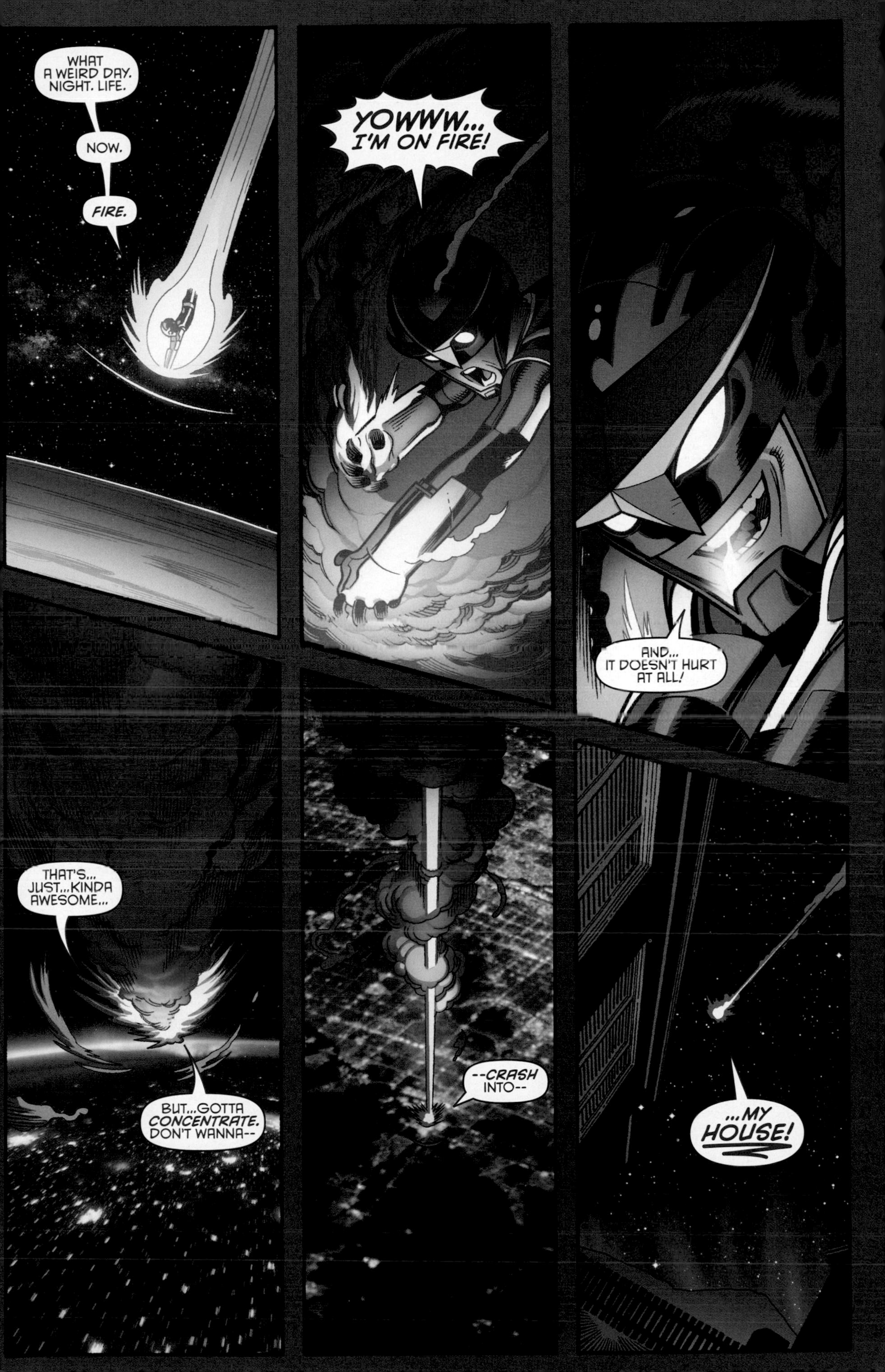
WHAT A WEIRD DAY. NIGHT. LIFE.
NOW.
FIRE.
YOWWW... I'M ON FIRE!
AND... IT DOESN'T HURT AT ALL!
THAT'S... JUST...KINDA AWESOME...
BUT...GOTTA CONCENTRATE. DON'T WANNA--
--CRASH INTO--
...MY HOUSE!

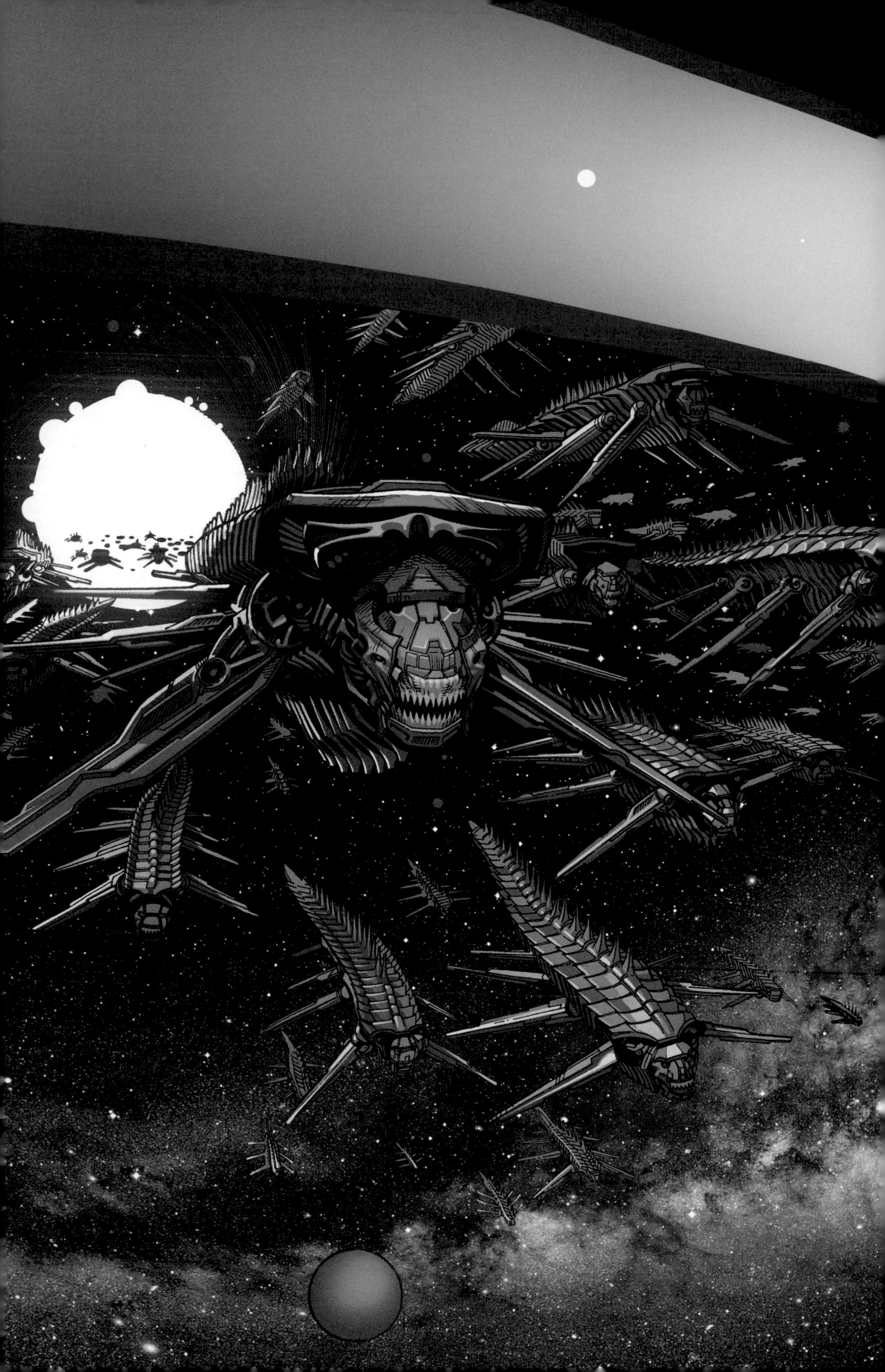

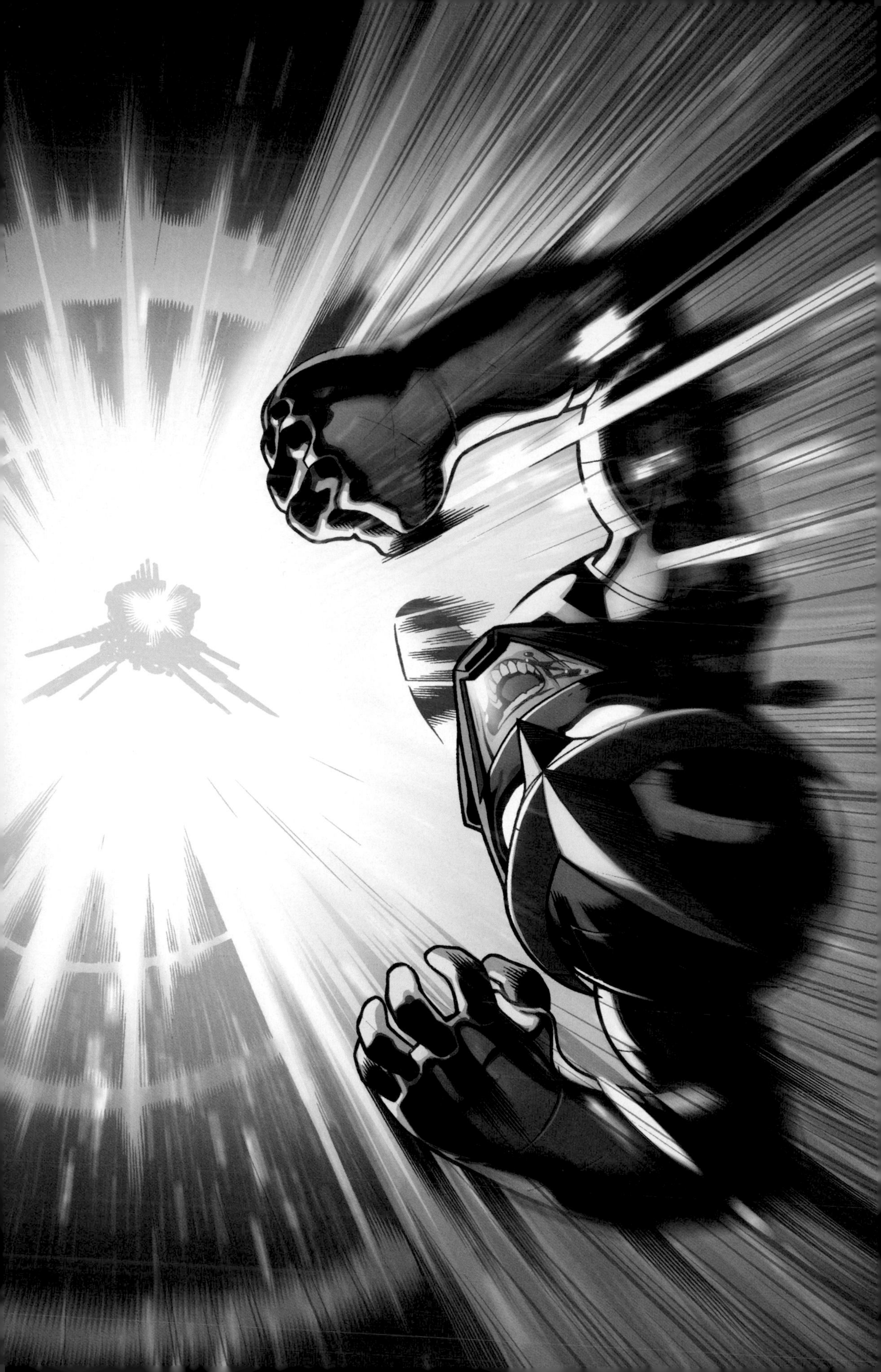

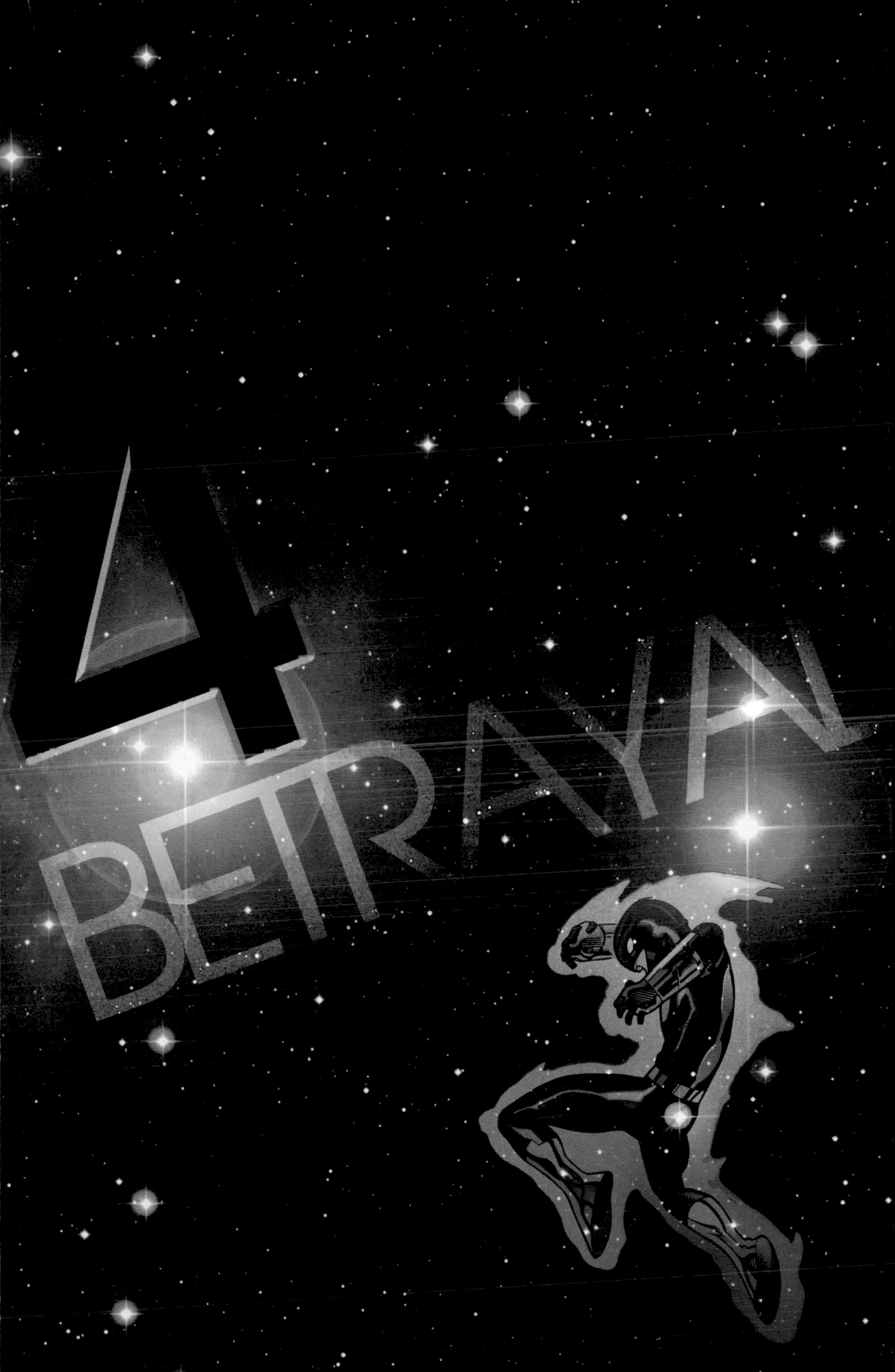
4
BETRAYAL

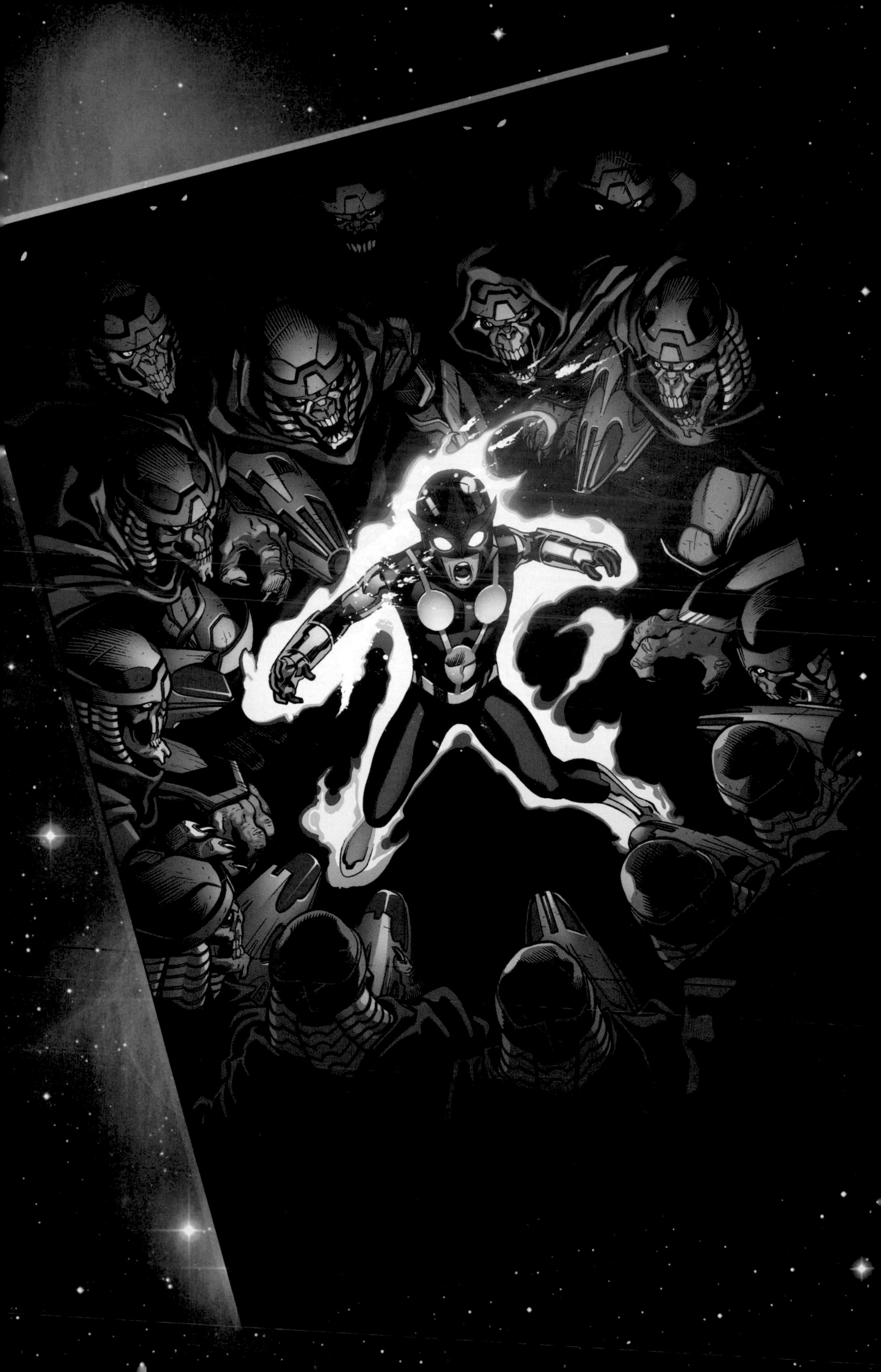

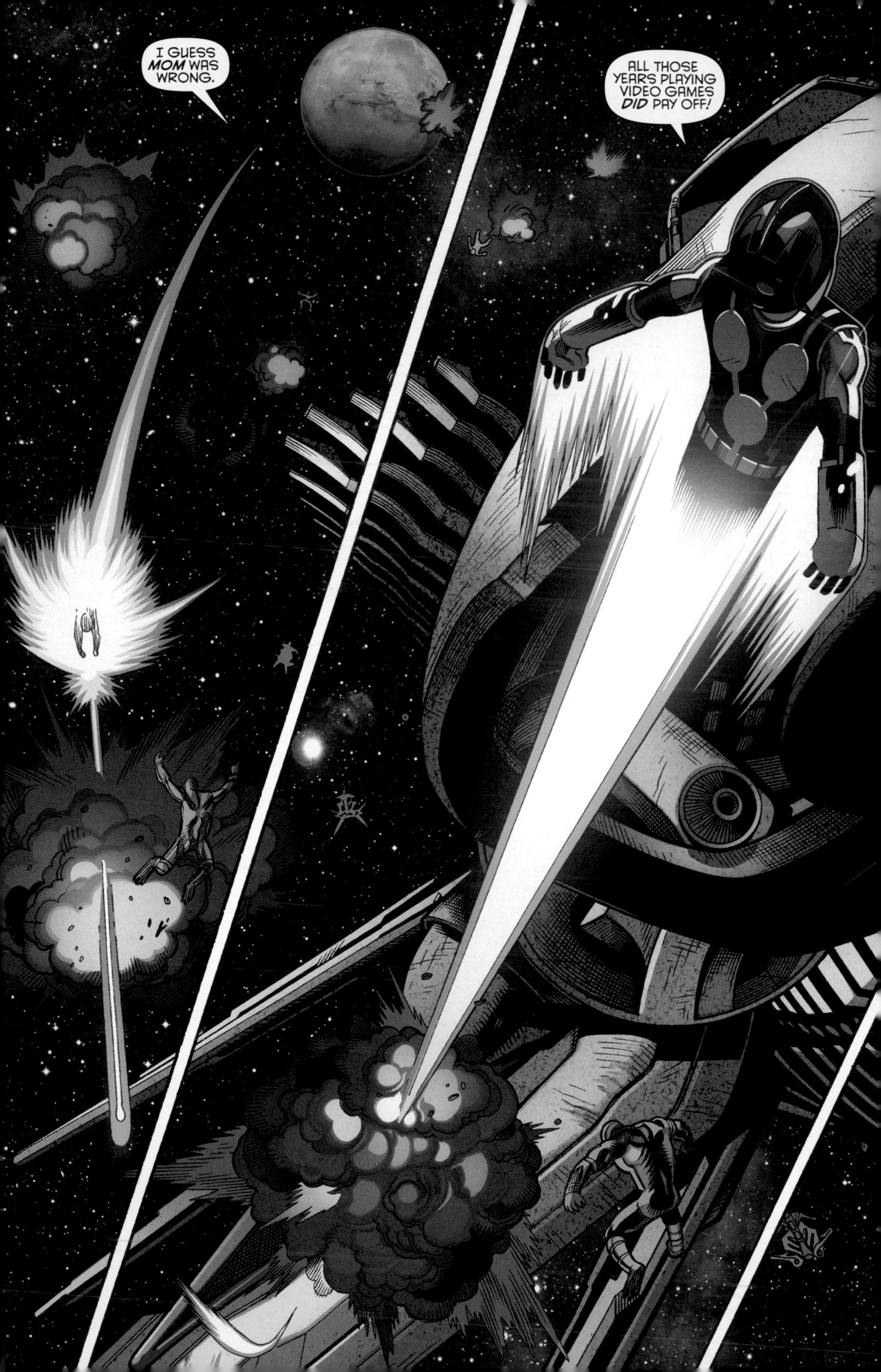
I GUESS MOM WAS WRONG.
ALL THOSE YEARS PLAYING VIDEO GAMES DID PAY OFF!

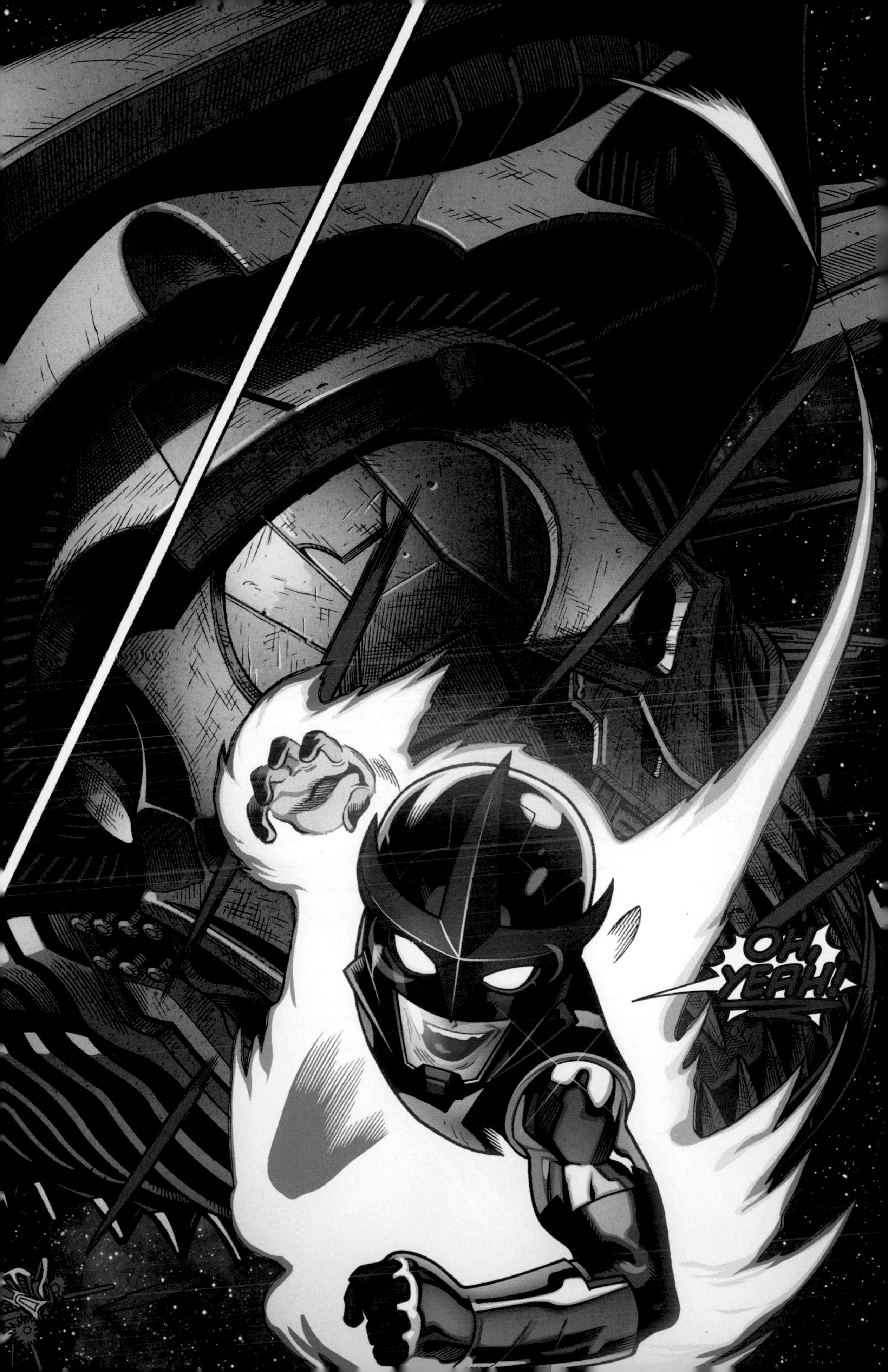
OH, YEAH!

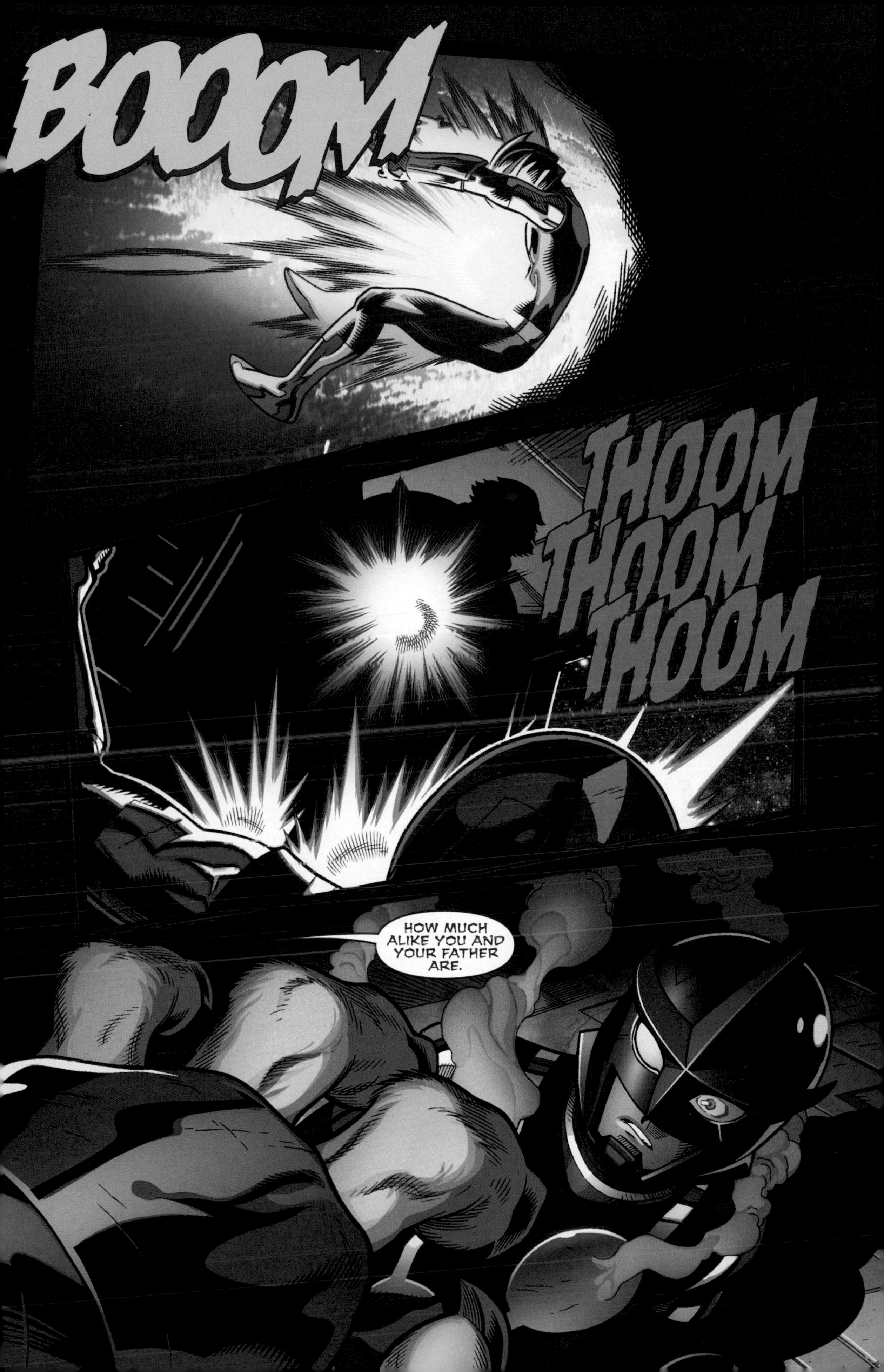
BOOOM
THOOM
THOOM
THOOM
HOW MUCH ALIKE YOU AND YOUR FATHER ARE.

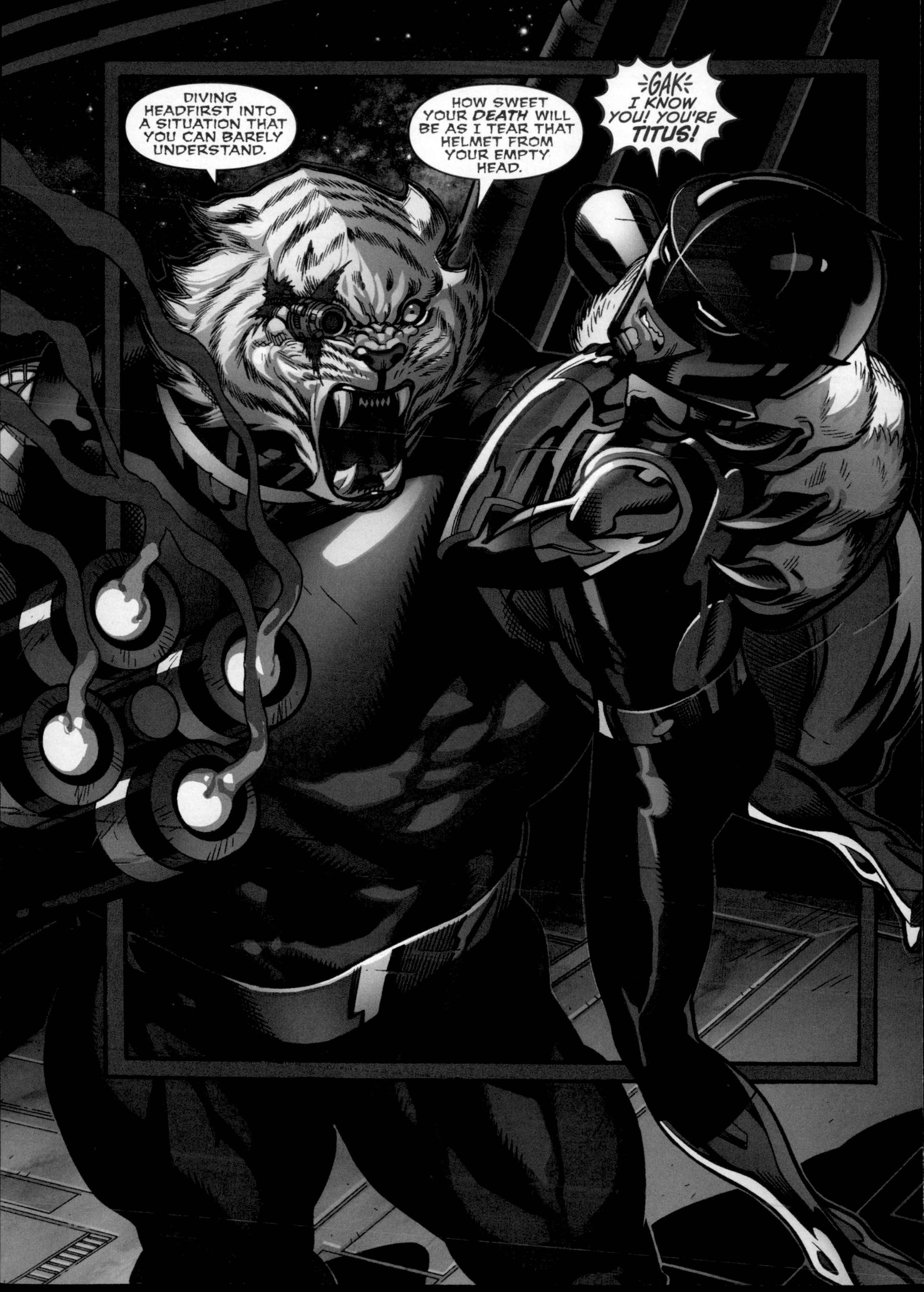
DIVING HEADFIRST INTO A SITUATION THAT YOU CAN BARELY UNDERSTAND.
HOW SWEET YOUR DEATH WILL BE AS I TEAR THAT HELMET FROM YOUR EMPTY HEAD.
GAK
I KNOW YOU! YOU'RE TITUS!

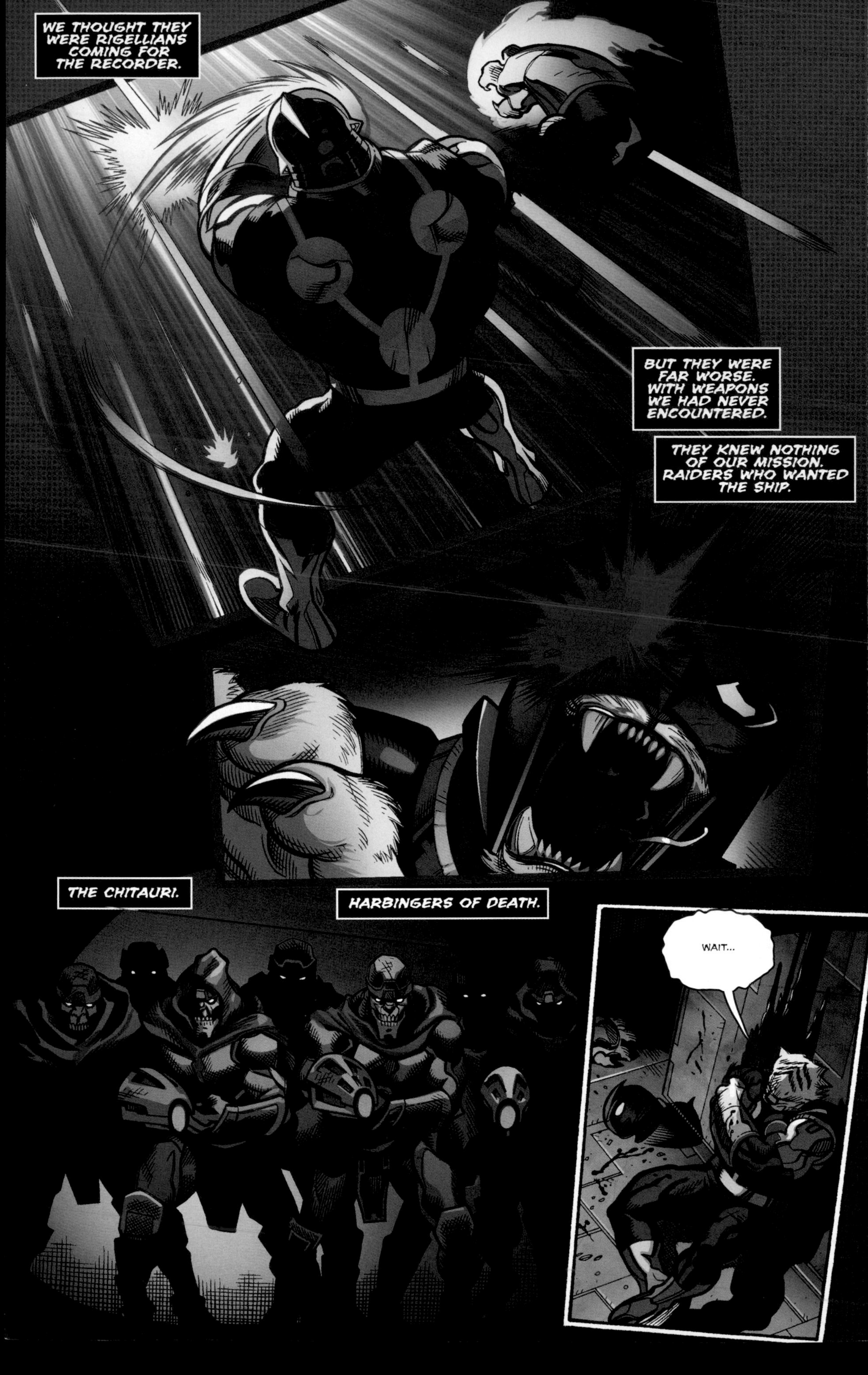
WE THOUGHT THEY WERE RIGELLIANS COMING FOR THE RECORDER.
BUT THEY WERE FAR WORSE. WITH WEAPONS WE HAD NEVER ENCOUNTERED.
THEY KNEW NOTHING OF OUR MISSION. RAIDERS WHO WANTED THE SHIP.
THE CHITAURI.
HARBINGERS OF DEATH.
WAIT...

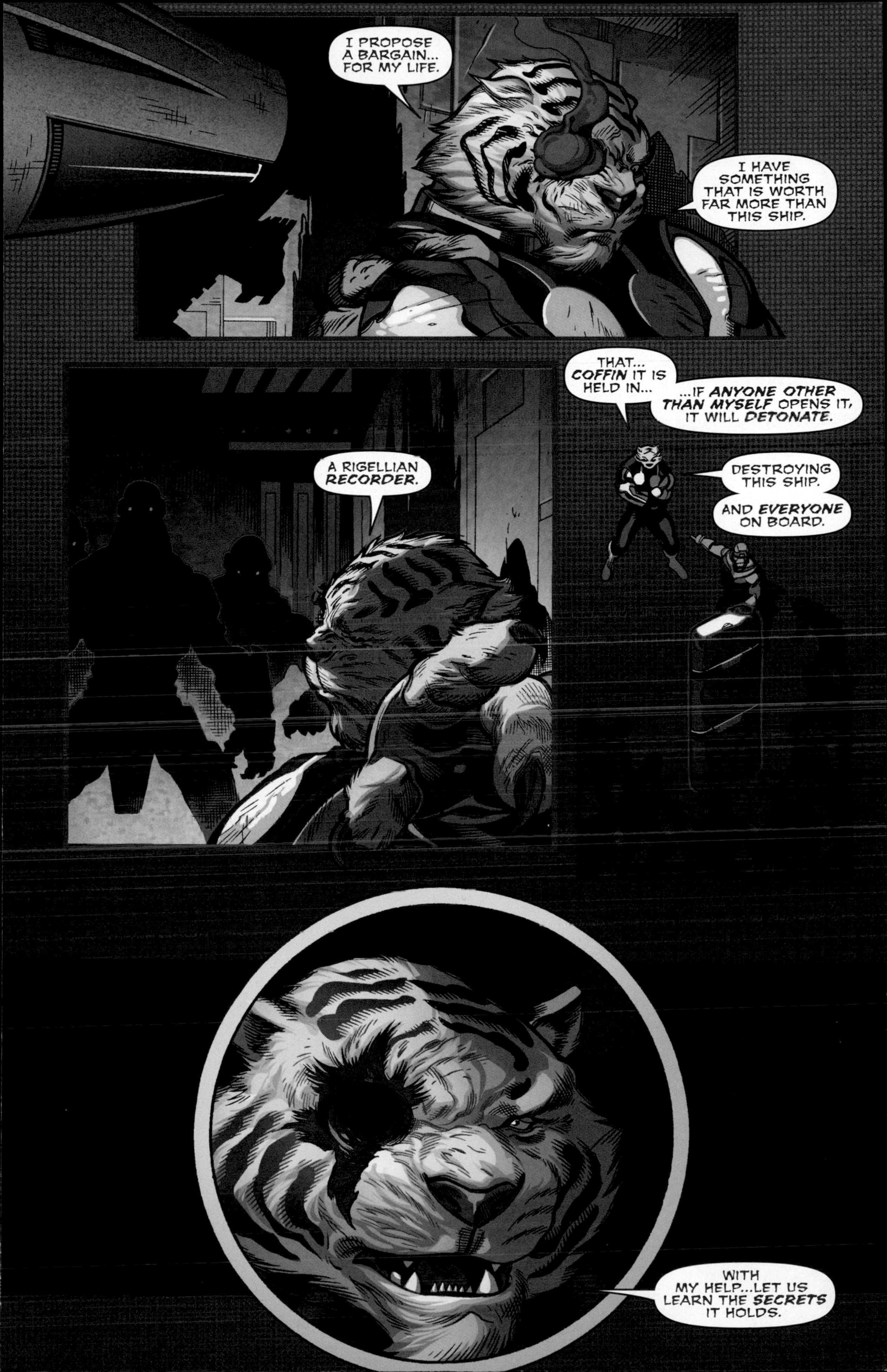
I PROPOSE A BARGAIN... FOR MY LIFE.
I HAVE SOMETHING THAT IS WORTH FAR MORE THAN THIS SHIP.
A RIGELLIAN *RECORDER*.
THAT... *COFFIN* IT IS HELD IN...
...IF *ANYONE OTHER THAN MYSELF* OPENS IT, IT WILL *DETONATE*.
DESTROYING THIS SHIP.
AND *EVERYONE* ON BOARD.
WITH MY HELP...LET US LEARN THE *SECRETS* IT HOLDS.

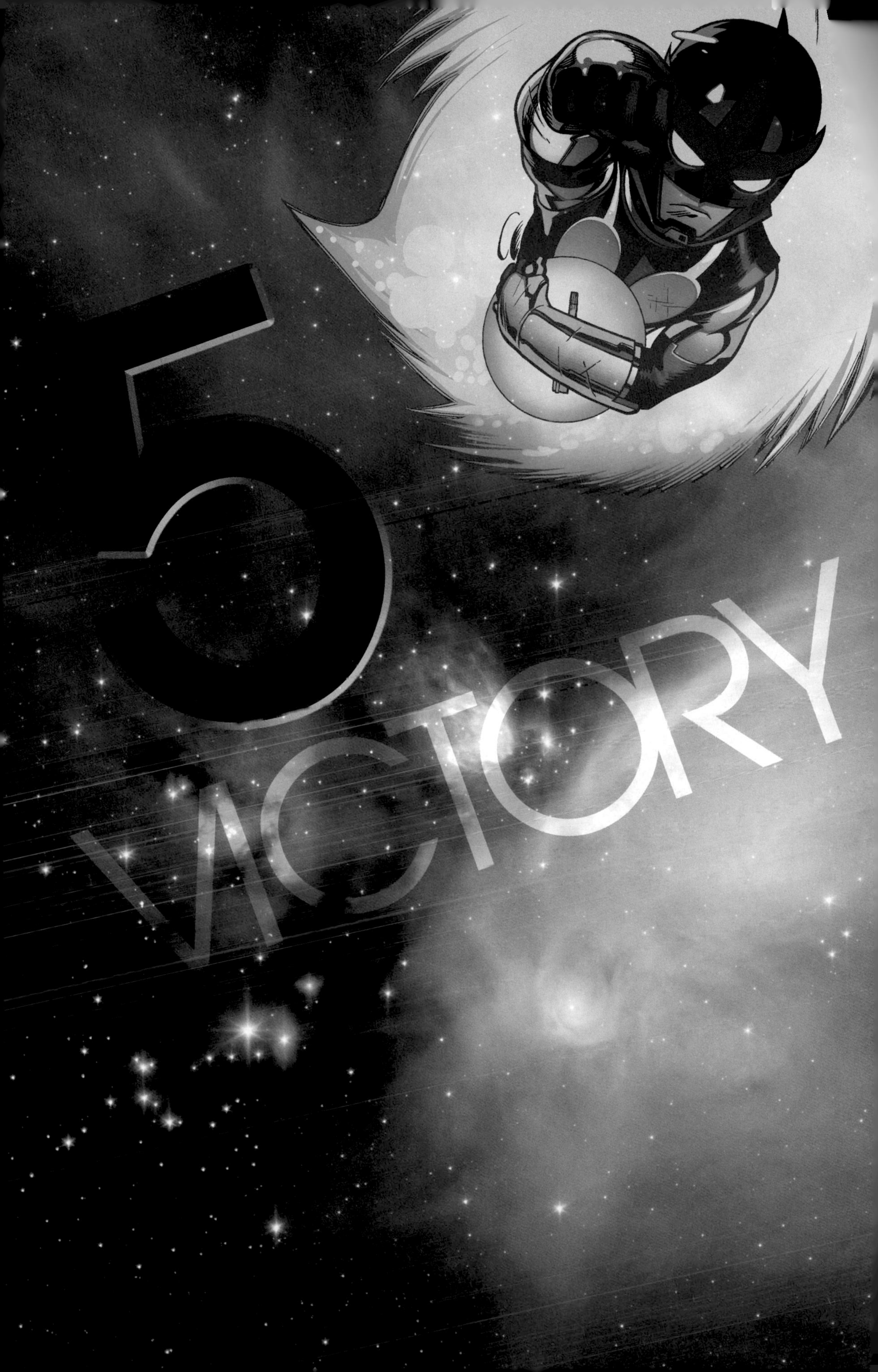
5
VICTORY

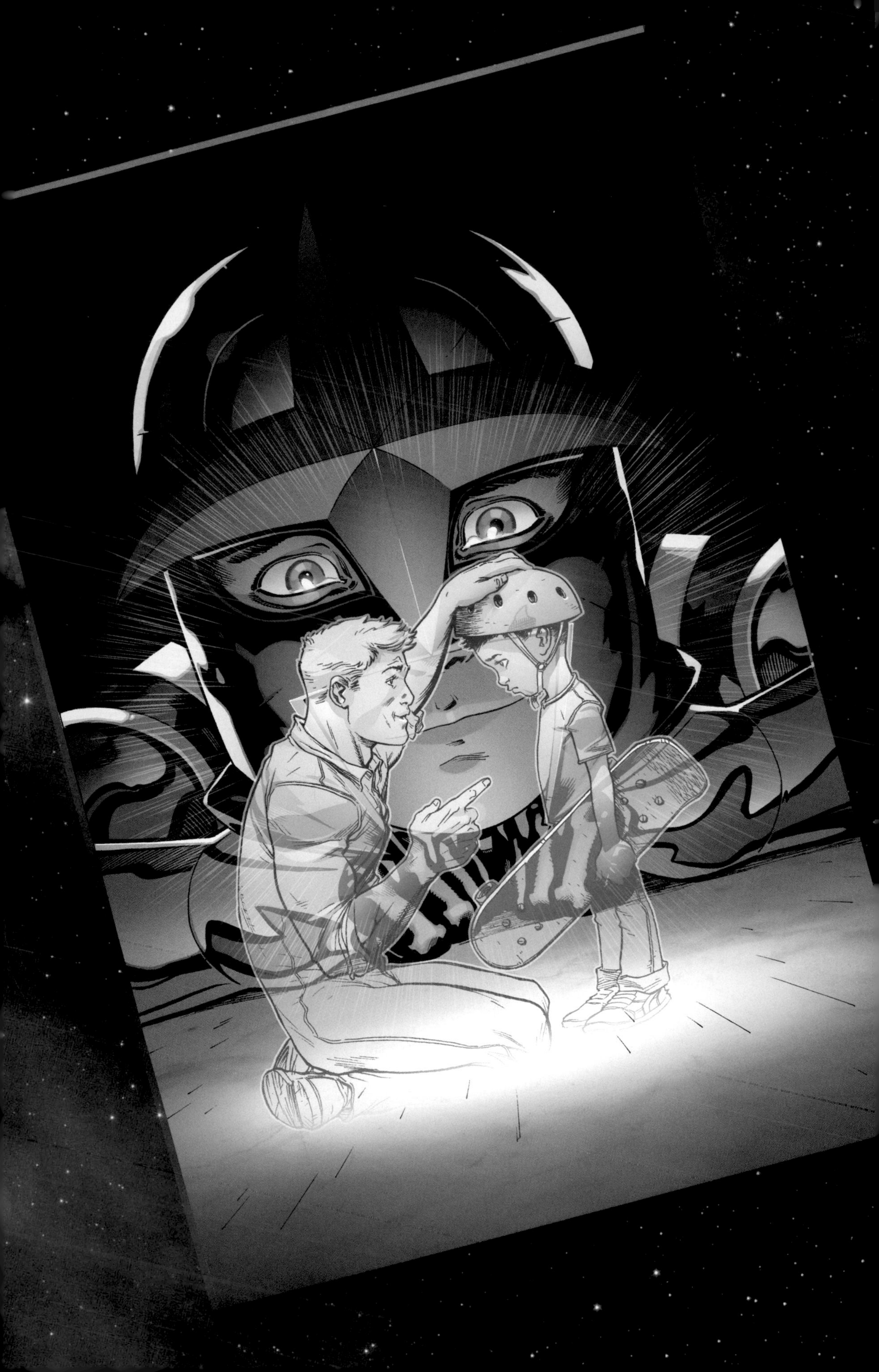

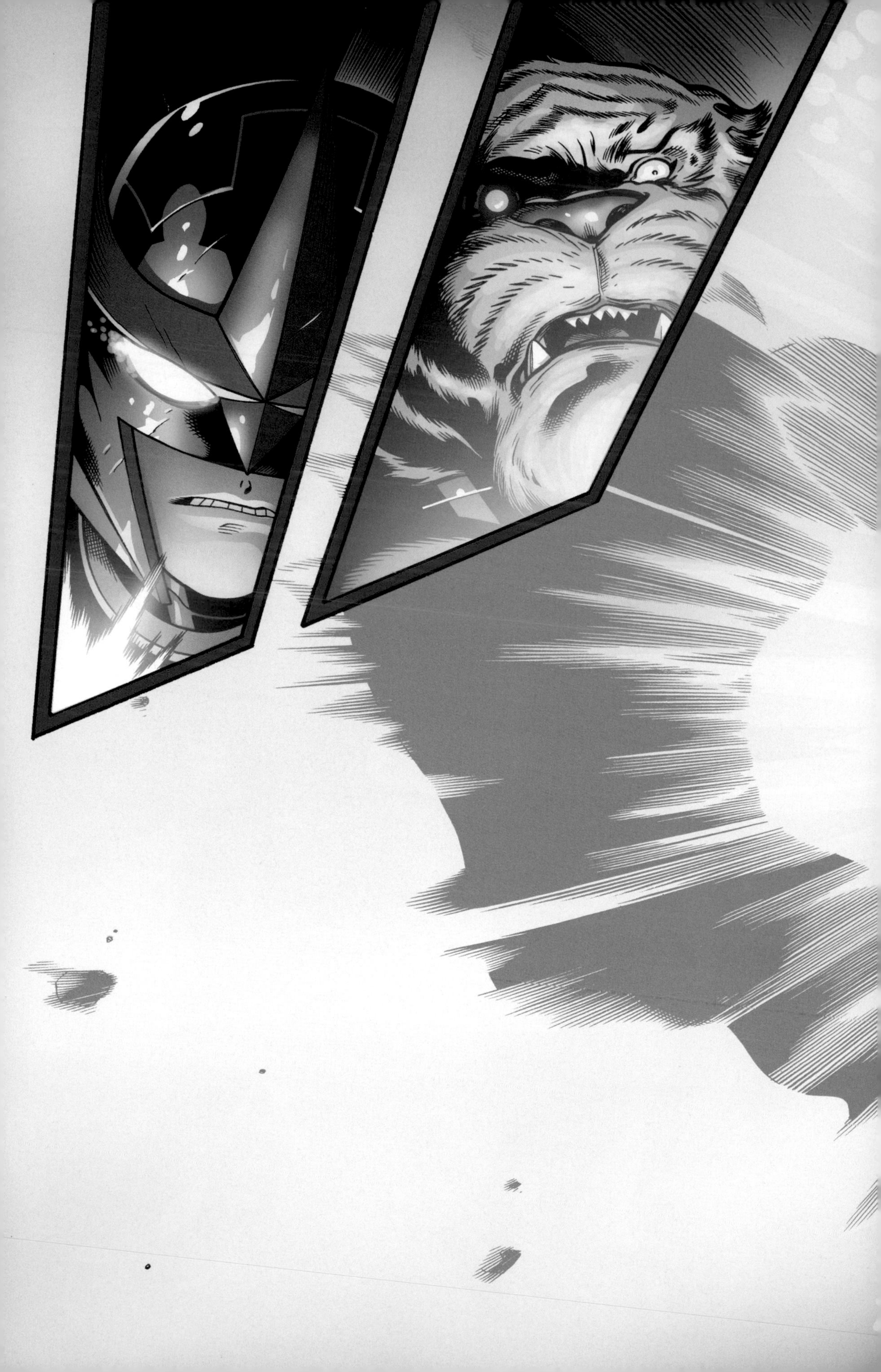

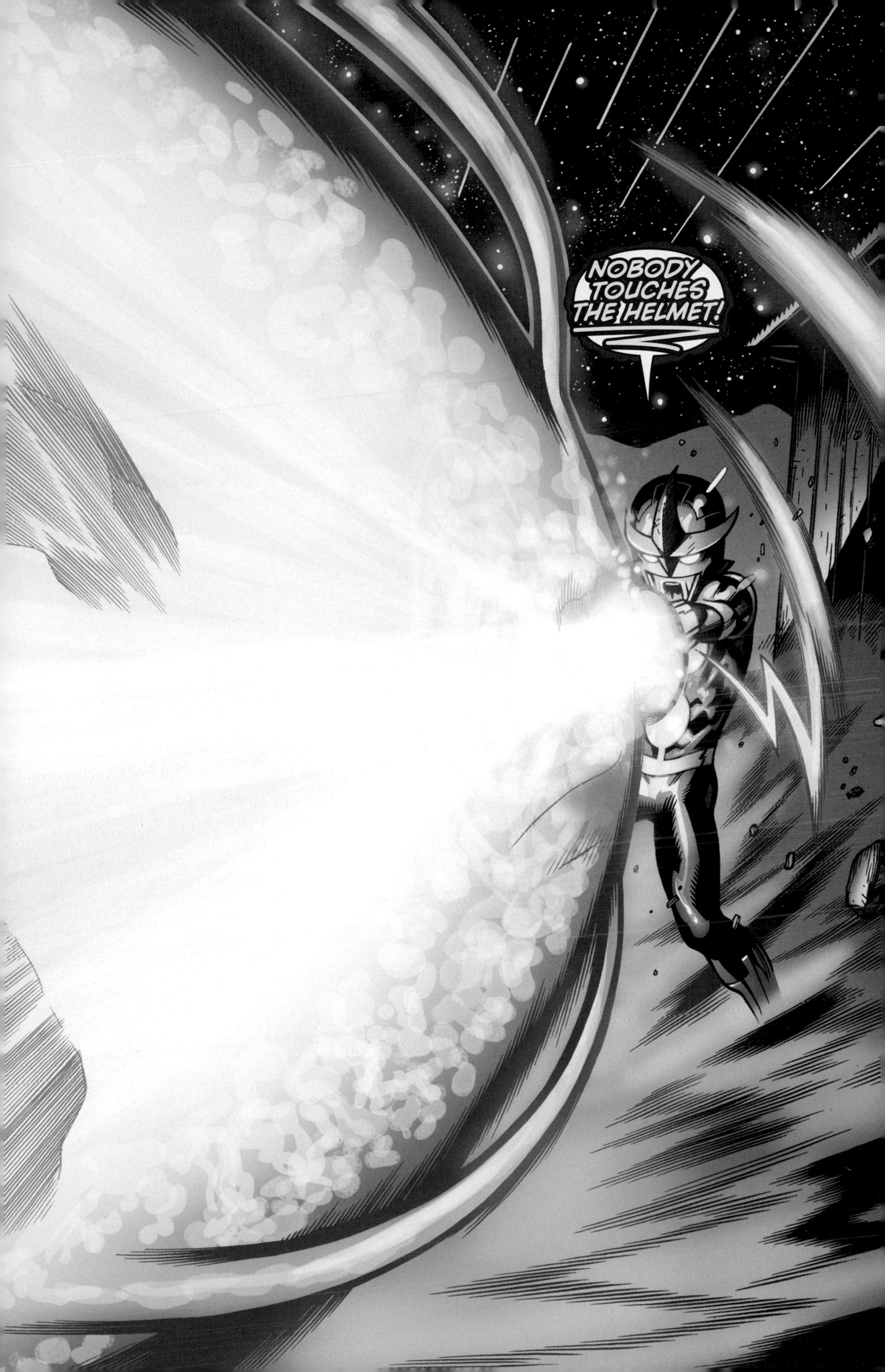
NOBODY TOUCHES THE HELMET!

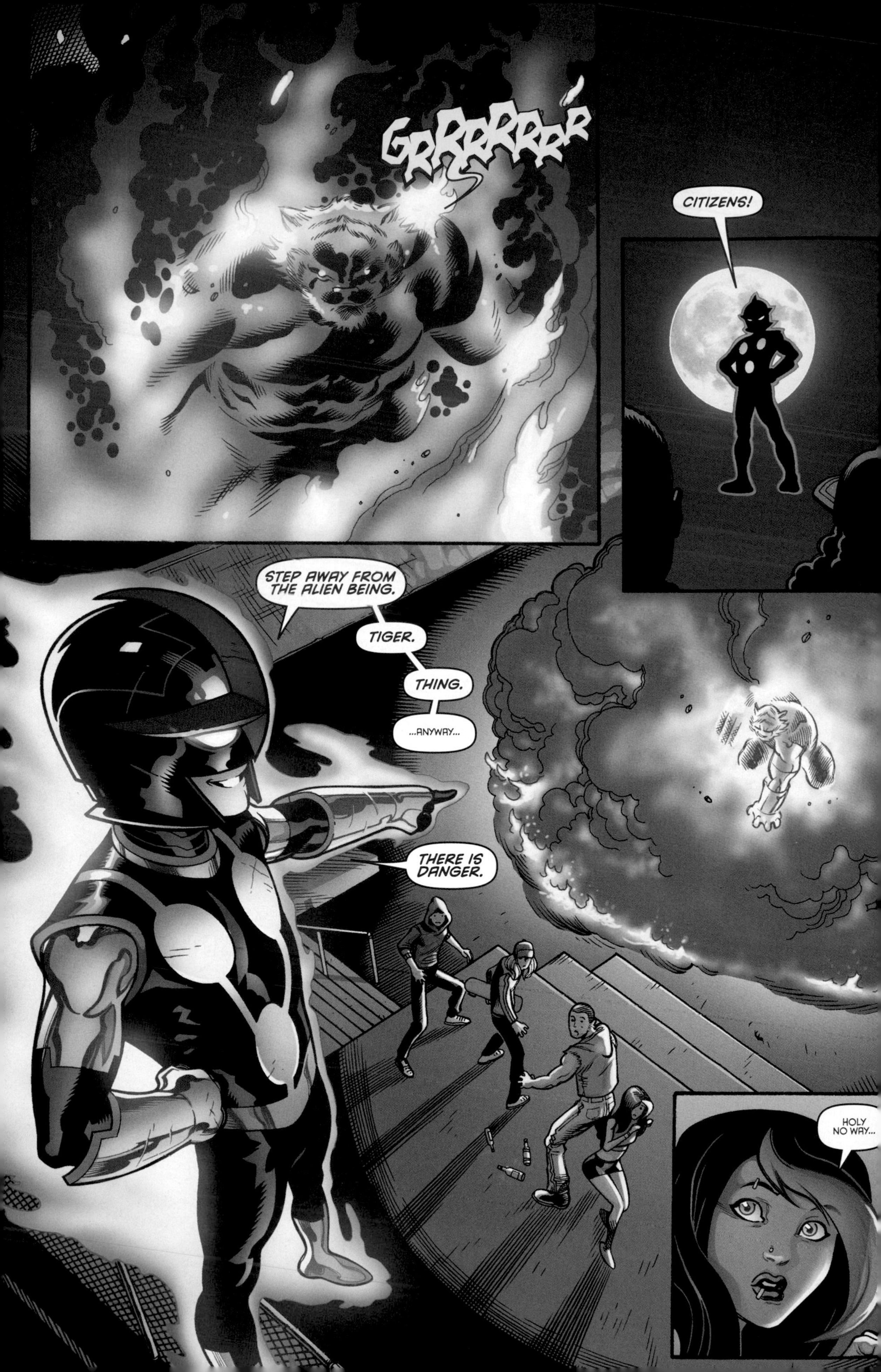
GRRRRRRR
CITIZENS!
STEP AWAY FROM THE ALIEN BEING.
TIGER.
THING.
...ANYWAY...
THERE IS DANGER.
HOLY NO WAY...

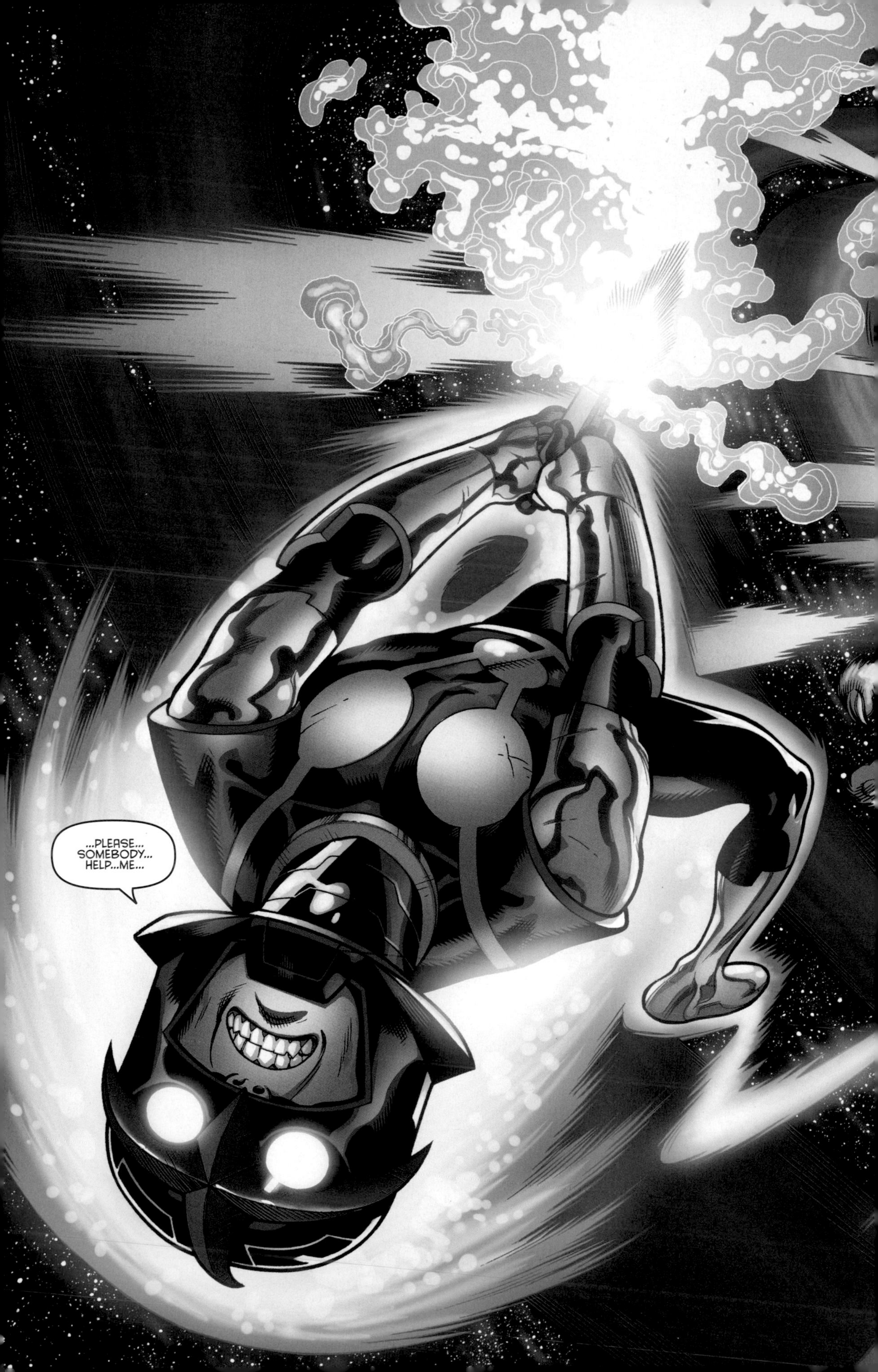
...PLEASE... SOMEBODY... HELP...ME...

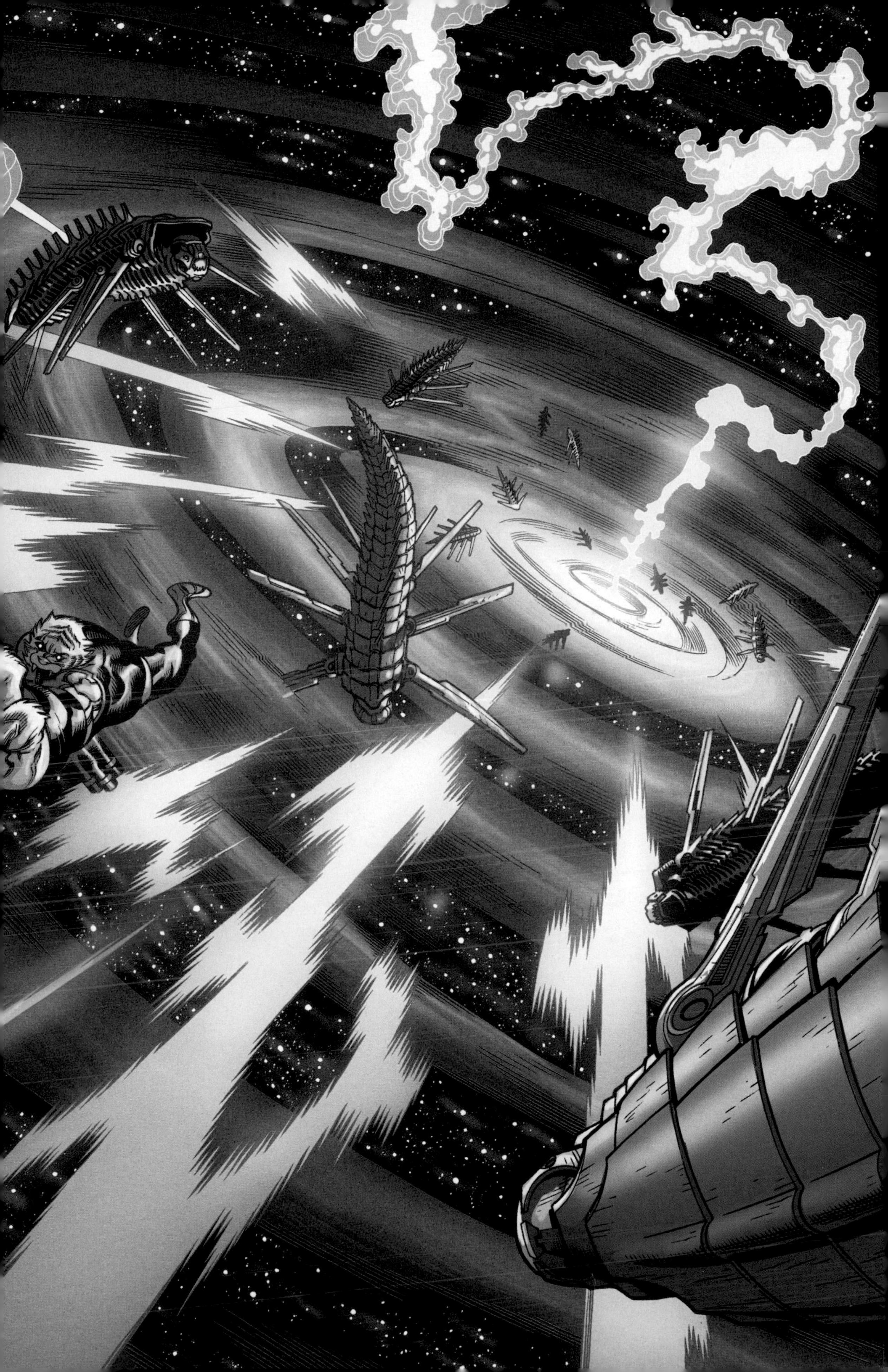

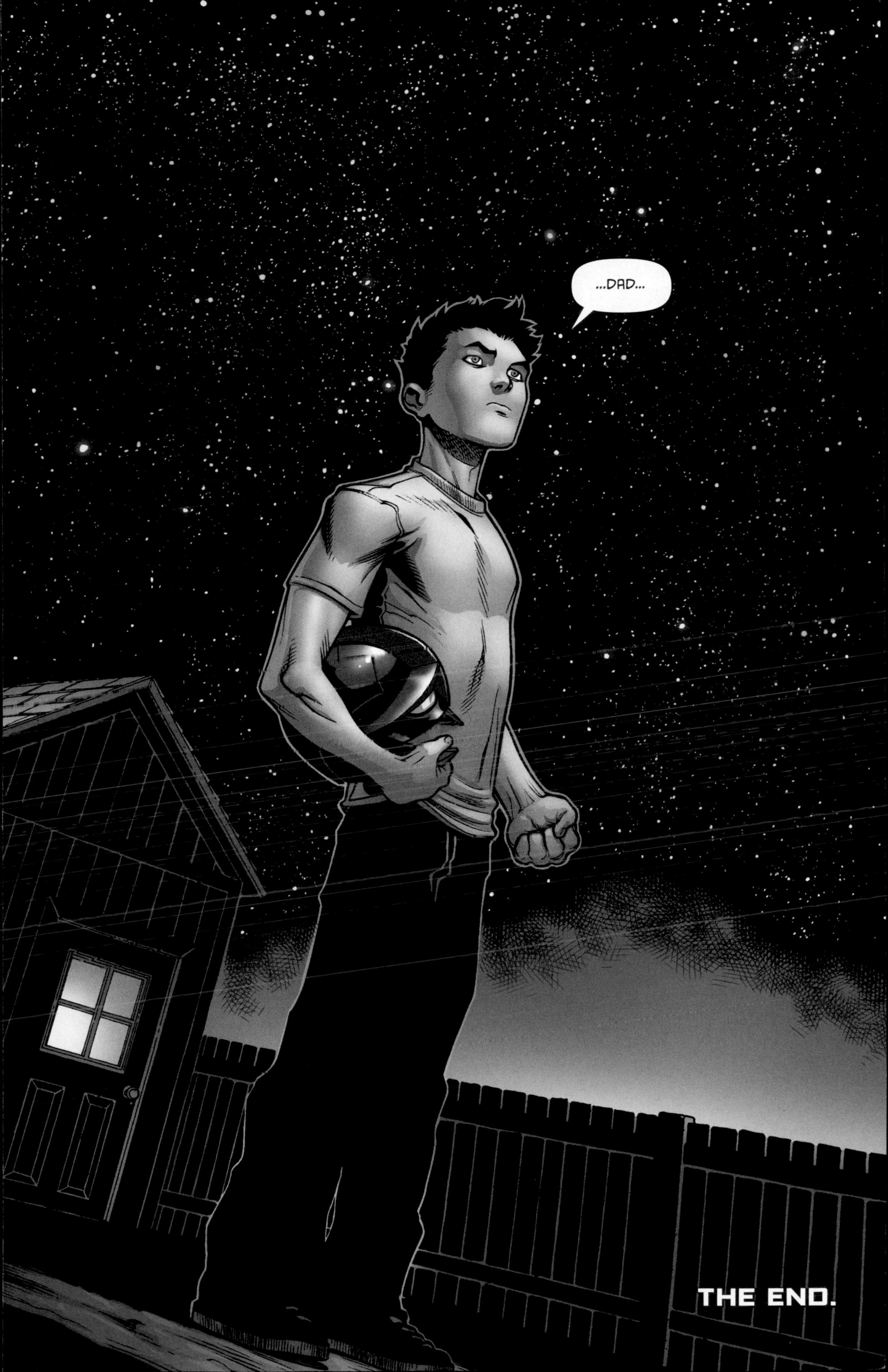
...DAD...
THE END.

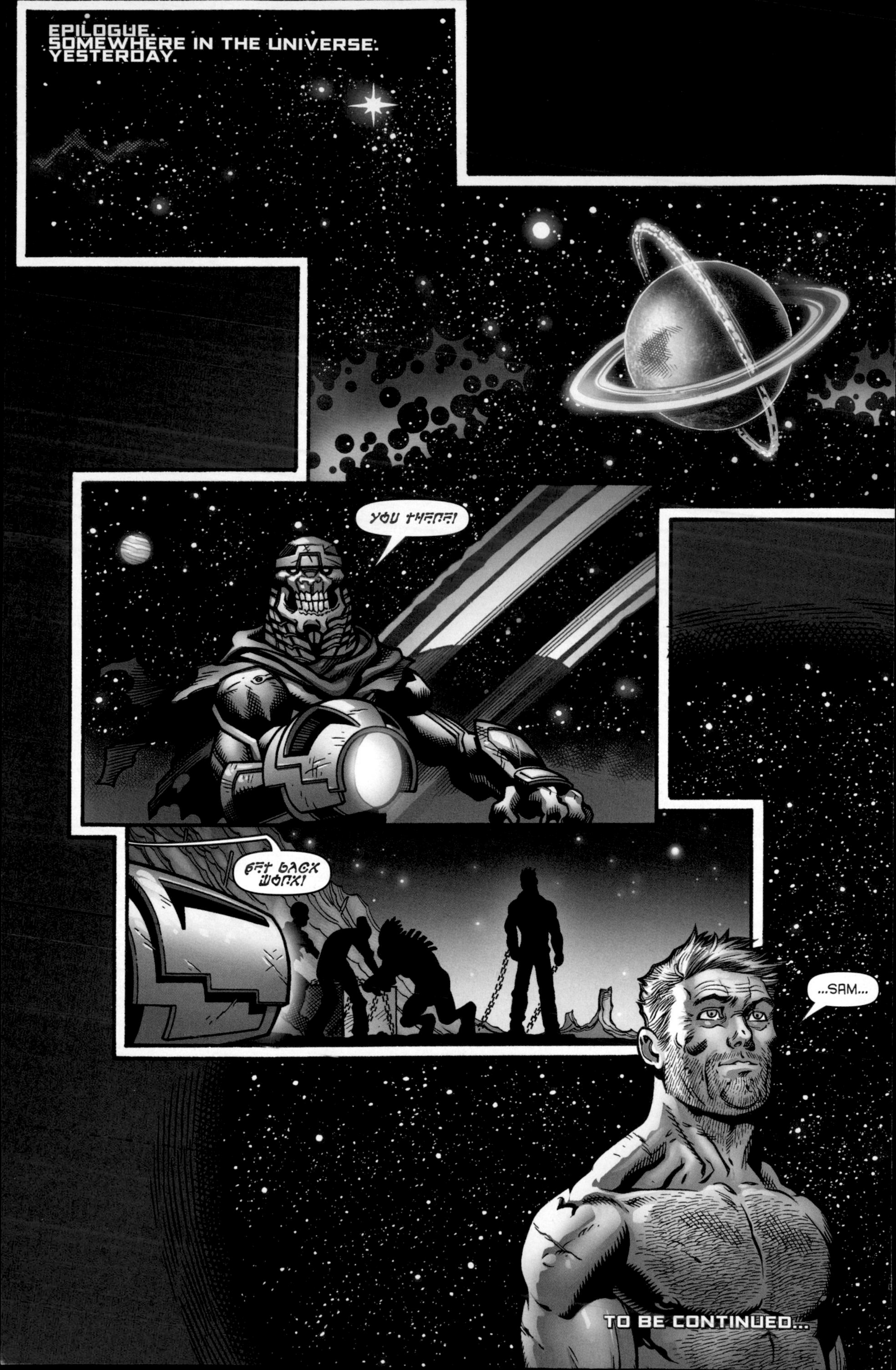
EPILOGUE.
SOMEWHERE IN THE UNIVERSE:
YESTERDAY.
YOU THERE!
GET BACK WORK!
...SAM...
TO BE CONTINUED...

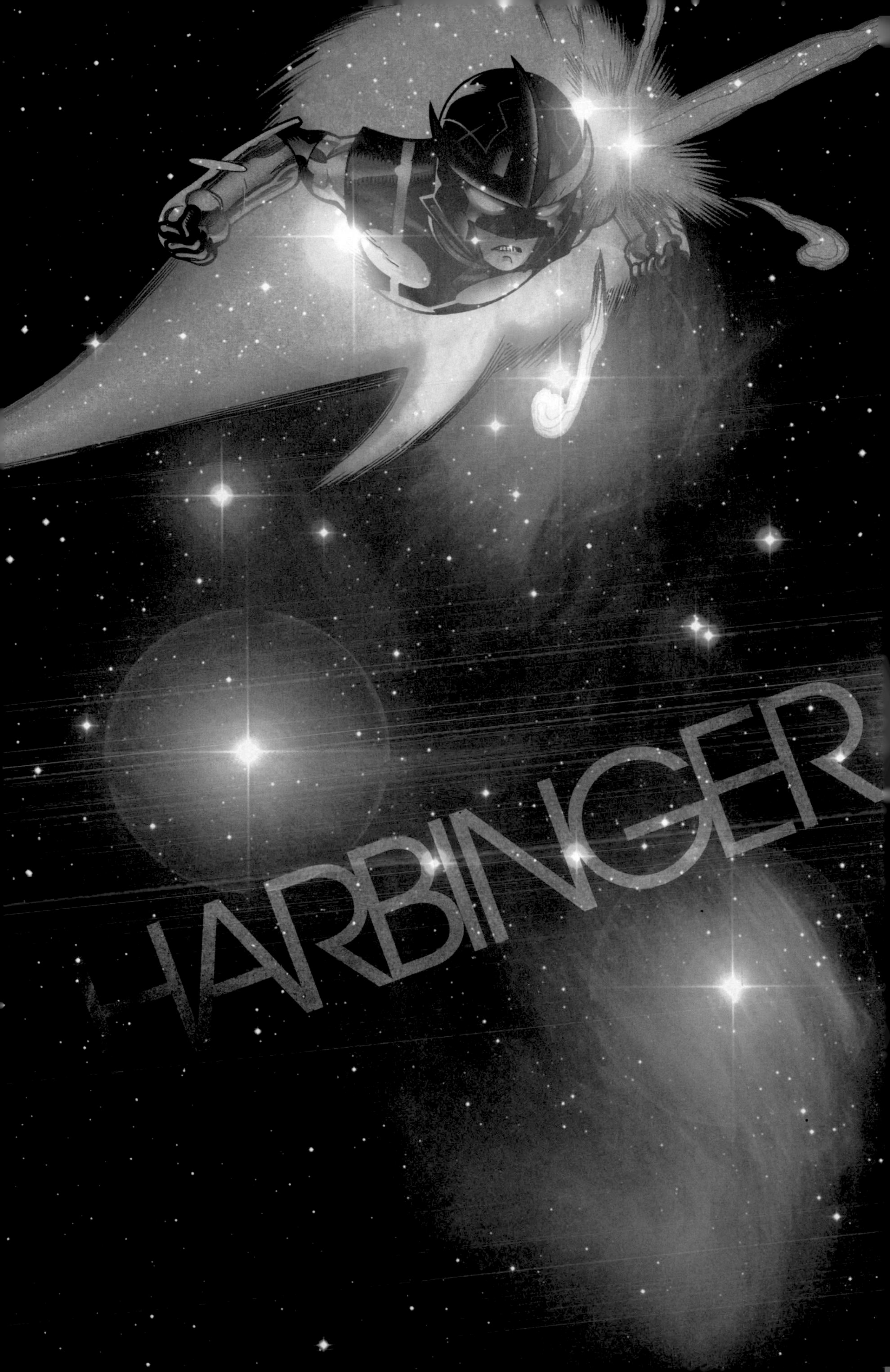
HARBINGER

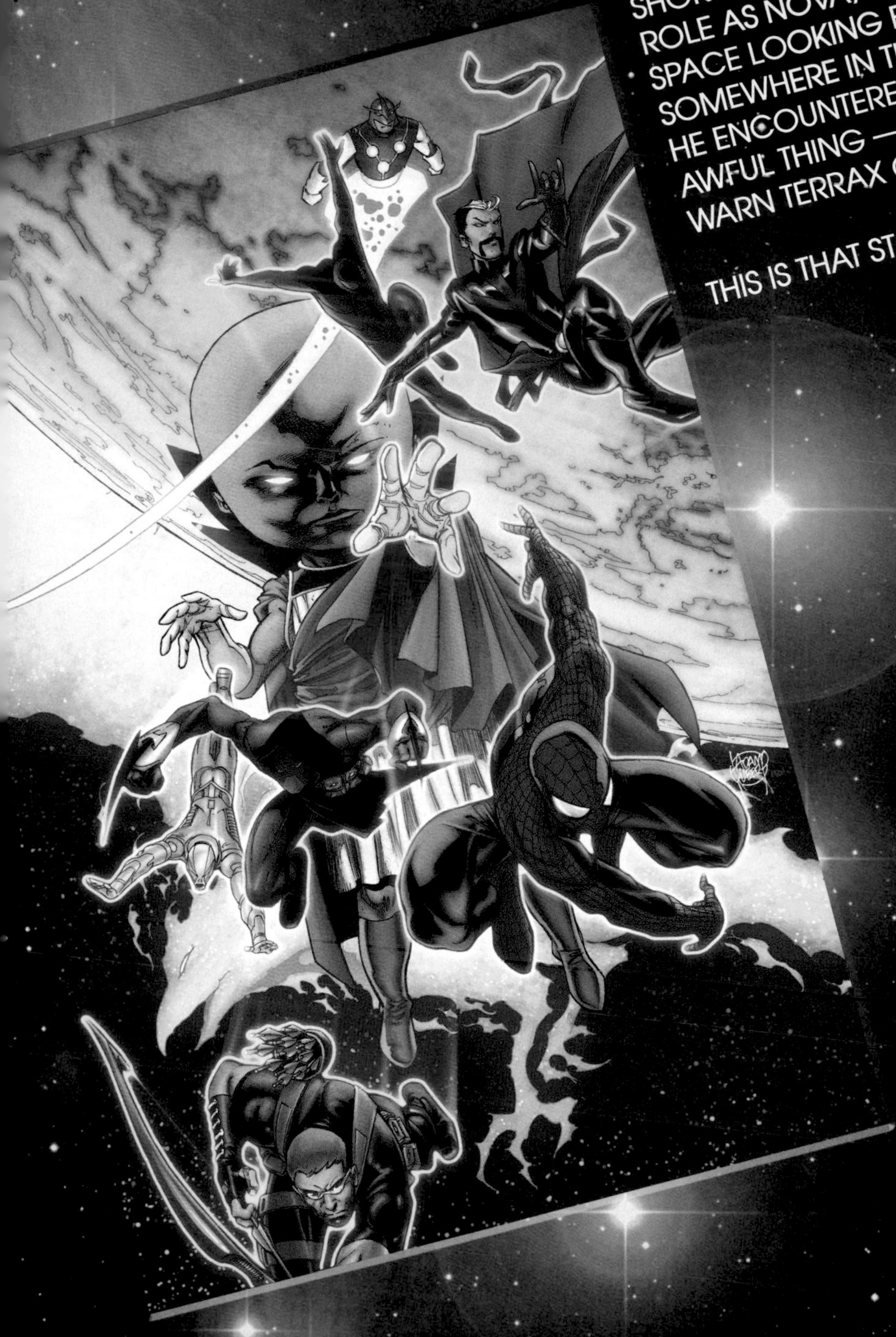

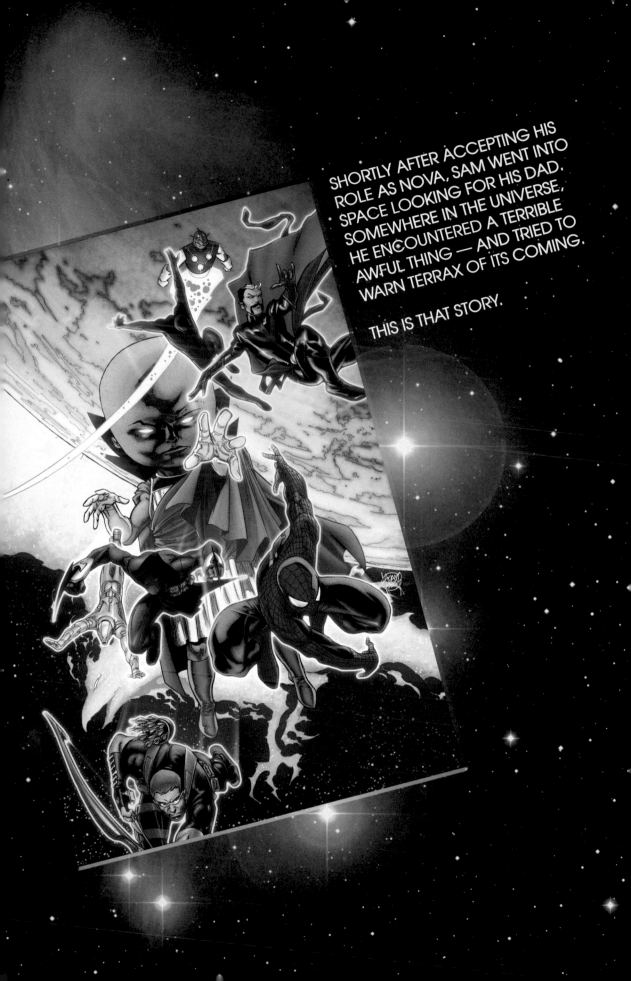

SHORTLY AFTER ACCEPTING HIS ROLE AS NOVA, SAM WENT INTO SPACE LOOKING FOR HIS DAD. SOMEWHERE IN THE UNIVERSE, HE ENCOUNTERED A TERRIBLE AWFUL THING — AND TRIED TO WARN TERRAX OF ITS COMING.

THIS IS THAT STORY.

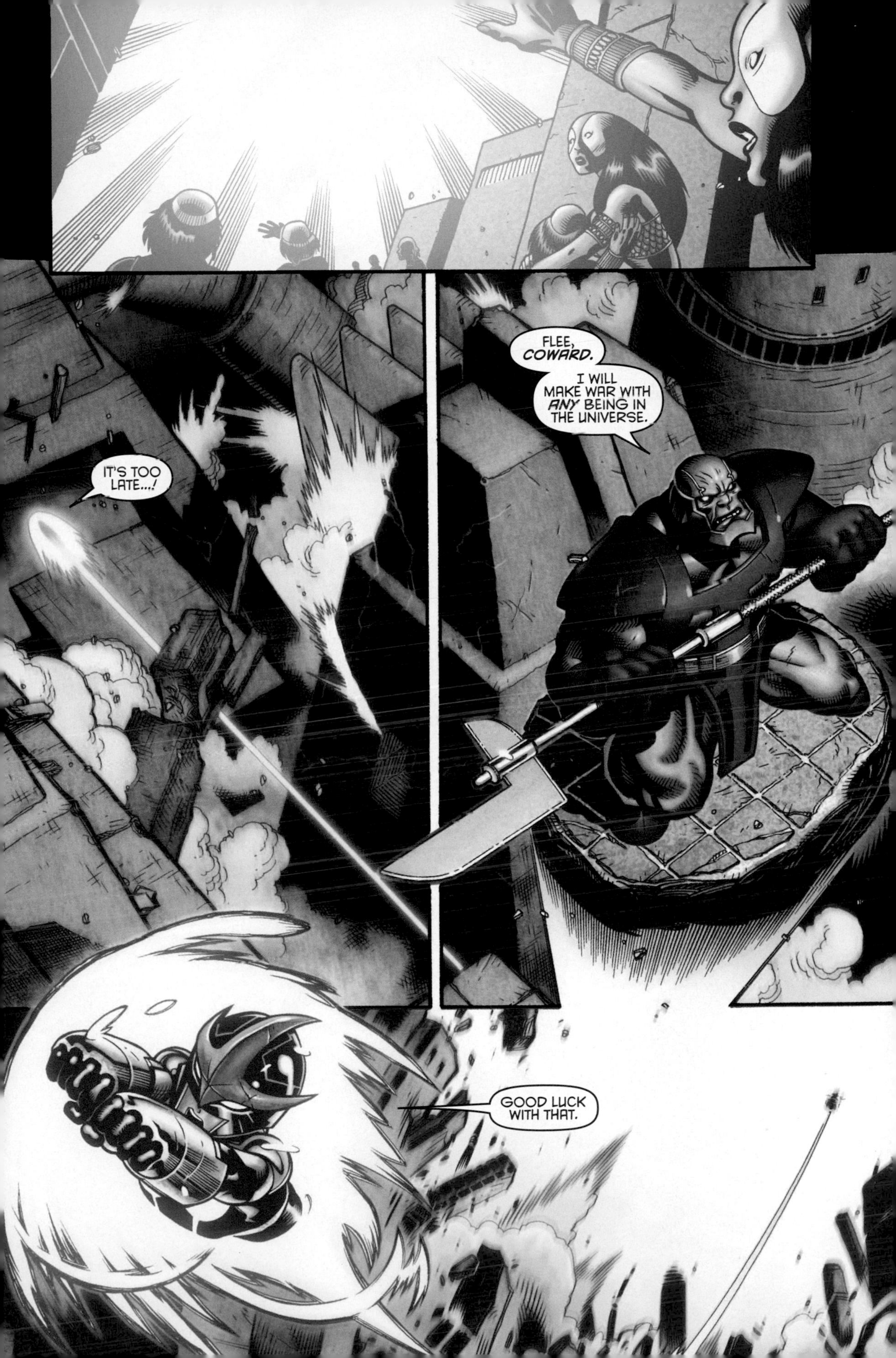
IT'S TOO LATE...!
FLEE, COWARD.
I WILL MAKE WAR WITH ANY BEING IN THE UNIVERSE.
GOOD LUCK WITH THAT.

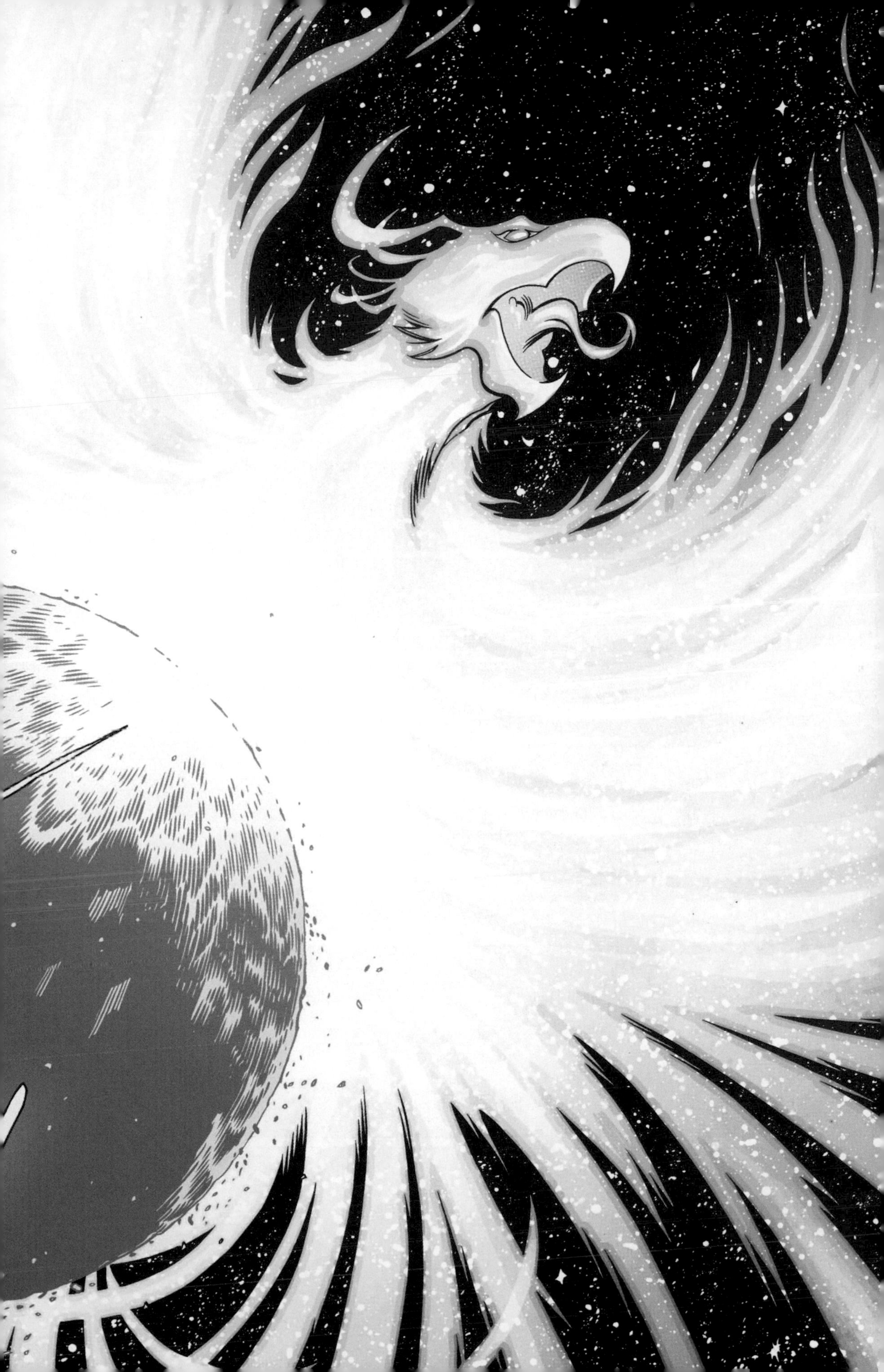

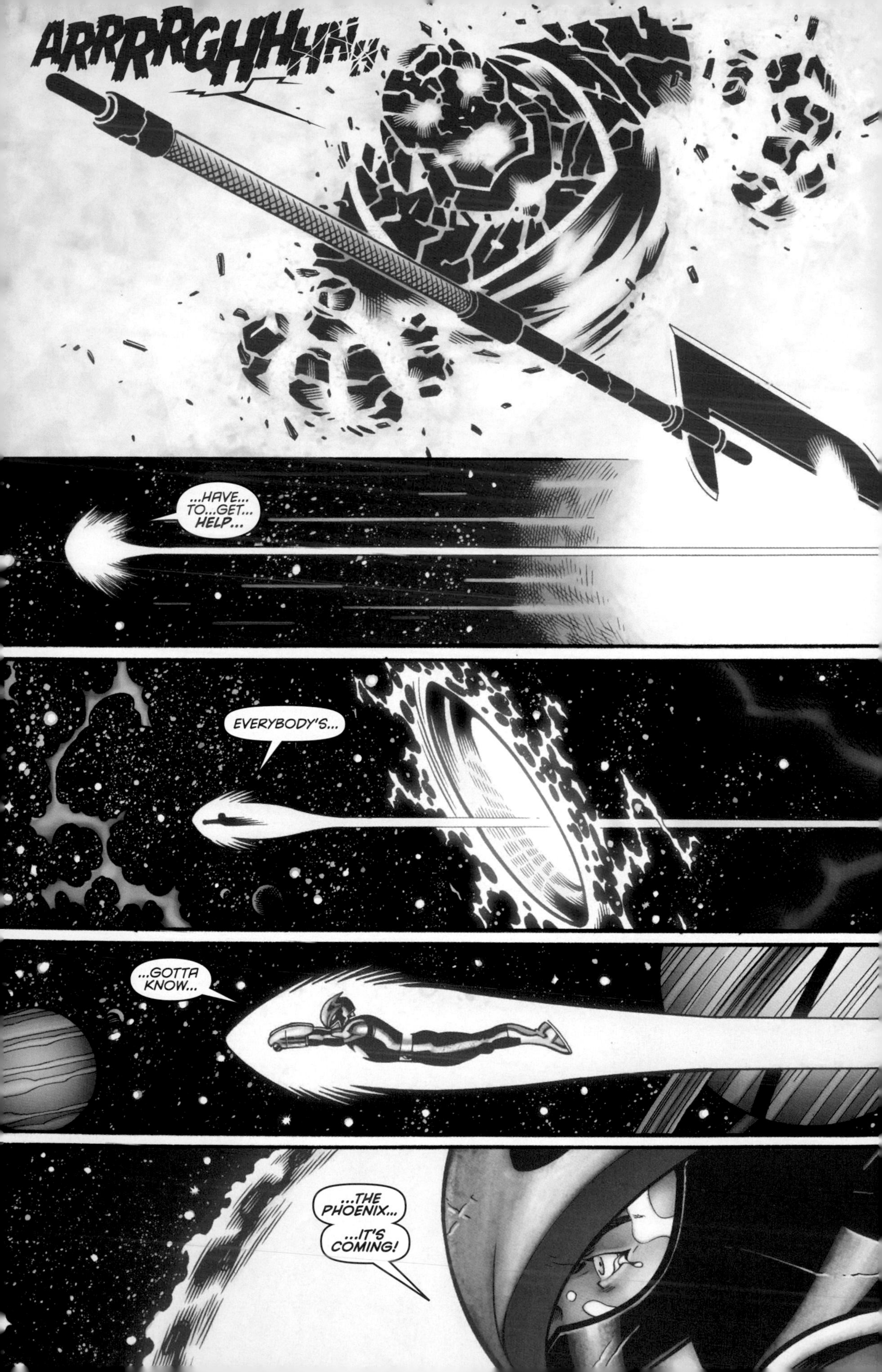
ARRRRGHHH!!
...HAVE... TO...GET... HELP...
EVERYBODY'S...
...GOTTA KNOW...
...THE PHOENIX...
...IT'S COMING!

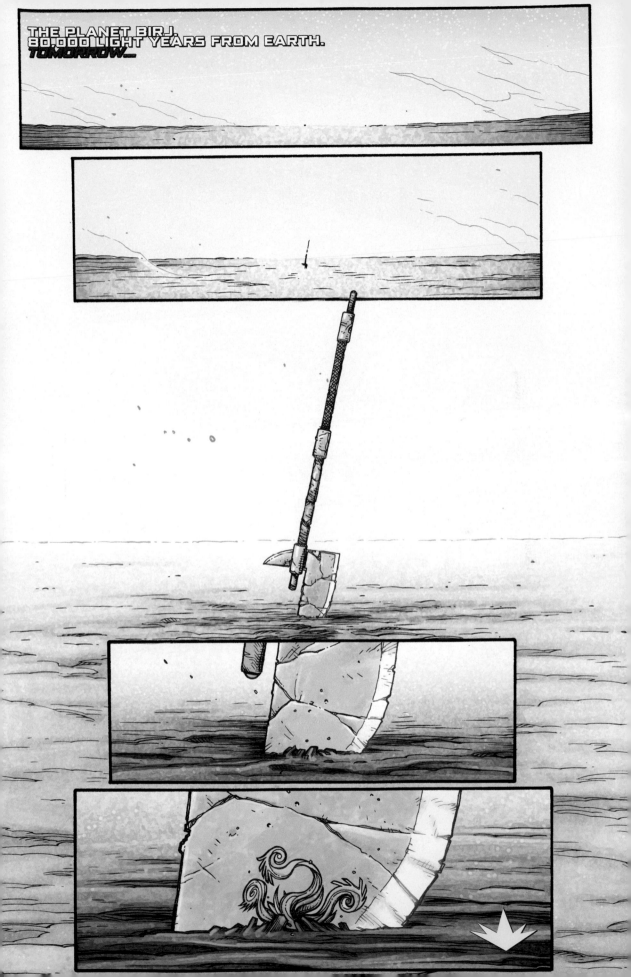

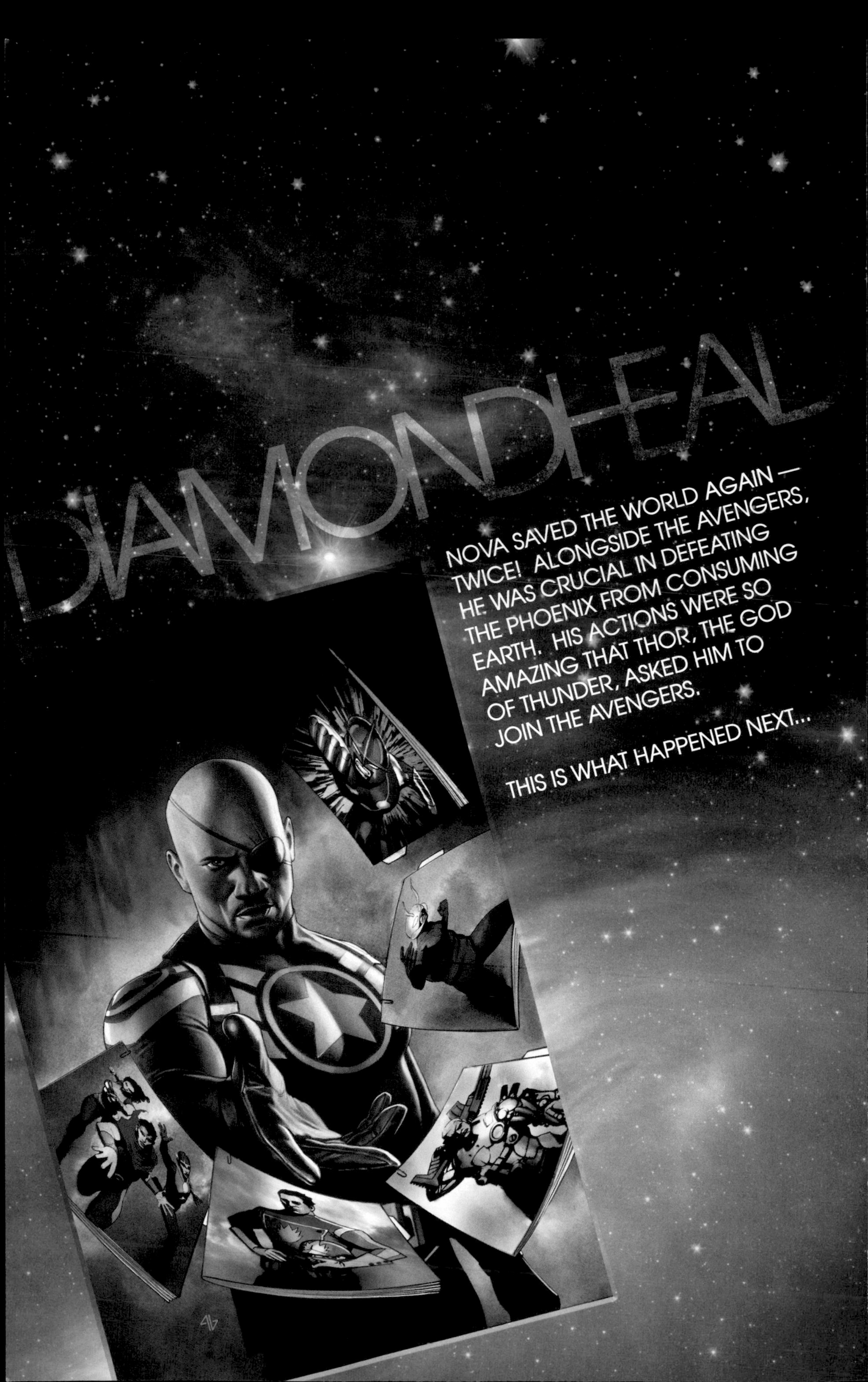
DIAMONDHEAL
NOVA SAVED THE WORLD AGAIN — TWICE! ALONGSIDE THE AVENGERS, HE WAS CRUCIAL IN DEFEATING THE PHOENIX FROM CONSUMING EARTH. HIS ACTIONS WERE SO AMAZING THAT THOR, THE GOD OF THUNDER, ASKED HIM TO JOIN THE AVENGERS.
THIS IS WHAT HAPPENED NEXT...

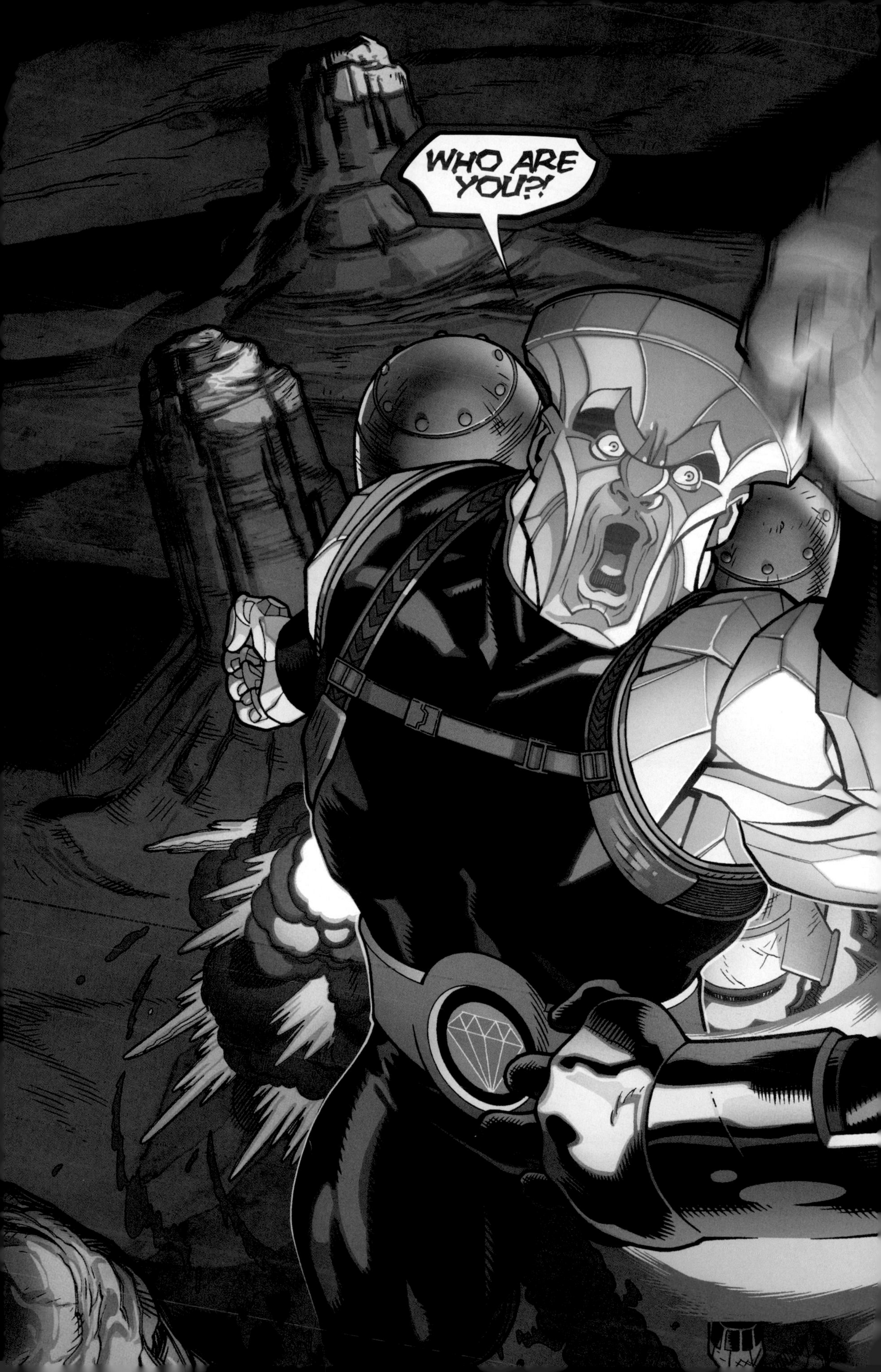
WHO ARE YOU?!

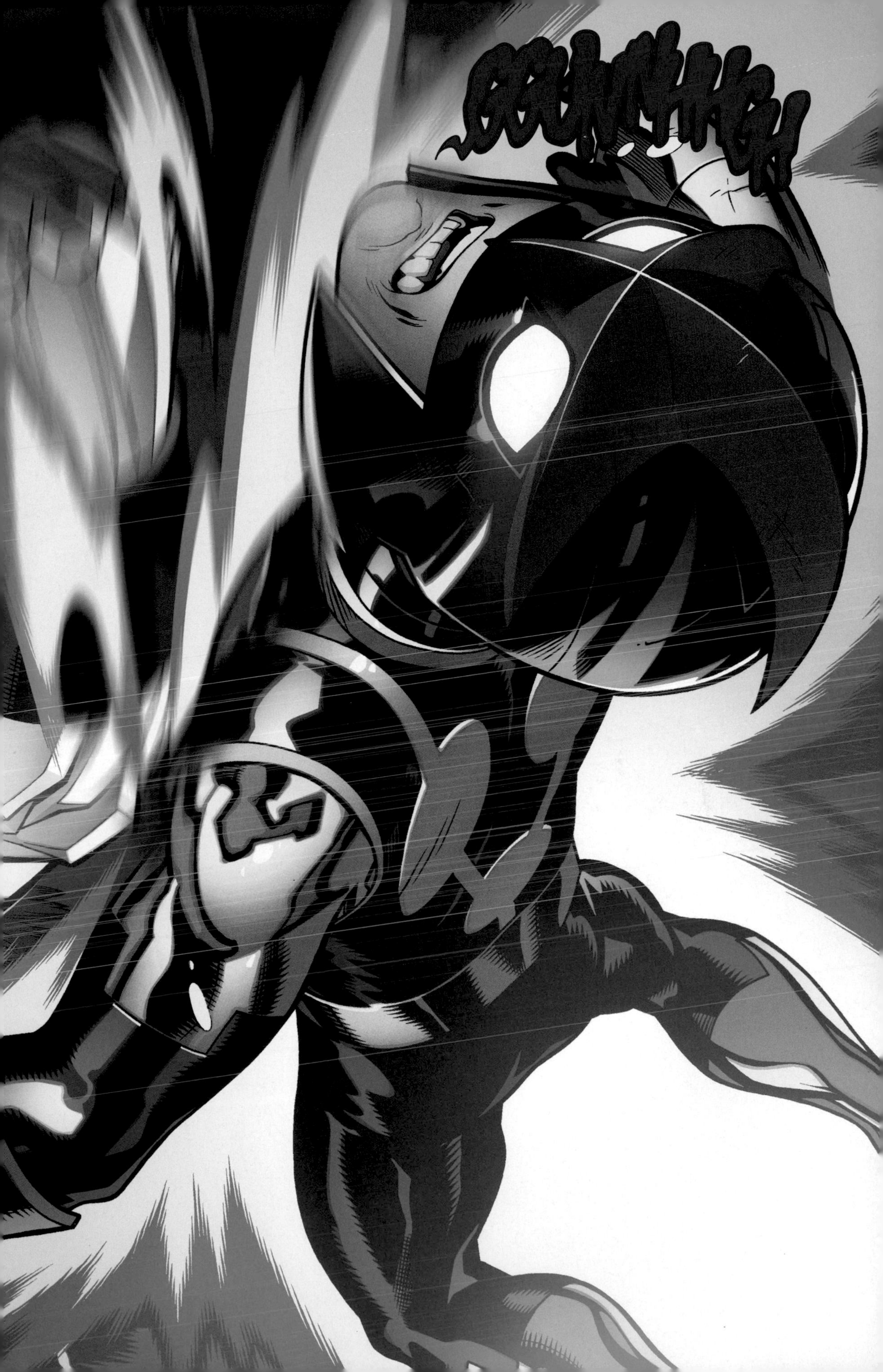
GGUNHHGH

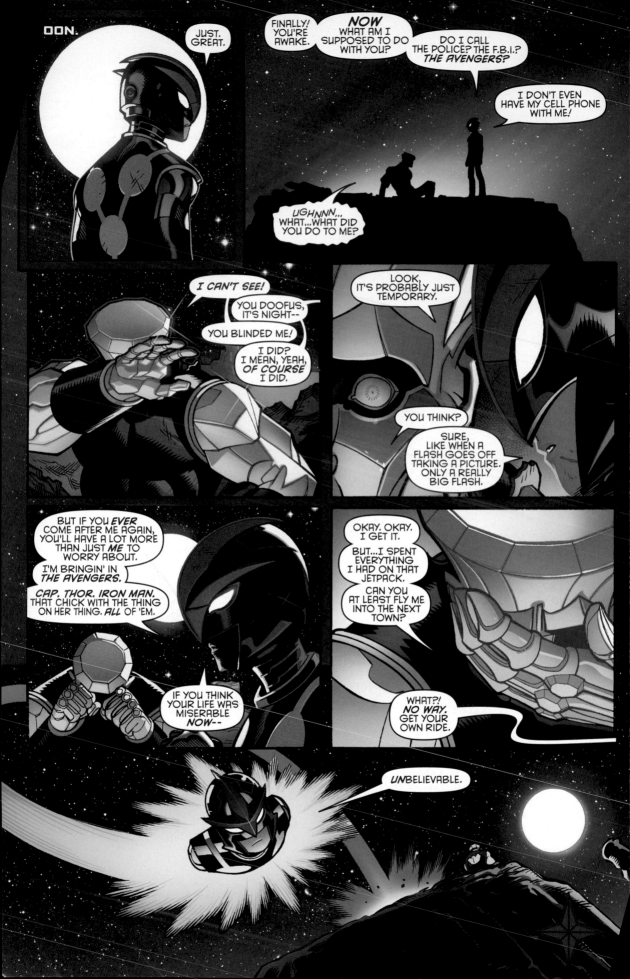

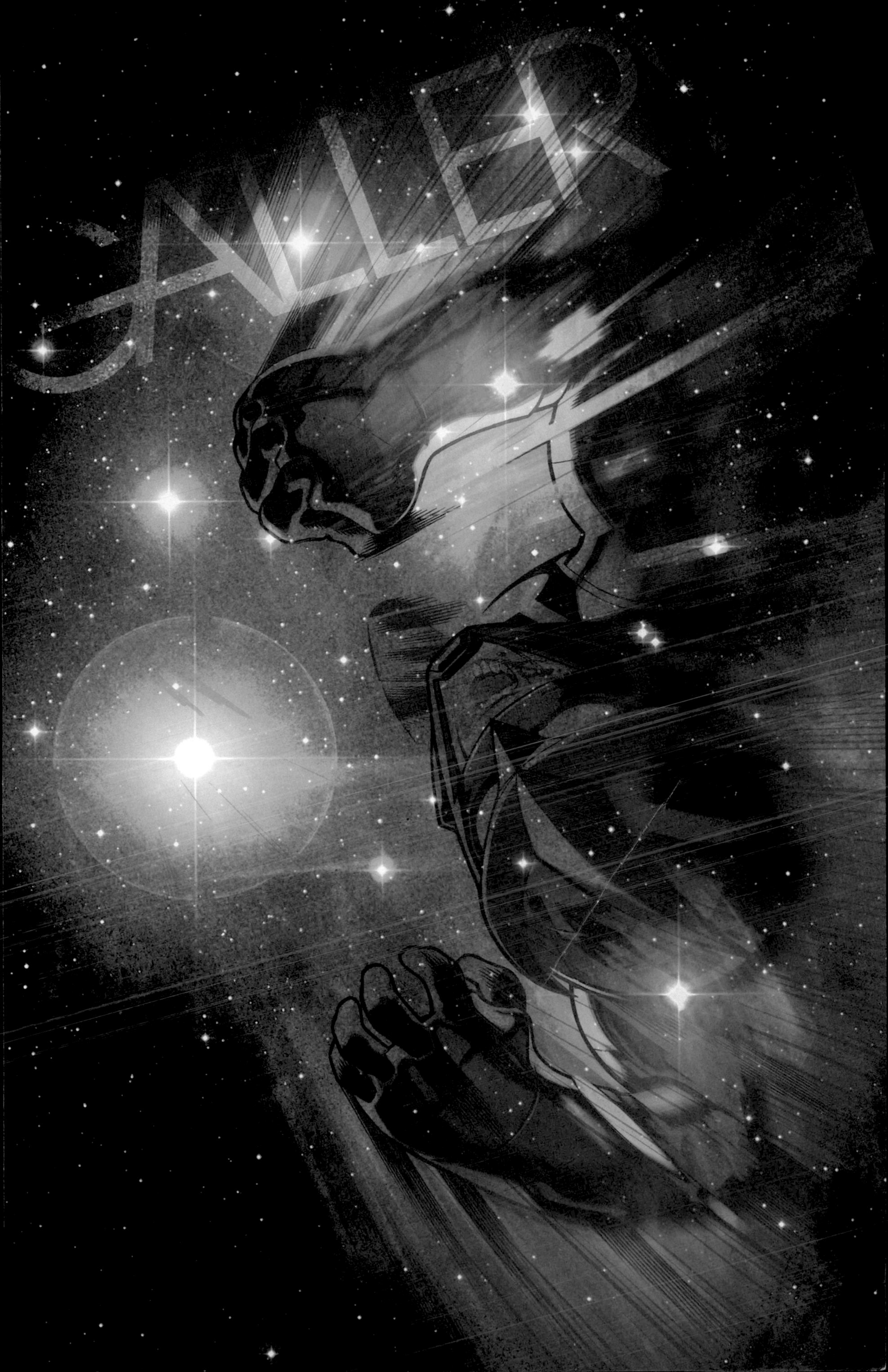

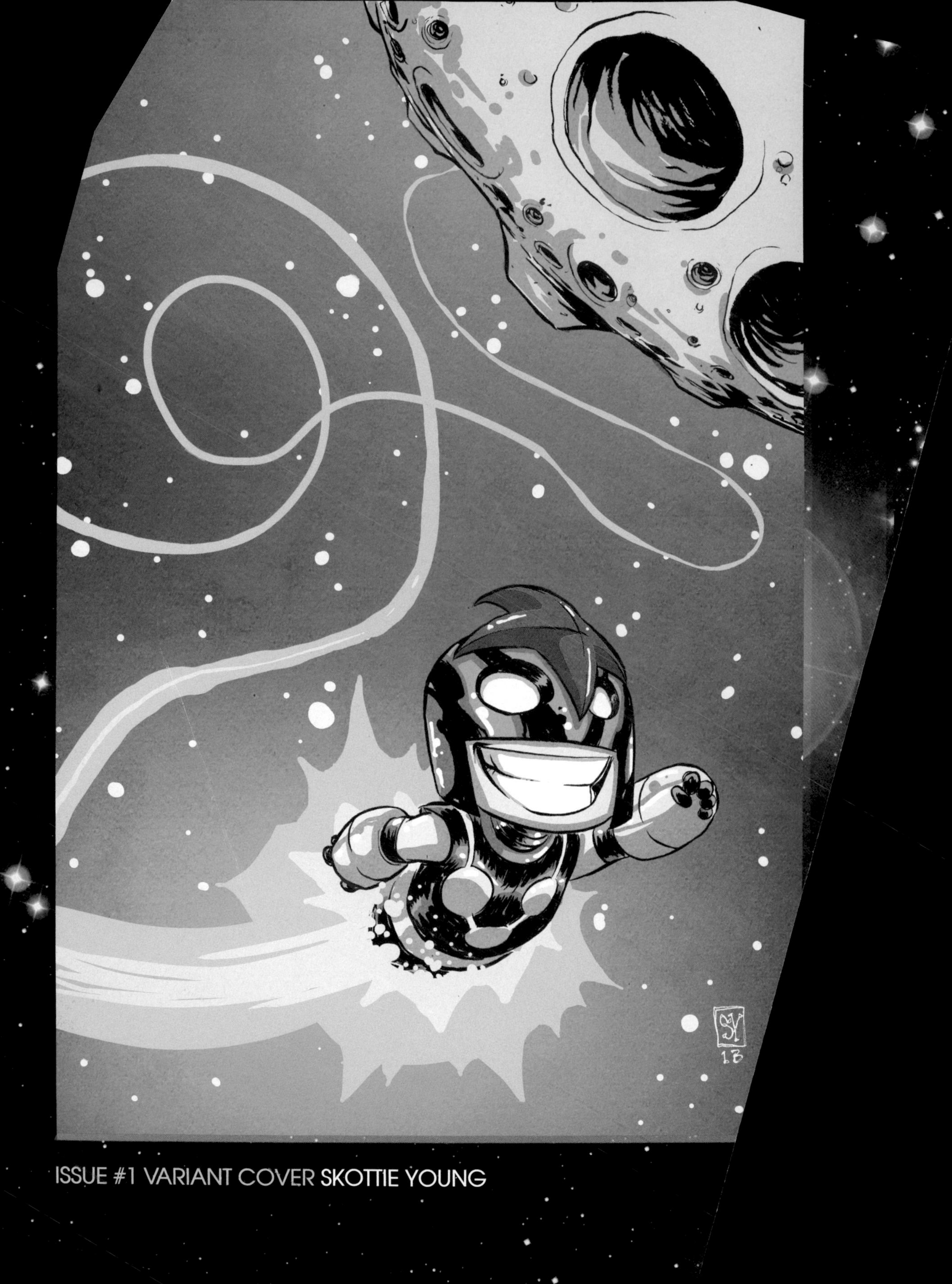

ISSUE #1 VARIANT COVER SKOTTIE YOUNG

ISSUE #1 VARIANT COVER
JOE QUESADA, DANNY MIKI & RICHARD ISANOVE

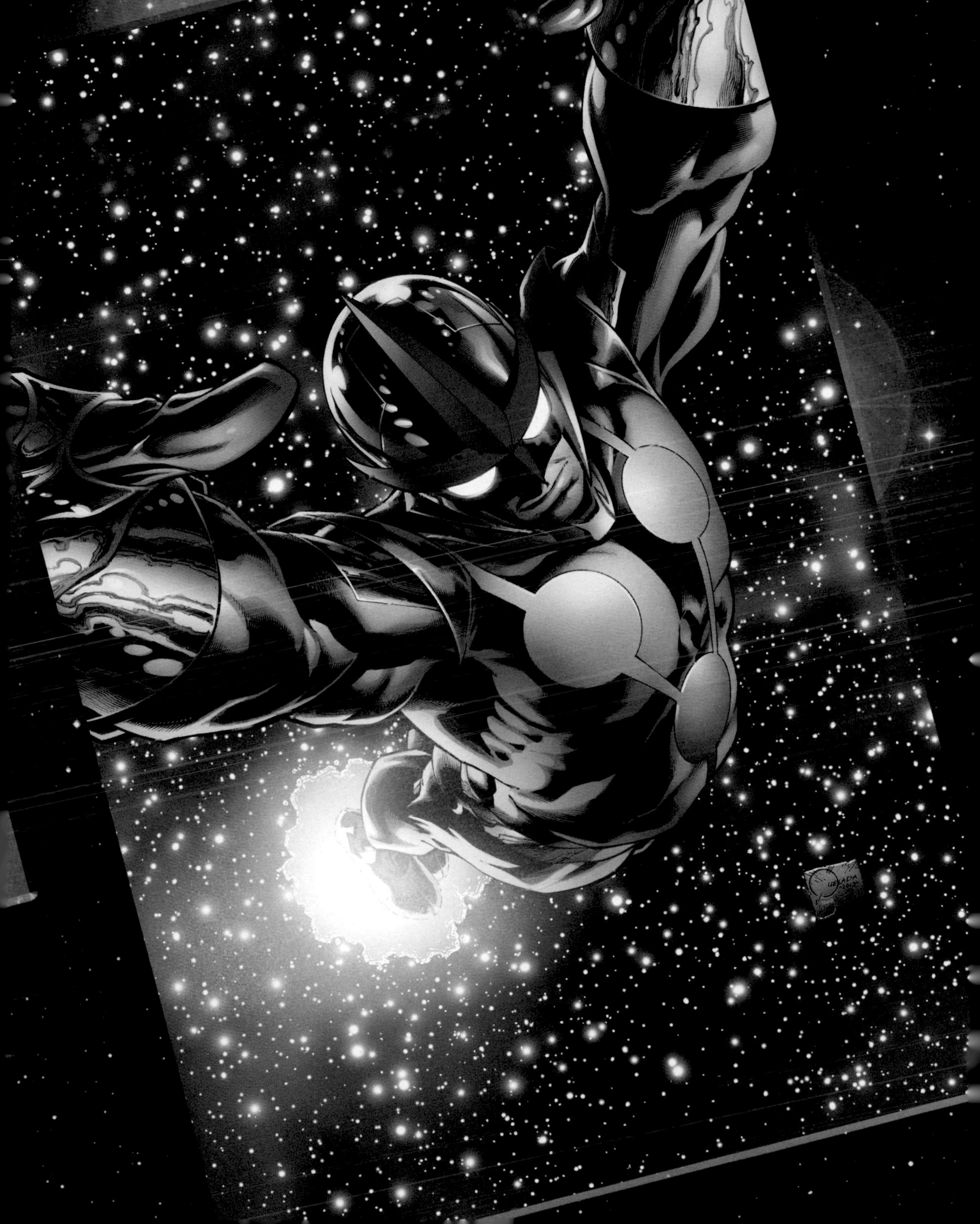

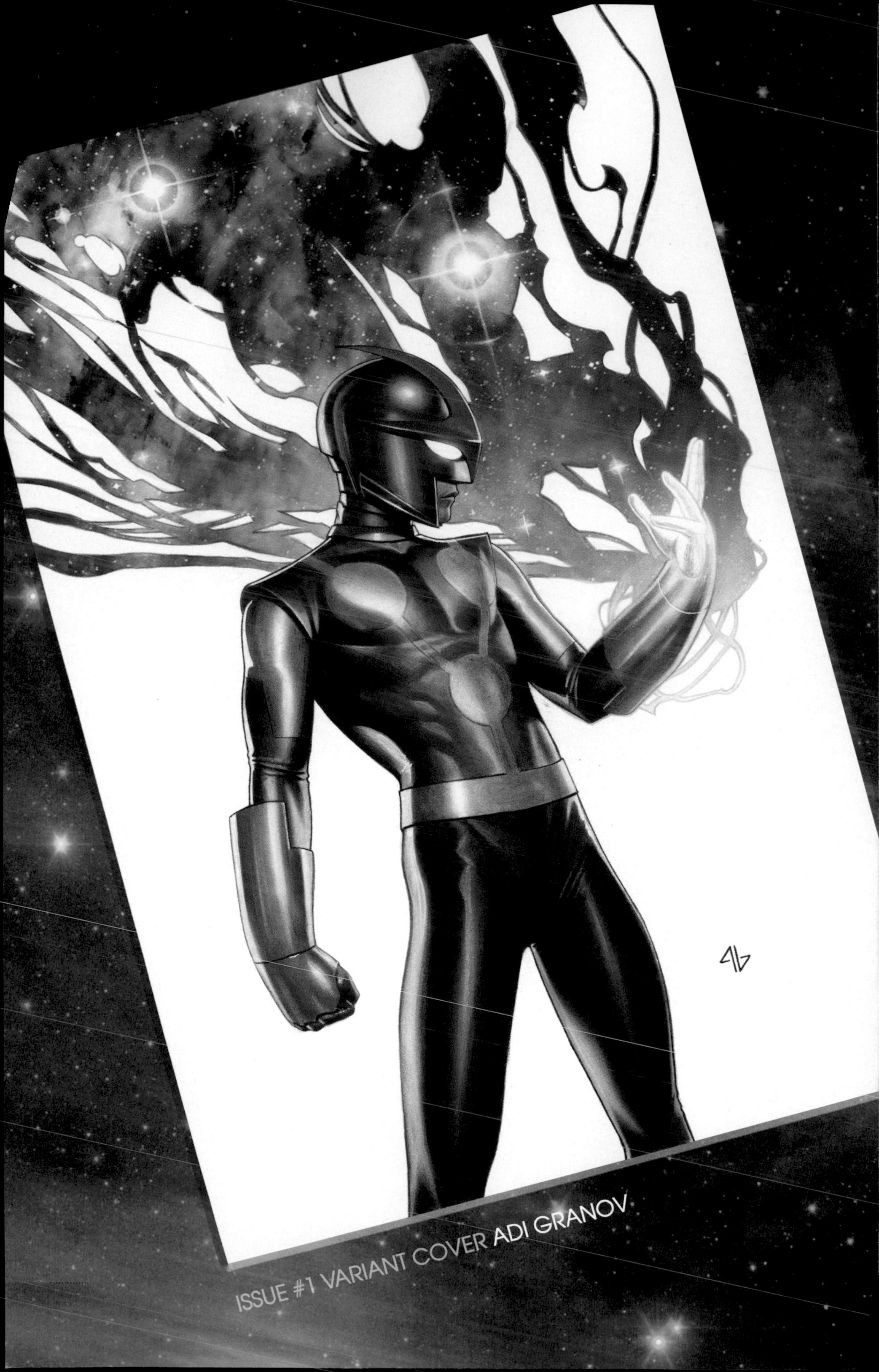

ISSUE #1 VARIANT COVER ADI GRANOV

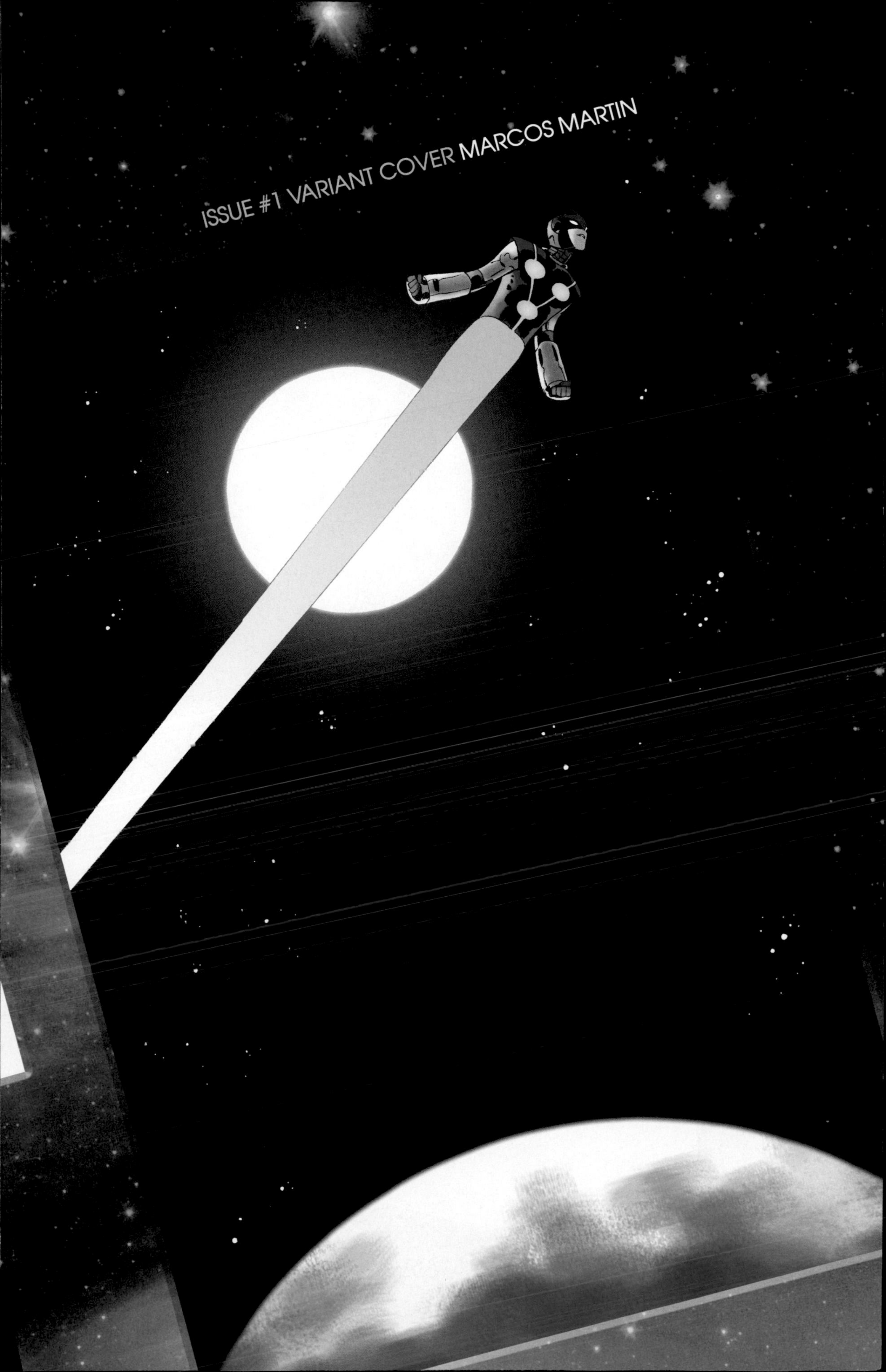
ISSUE #1 VARIANT COVER MARCOS MARTIN

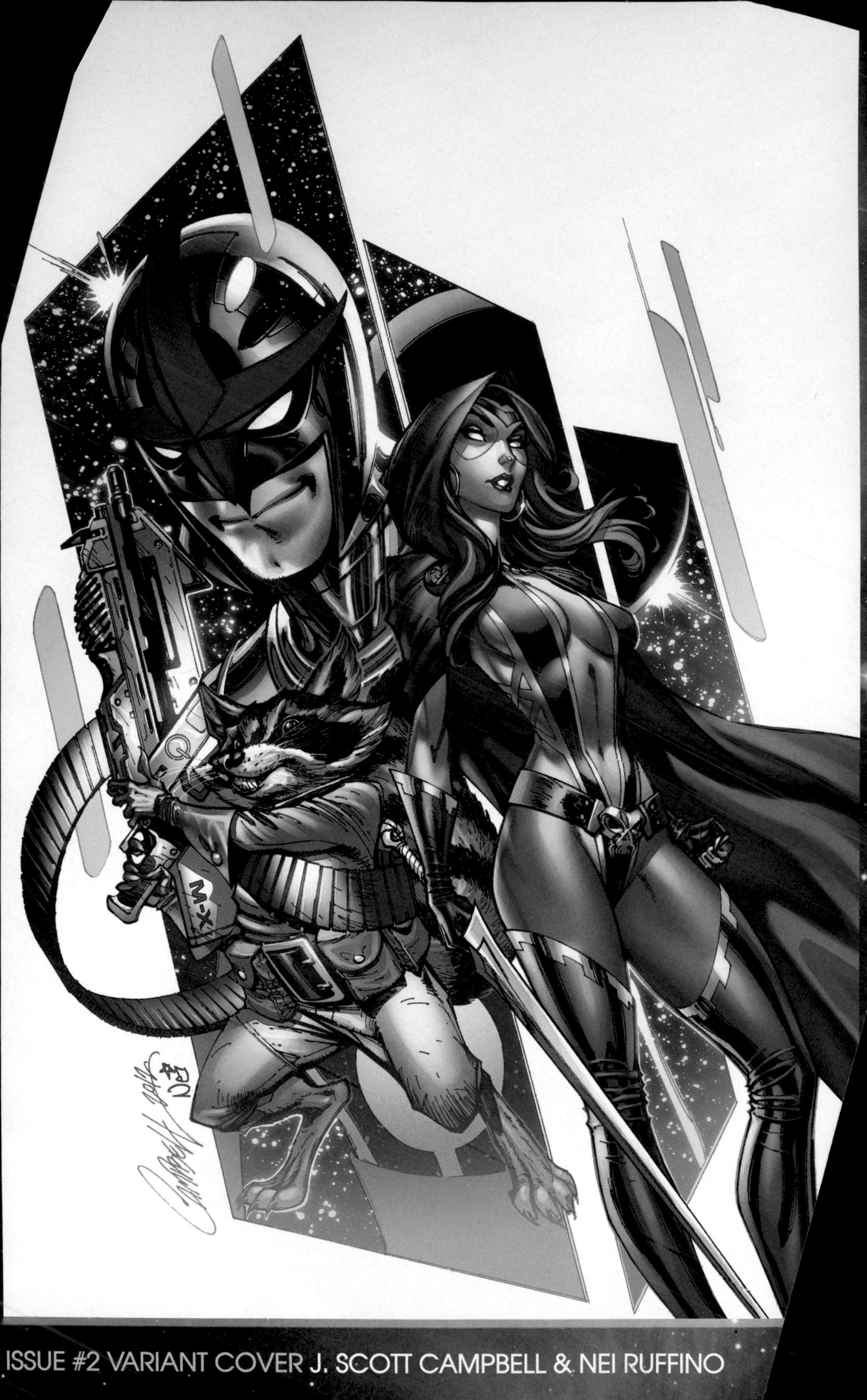
M-X

ISSUE #2 VARIANT COVER J. SCOTT CAMPBELL & NEI RUFFINO

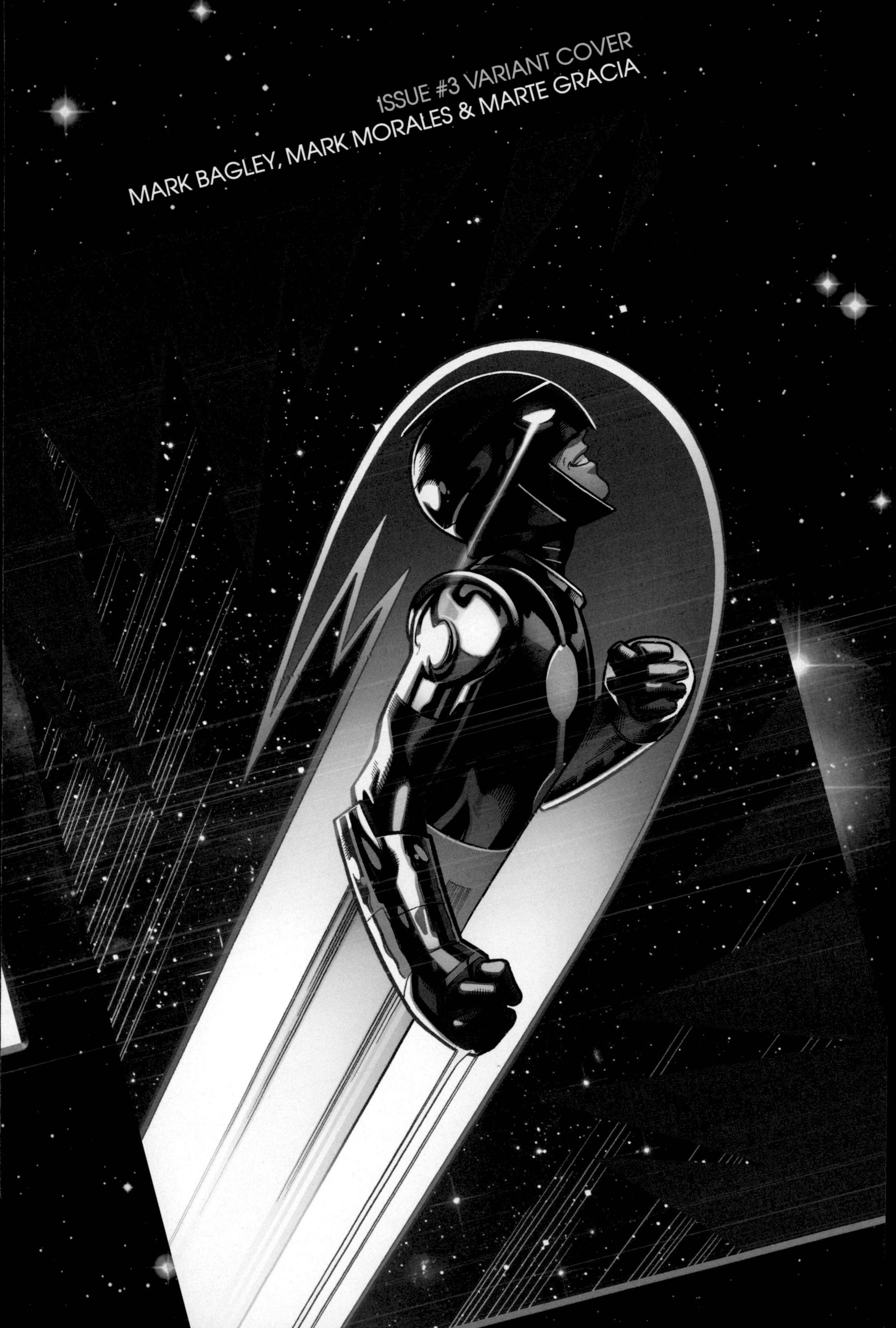

ISSUE #3 VARIANT COVER
MARK BAGLEY, MARK MORALES & MARTE GRACIA

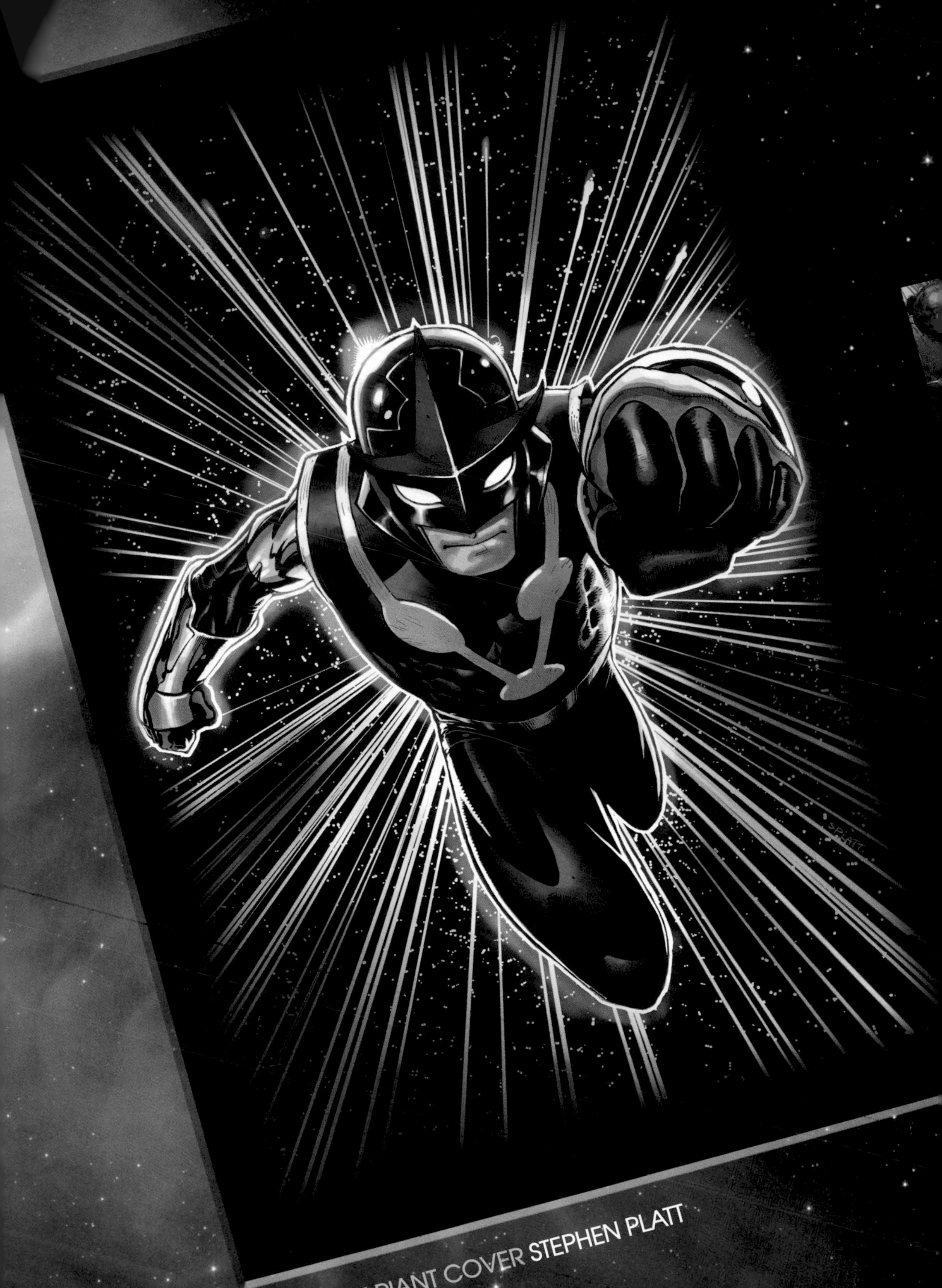

ISSUE #4 VARIANT COVER STEPHEN PLATT

ISSUE #5 VARIANT COVER MR GARCIN

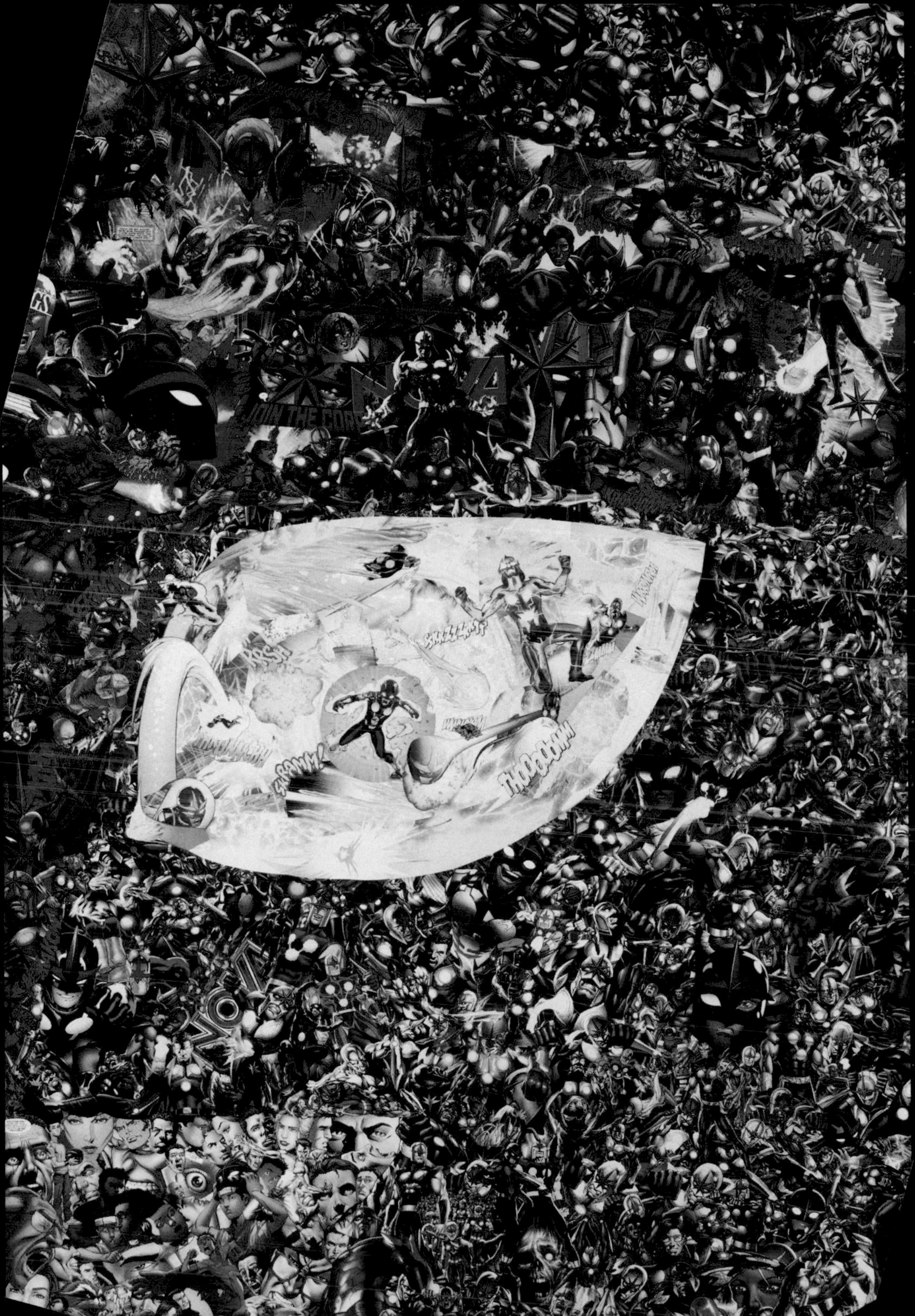

ED McGUINNESS' SKETCH

DAREDEVIL GLINT IN EYES (NO PUN INTENDED)

SHORT - WILD HAIR

AN UNHAPPY BOUNCY EYEBROWS HE COULD SLIGHTLY UNPREDICTABLE

MARIO LOPEZ DIMPLES

GOLD —

BLACK —

GOLD —

BLACK —

BLACK NECK

GOLD BELT

GOLD —

BLACK —

ALL HIGHLIGHTS ON SUIT ARE WHITE NOT BLUE.

GOLD —

CHIN PIECE MOVES UP FROM NECK AND CLEAR GOLD SHEILD COMES DOWN OVER MOUTH FOR SPACE AND UNDER-WATER BREATHING.

BLACK WITH WHITE HIGHLIGHTS

BLACK

GOLD —

EMZKID!

These were among Ed's first attempts at Nova. What's so delightful is that Sam looked like a kid — not a small adult (as it often happens in comics). There was more of Ditko's Peter Parker in him than Jack Kirby, who influences Ed in most things we do.

BOOK

WATCH IT PAL!

Ed had a very dynamic challenge when he designed Nova's costume. From the beginning we knew it had to work in a comic — but we had the added pressure that it needed to be animated for ULTIMATE SPIDER-MAN which was beginning production around the same time.

We talked a lot about adding more black to the look and particularly to the Helmet. It was integral to the story as a new (and so far unknown) division of the Nova Corps and at the same time had to be functional as a moving piece of artwork and animation.

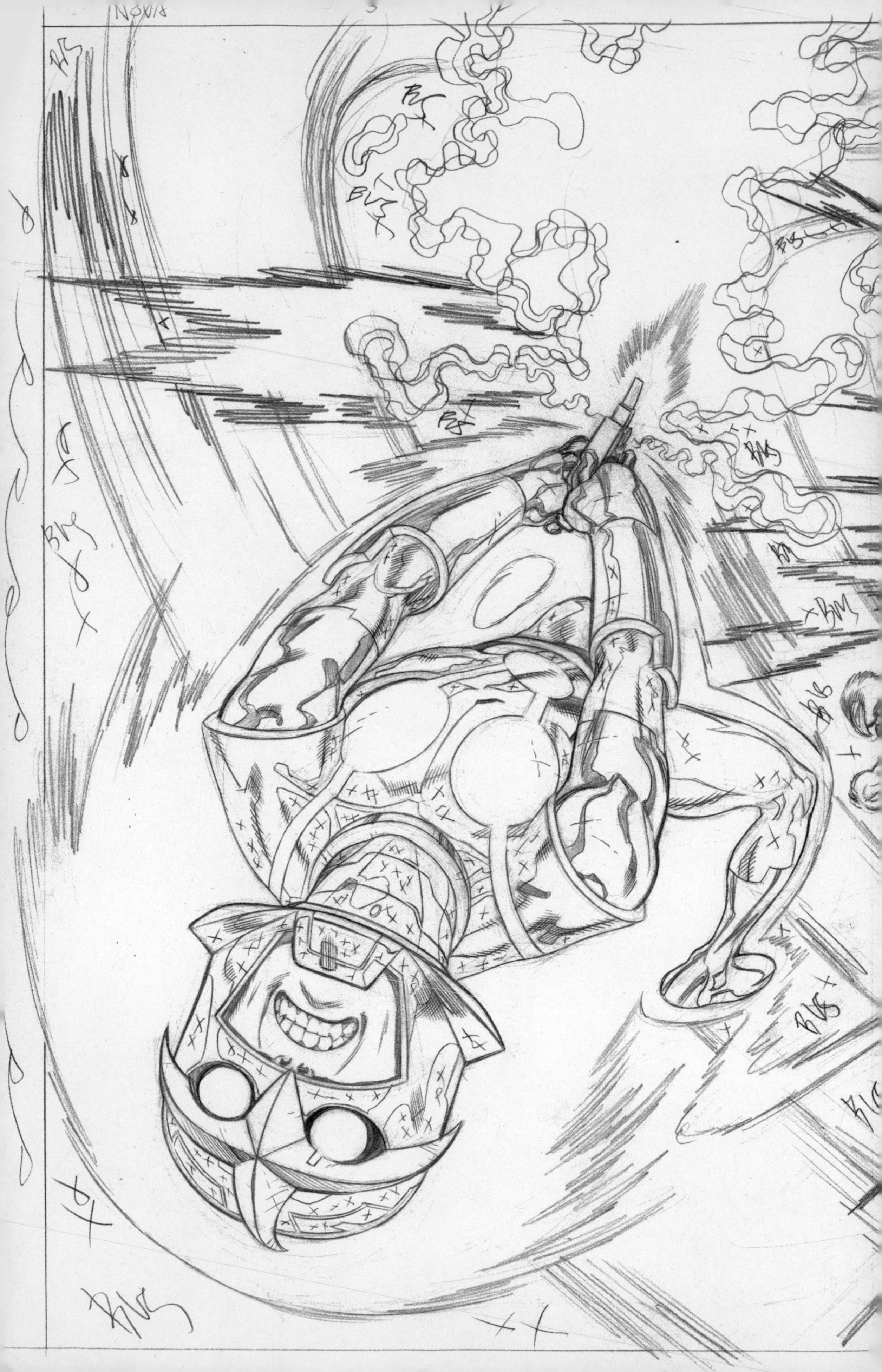

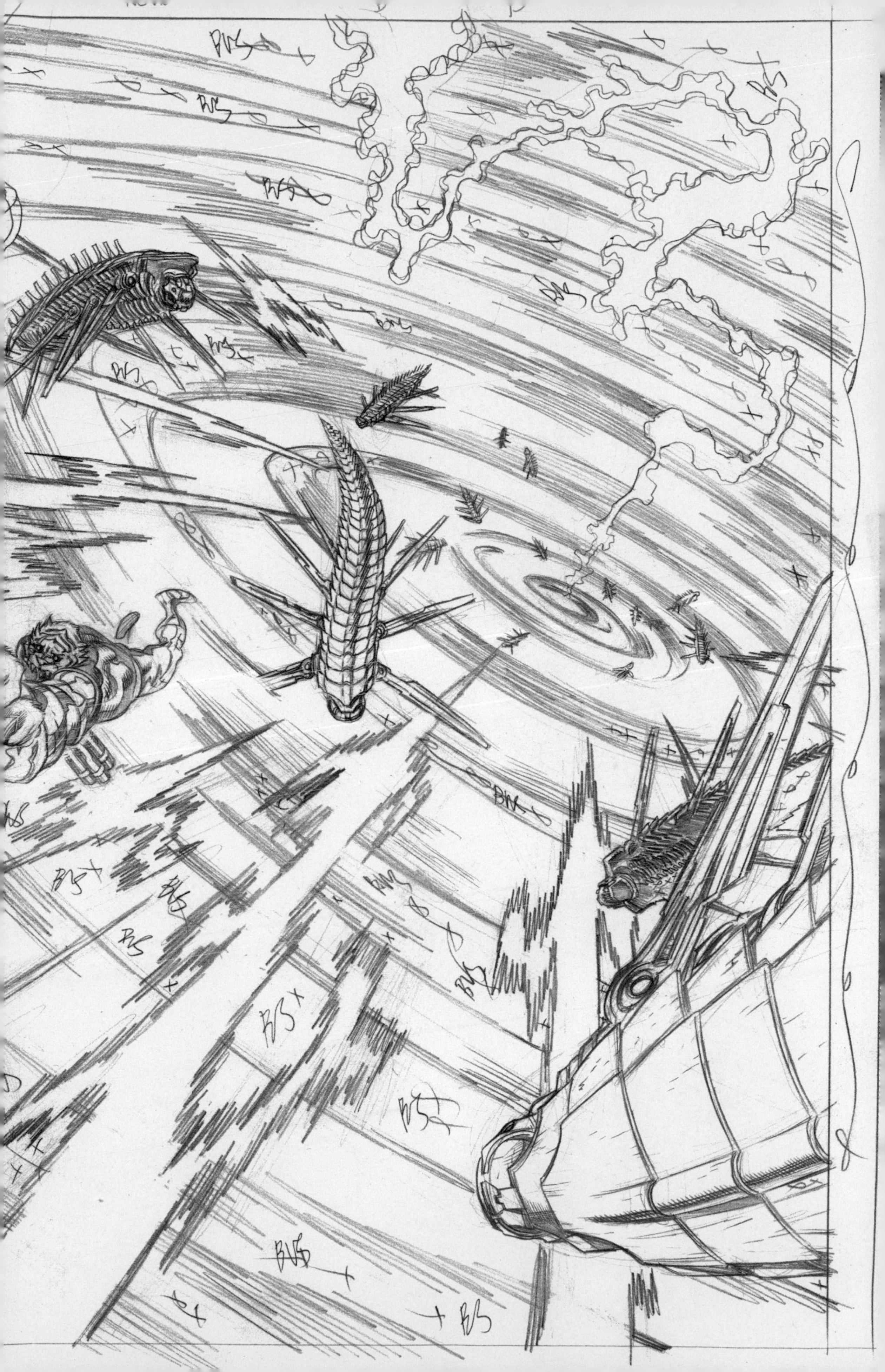

COVER DESIGN

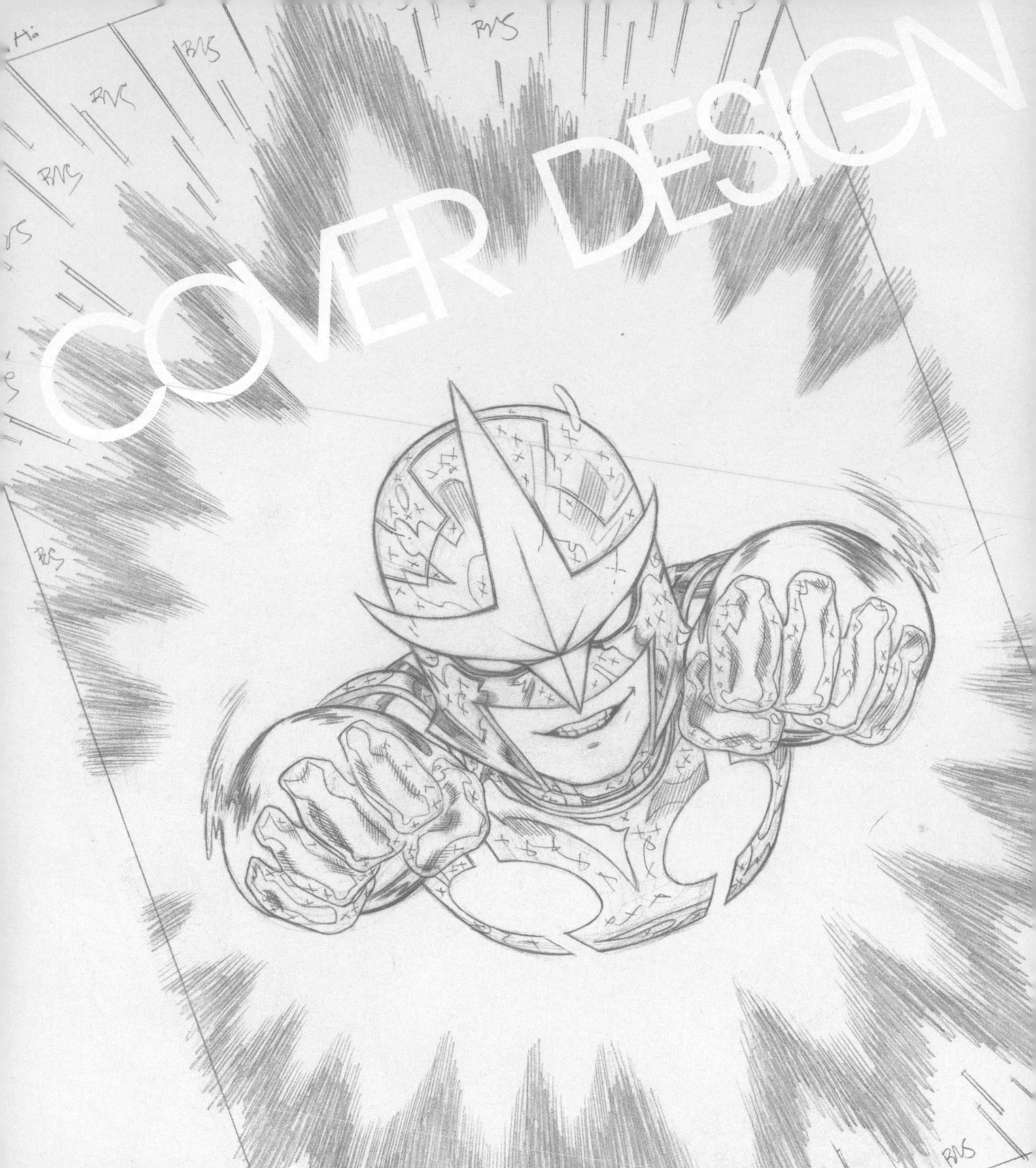

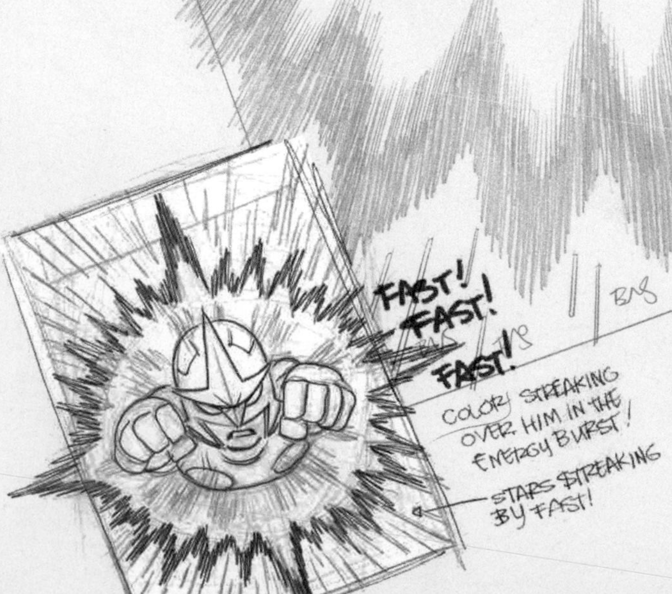
FAST!
FAST!
FAST!
COLOR STREAKING OVER HIM IN THE ENERGY BURST!
STARS STREAKING BY FAST!

Covers are one of Ed's many strengths: bold, clean images. When talking about the first issue, we wanted Nova to be coming right at you and Ed nailed it. But what makes the cover so much fun (as editor Steve Wacker loves to point out) is the sly grin on Sam's face. It's a small, pure character thing that really gives you a sense that he's not like any Nova we've seen before.

STUFF......

For our last issue, Ed pitched the idea of seeing Sam and his Dad when Sam was very little. As fathers, both Ed and I have lots of photos of us with our kids when they were little and this was an attempt to capture some of that. Because the ending was hopefully going to be very emotional, Ed wanted a cover that would depict one of those quiet, sweet moments between a father and a son.

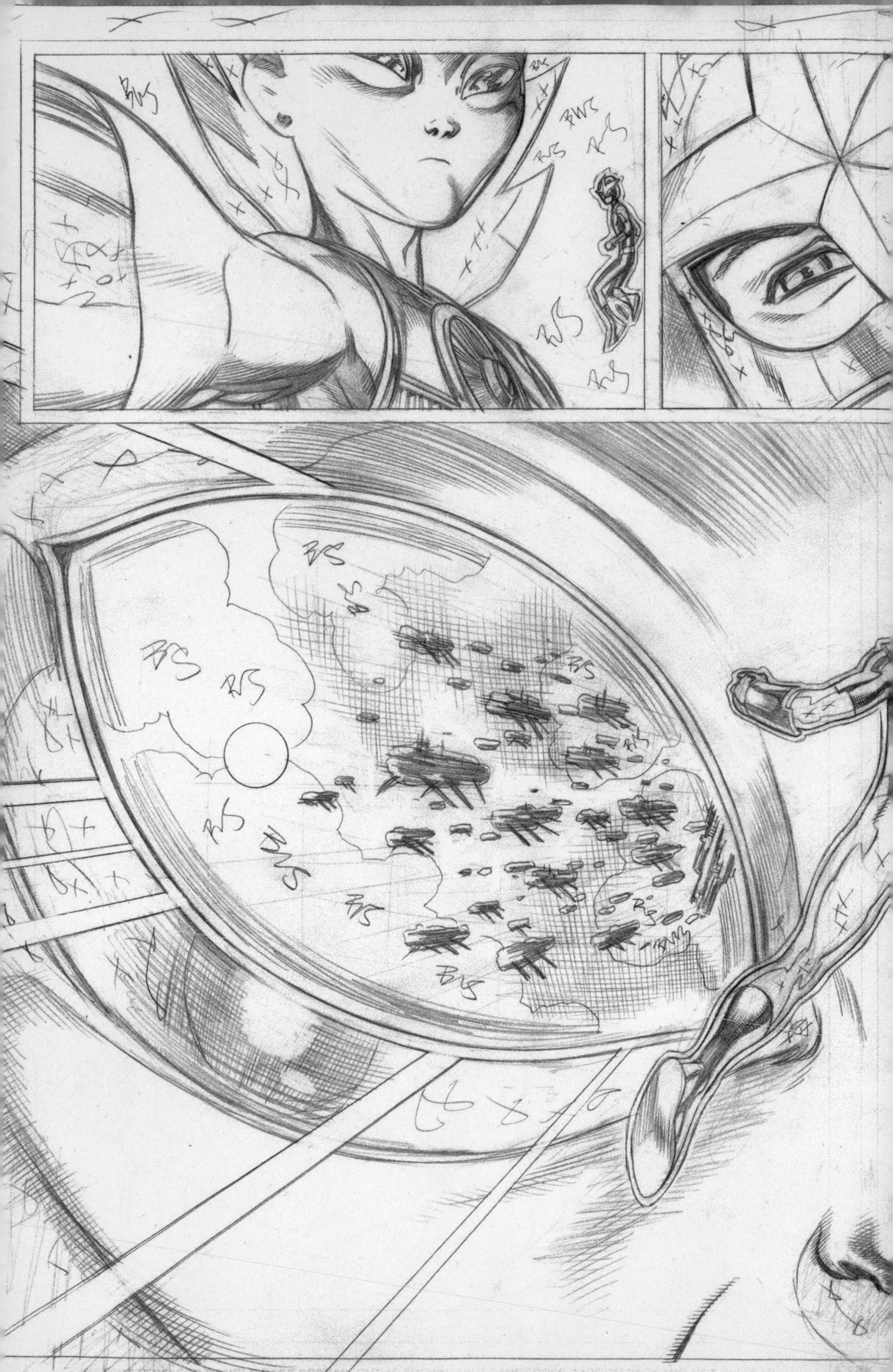

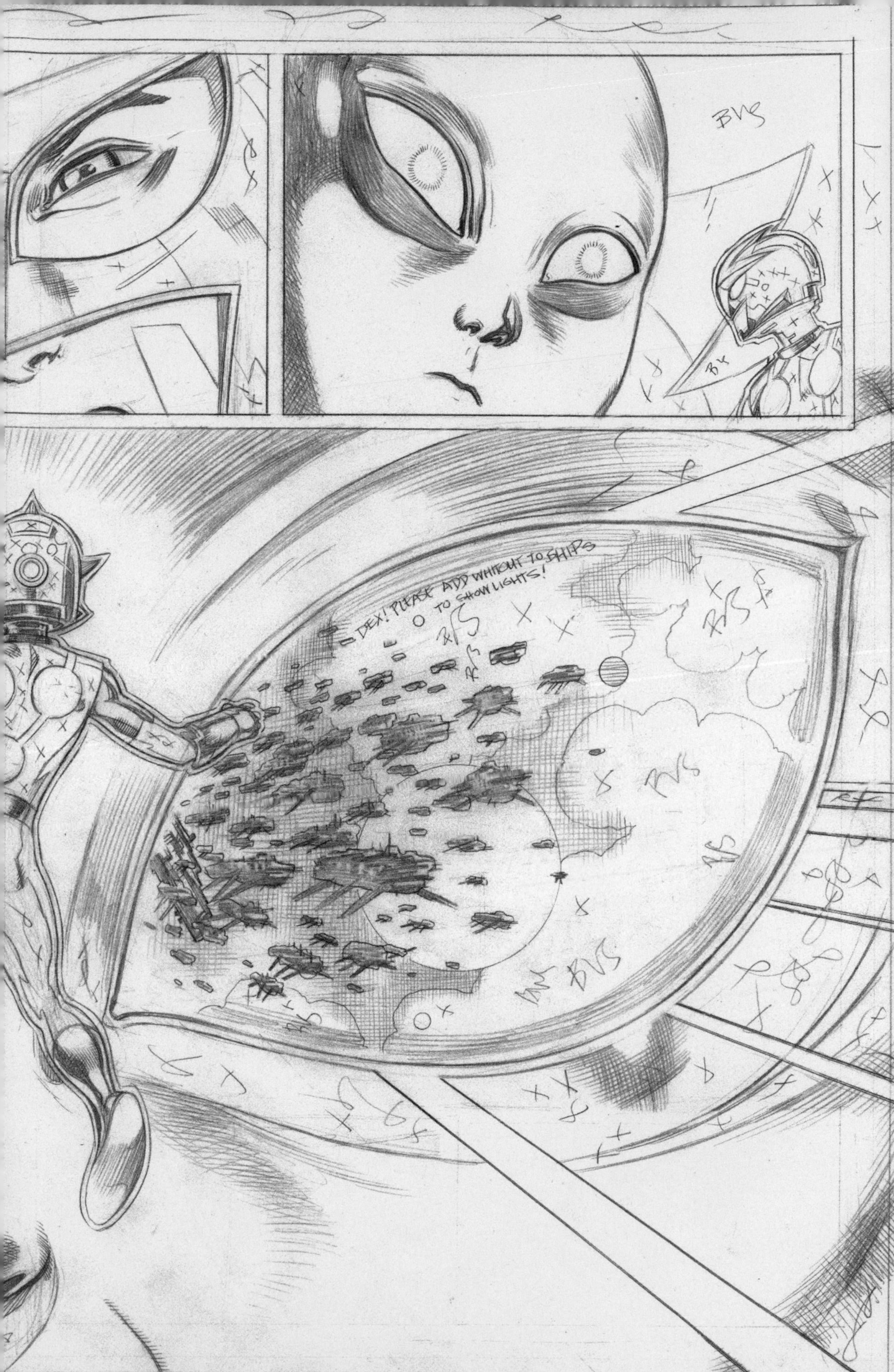
DEX! PLEASE ADD WHITOUT TO SHIPS TO SHOW LIGHTS!

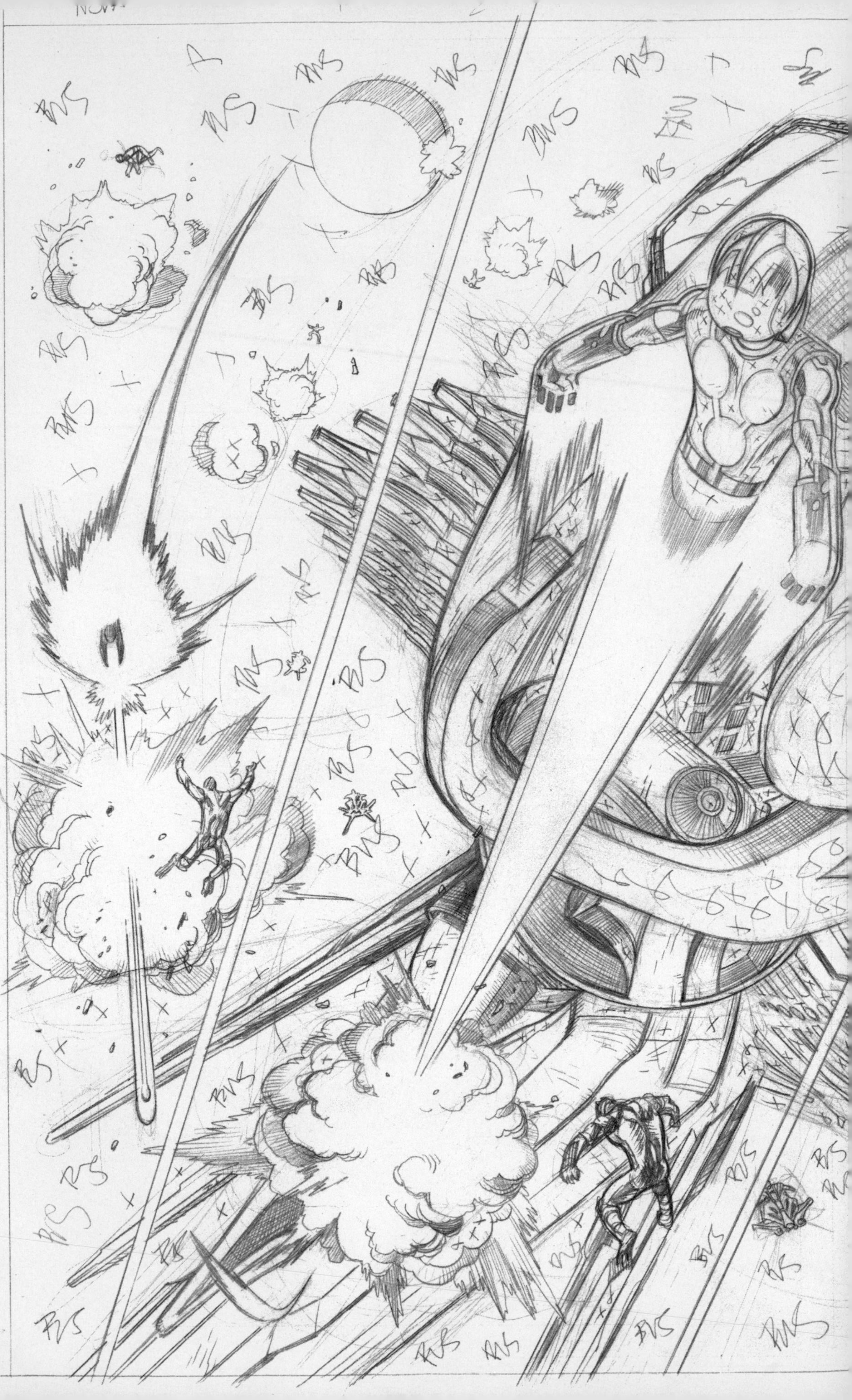

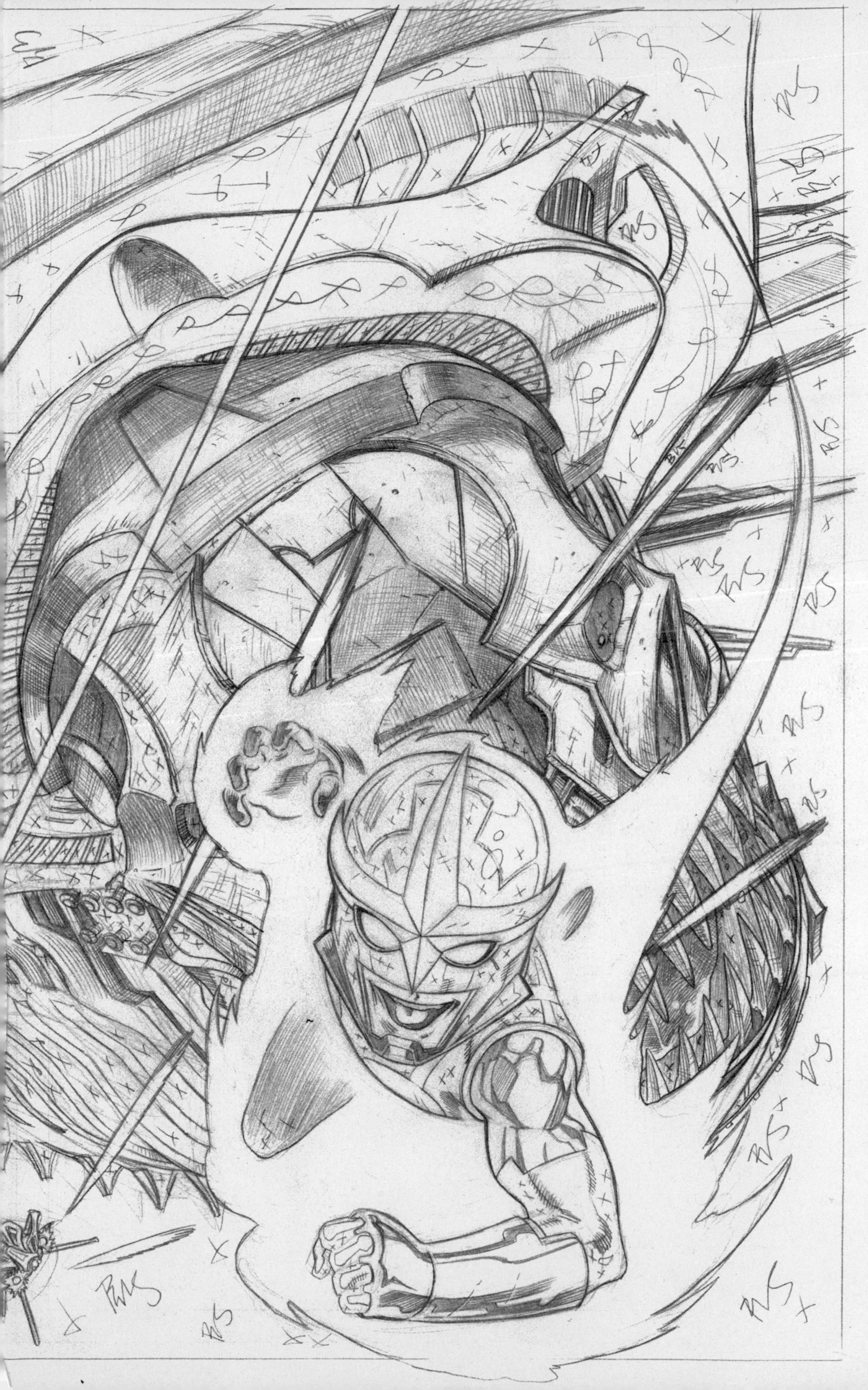

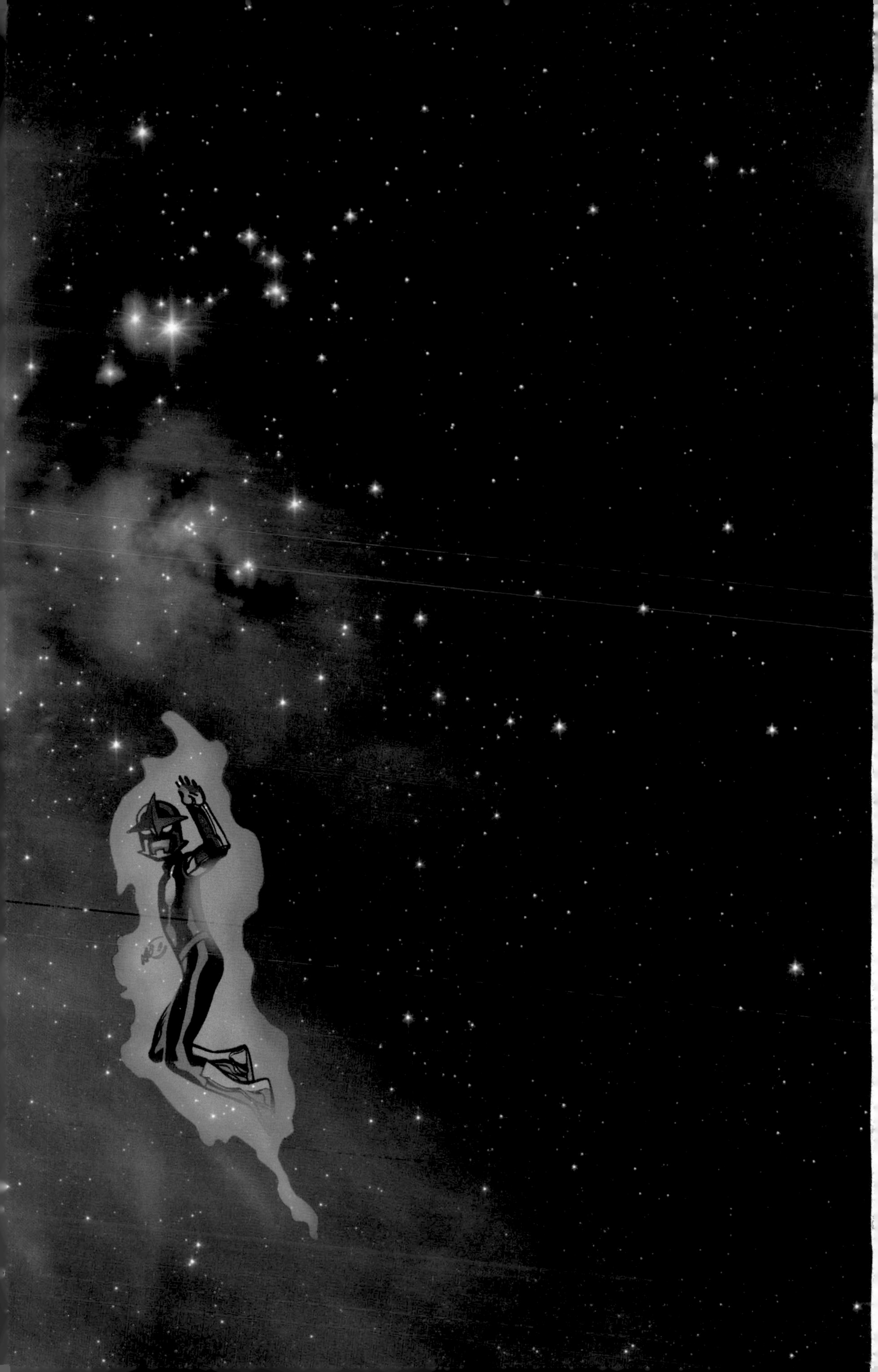